THE ENIGMA OF SC

Drawing on a novel blend of moral philosophy, social science, psychoanalytic theory and continental philosophy, this book offers up a diagnosis of contemporary liberal-capitalist society and the increasingly febrile culture we occupy when it comes to matters of harm. On what basis can we say that something is harmful? How are we supposed to judge between competing opinions on the harmfulness of a particular behaviour, practice, or industry? Can we avoid drifting off into relativism when it comes to judgements about harm? In an age of deep cultural and political discord about what is and is not harmful, providing answers to such questions is more important than ever.

Appraising the current state of the concept of social harm in academic scholarship and everyday life, Thomas Raymen finds a concept in an underdeveloped state of disorder, trapped in interminable deadlocks and shrill disagreements about what should and should not be considered harmful. To explain the genesis of this conceptual crisis and identify what we need to do to resolve it, The Enigma of Social Harm travels from Graeco-Roman antiquity to the present day, exploring trends and developments in moral and political philosophy, religion, law, political economy, and culture. Along the way, we see how such trends and developments have not only made it more difficult to establish a shared basis for evaluating harm, but that the tools which might enable us to do so are now outright prohibited by the political-economic, cultural, and ethical ideology of liberalism that dominates contemporary society.

Written in a clear and accessible style, it is essential reading for all those interested in matters of social harm, justice, politics, and ethics.

Thomas Raymen is an Associate Professor of Criminology in the Department of Social Sciences at Northumbria University.

'This book is a landmark in the study of zemiology and social harm. Surveying the zemiological landscape, Raymen finds the concept of social harm to be in a state of disorder, and takes us on a historical, philosophical, political, and psycho-analytic journey of remarkable scale and scope. Arriving back at the present, this book equips its readers with a new set of questions, tools, and insights to categorise and critique myriad zemiological positions as well as a powerful perspective from which to ask questions about social harm in the 21st century. Required reading for anyone interested in social harm.'

Anthony Lloyd, *Associate Professor of Criminology and Sociology, Teesside University*

'If by chance this book does not receive classic status and act as a new foundation for the study of social harm, it will be yet another indication that the social sciences are in terminal decline, and nothing can be done to slow the descent.'

Simon Winlow, *Professor of Criminology, Northumbria University*

'New criminology books are commonplace, but theoretically ground-breaking ones that make a significant leap forward in a core area of our discipline are truly rare. This book falls into the latter category. It is a book that will either make you think again, or it will give clarity and coherence to those inchoate thoughts that have been in the back of your head but that you have never managed to articulate. Either way, it is a book that everyone interested in social harm must read.'

James Treadwell, *Professor of Criminology, Staffordshire University*

THE ENIGMA OF SOCIAL HARM

The Problem of Liberalism

Thomas Raymen

Routledge
Taylor & Francis Group

LONDON AND NEW YORK

Cover image: © DNY59/Getty Images

First published 2023
by Routledge
4 Park Square, Milton Park, Abingdon, Oxon OX14 4RN

and by Routledge
605 Third Avenue, New York, NY 10158

Routledge is an imprint of the Taylor & Francis Group, an informa business

© 2023 Thomas Raymen

The right of Thomas Raymen to be identified as author of this work has been asserted in accordance with sections 77 and 78 of the Copyright, Designs and Patents Act 1988.

British Library Cataloguing-in-Publication Data
A catalogue record for this book is available from the British Library

Library of Congress Cataloging-in-Publication Data
Names: Raymen, Thomas, author.
Title: The enigma of social harm : the problem of
   liberalism / Thomas Raymen.
Description: Abingdon, Oxon ; New York,
   NY : Routledge, 2023. | Includes bibliographical
   references and index. |
Identifiers: LCCN 2022022893 | ISBN 9780367565930
   (hardback) | ISBN 9780367565947 (paperback) |
   ISBN 9781003098546 (ebook)
Subjects: LCSH: Social problems. | Social justice. |
   Liberalism—Social aspects.
Classification: LCC HN18.3 .R39 2023 | DDC
   361.1—dc23/eng/20220705
LC record available at https://lccn.loc.gov/2022022893

ISBN: 978-0-367-56593-0 (hbk)
ISBN: 978-0-367-56594-7 (pbk)
ISBN: 978-1-003-09854-6 (ebk)

DOI: 10.4324/9781003098546

Typeset in Bembo
by KnowledgeWorks Global Ltd.

To my son, Oscar

CONTENTS

ACKNOWLEDGEMENTS

I would like to take this opportunity to thank a number of professional colleagues who have provided a great deal of inspiration and support for this book. Perhaps my biggest debt is to Steve Hall and Simon Winlow, who have served as the best kind of professional mentors. Over a number of years, they have posed challenging questions, offered illuminating suggestions, and exposed me to a number of the otherwise disparate intellectual influences that inform this book, significantly enhancing its overall argument. But they have done so with a great deal of patience, resisting the temptation to impose their ideas and instead afforded me the space to connect the dots and discover my own lines of argument in my own time. These are arguments which, while a revelation to me, have probably been obvious to them for years. Thanks for leaving the 'penny in the air', so to speak. Anth Lloyd and Tereza Kuldova deserve particular mention for indulging my tendency to send long exploratory emails full of half-formed ideas, always responding with a pearl or two that would bring them into sharper focus. Oliver Smith always deserves a mention for both our professional and personal relationship. It is questionable whether I would have a career in academia without him. James Treadwell has been an inspiration for his courage to never be silent on important matters, and also a great source of humour and comradeship as well. All of the above have also read the manuscript and offered thoughtful comments which have certainly enhanced its overall quality. I'll break with custom and blame any shortcomings on them. Thank you to Northumbria University for the sabbatical that made it possible to finish this book and to Tom Sutton and Jess Phillips at Routledge for both believing in the book and putting up with my missed deadlines.

The dedication of this book is itself a form of thanks. The experience of becoming a father is not only the best thing that will ever happen to me, but it has also informed and solidified some of the thinking behind this book as much as any academic text. Thank you to my mum and dad for their endless enthusiasm, love, and support. But most of all, I consider myself truly blessed to have a wonderful partner (and colleague) in Sam. She knows more than anyone of what a truly good life consists and, most importantly, she knows how to live one. I consider myself privileged to have the opportunity to learn from her example. She has sacrificed in so many ways in order to accommodate my desire to write this book. Thank you for everything.

This book was written with the support and funding of The Research Council of Norway as part of the research project *Luxury, Corruption, and Global Ethics: Towards a Critical Cultural Theory of the Moral Economy of Fraud (LUXCORE)* [Project No. 313004].

FOREWORD

The social sciences were founded on the general assumption that we could set aside myth, superstition, religious doctrine, and individual interpretation to objectively appraise the reality of human societies. The cold rationality of an adapted scientific method could be deployed to depict the world as it was, free from the tyranny of archaic lore, the cloying sensitivities of cultural elites, and the self-interested manipulation of vested interests. Beneath what seemed to be the chaos of everyday life lay patterns, processes, and contexts that could be rendered visible and explained. The discourse on social harm promised to continue this tradition of objective investigation. The scholars who first began to popularise the study of social harm were keen to move beyond a narrow focus on acts that contravened criminal law to begin the process of acknowledging and explaining the boundless diversity of harms that litter our social, cultural, and economic life.

Interest in forms of social harm grew steadily during the first two decades of the 21st century. Much of the material produced by this rapidly growing field has ignored the obvious limits of empiricism to offer critical accounts of the forms of injustice that appear to underpin the experience of harm, and consequently the study of social harm has often been understood as a branch of critical criminology. However, the study of social harm certainly does not necessitate a focus on criminal law, contraventions of criminal law, and responses to contraventions of criminal law. Many notable works have moved well beyond the confines of criminology, and it may well be that going forwards the study of social harm remains a diverse and inter-disciplinary endeavour that draws nourishment from established disciplines in the social sciences and supplementary resources from across the entire vista of contemporary intellectual life.

But if the study of social harm is indeed to go forwards, it must proceed from a firm ontological and epistemological base. It is remarkable that so many working in this field seem to intuitively grasp what harm is despite the fact that no robust framework has emerged that might enable us to clearly determine the actual con-stitution of social harm, or indeed delineate clearly between what is and is not socially harmful. Most are just keen to press on with their analysis of the form of harm that most interests them and therefore sidestep what is in truth a thorny intellectual problem. To solve the problem, or even address it in a rational and productive manner, we cannot rely upon the comforting tools of empirical investigation and a strident critique of structures of power and privilege. These tools can enable us to grasp the probabilistic contexts that appear to shape the experience of social harm, and they can also shed a degree of light upon the generative mechanisms that seem to underpin it. But if we hope to logically determine what social harm is and what it is not, we must extend ourselves a little further and learn to wield new tools. We need to rummage around continental philosophy's toolbox and pick out the implements that will allow us to develop trustworthy forms of ethical and moral critique.

All forms of logical evaluation must first establish a form of meas-urement and a benchmark from which to proceed. Our collective failure to establish these things means that, in the present climate of compulsory liberalism, all claims related to the experience of social harm neatly avoid critical interrogation and tend to be understood as self-evident truths. The study of social harm seems to have been defanged and neutralised, reduced to a simple agglomeration of bespoke studies in which data and standard forms of critical analysis are used to address a range of behaviours and events that appear red-olent of injustice or unfairness. Progressive, left-leaning liberalism is an absent presence across the field – usually disavowed, only rarely discussed, and yet perversely everywhere in social harm literature – and subtly determines what can be added to the established list social harms. But how can liberalism be everywhere when so many social harm scholars offer radical forms of critique and advocate a range of deep interventions into the foundations of our present way of life? Liberalism is, we should keep in mind, the ruling ideology. It is the default ideology of most aspects of contemporary intellectual culture, and the same is true of contemporary popular culture. In the absence of moral and ethical critique built upon a reasonably robust understanding of established moral and ethical systems, the study of social harm runs the risk of wasting its potential by accepting the disabling logic that anything judged by the individual to be harmful or harmless is in fact the case, and that any critical interrogation of such a judgement strips the claimant of their subjective experience and their right to interpret their own reality in any way they see fit. Of course, to proceed in this manner deprives the field of genuine intellectual forward motion. Harm is relativised, and in accepting the logic of relativism, social harm scholars surrender the great utility of their founding concept.

In the book you're about to read, Thomas Raymen gently cajoles social harm scholars to fight their way free from compulsory liberalism to think more deeply about what we mean when we talk about harm. How can we evaluate often highly diverse claims about the experience of harm? In the absence of any acknowledged moral or ethical commitments, how can we truly know that what has occurred is indeed harmful? Can we continue to simply relativise harm, to the extent that harm means whatever one wants it to mean? Can we develop new typologies of harm in which obviously huge and consequential harms are given precedence over relatively minor forms of subjective harm? Raymen is courageous enough to discard tools familiar to social scientists and pick up those usually deployed by psychoanalysts, continental philosophers, and theologians. Using an admirably broad frame of reference, he takes the reader on an edifying sight-seeing tour of aspects of our intellectual history too often overlooked by social scientists. The work of the great philosopher Alasdair MacIntyre is a key touchstone, as is the work of the psychoanalyst Jacques Lacan. Inevitably, Raymen deals with forms of abstract thought, but it is only by engaging in such thought that we can truly extend our understanding of harm. Despite the often philosophical nature of his analysis, Raymen's prose is crystal clear and not at all showy. His hope is, clearly, to open up this crucial field of study and invite all to assist in the task establishing a framework that can enable us, at long last, to firmly grasp what harm is and how its occurrence might enable us to better understand the world we live in.

Thankfully, Raymen's detailed investigation of the harms of the world does not lead him towards the negative politics that seems ubiquitous today. Rather than angrily composing an exhaustive list of those things we should be against, he hopes to encourage us to think carefully about what we are for, and how we might construct a politics that seeks to create a world of common social goods. Raymen's analysis is hopeful without being optimistic and centres upon knowing what it is that is truly valuable to human existence. It is a masterful, confident, and illuminating read that has the potential to re-establish the study of social harm on a firm epistemological and ontological foundation. On that note, I warmly welcome you to the book.

Professor Simon Winlow
Department of Social Sciences, Northumbria University
March 2022

PREFACE

This is a book about the concept of social harm. It is concerned with understanding the nature and genesis of the current problems we seem to have in establishing some clear conceptual parameters and criteria for establishing whether or not something should be considered socially harmful. The idea for the book originated from my own work with Oliver Smith, which we (mis)named the 'deviant leisure perspective' (Raymen and Smith, 2019; Smith and Raymen, 2016). I say misnamed because we had never been interested in 'deviance' whatsoever. Rather, following a broader turn towards the concept of harm within critical criminology, we were interested in pushing past criminology's traditional focus on those leisure practices which, if not outright illegal, carried enough of a transgressive veneer or operated close enough to the boundaries of legality to invoke considerations of 'social deviance'. Things like joyriding, graffiti, recreational drug use, skateboarding in public places, football hooliganism, music cultures and so on have long been the stock and trade of criminologists interested in youth leisure and subcultures, as they wander the post-political savannah of late-modern consumer culture and urban life. These topics had not only been researched to death, but in the contemporary context, we also questioned whether they constituted a form of 'deviance' at all. To label something as 'deviant' suggests that the practice under consideration *deviates* from dominant social norms and values. But in a culture predicated on cool individualism, in which rebellion and anti-authoritarianism have become dominant marketing tropes, and in which there is a need to 'fit in' whilst simultaneously distinguishing oneself from the herd, cultural transgression has arguably become the quintessential form of conformity in late-modern consumer capitalism (Hall et al, 2008; Heath and Potter, 2006; Miles, 1998; Raymen, 2018).

Besides, as we surveyed the landscape of leisure and consumerism, it was the most normalised, mainstream, and culturally celebrated aspects of leisure and consumer culture that appeared to be most harmful. So we began to research and write about the normalised harms of contemporary leisure and consumer culture. Our topics of focus became the night-time economy, gambling, shopping, fashion, tourism, 'eco-consumerism', and Instagram culture to name a few. Senior colleagues, early-career researchers, and PhD students joined us, drawing on the deviant leisure perspective to look at things like the cosmetics industry and lifestyle pharmaceuticals, image and performance-enhancing drugs, the fitness and wellness industry, 'volun-tourism', ticket touting, children's sport, loot boxes, video games, and pornography among other areas of cultural life. Collectively, we appeared to be challenging a dominant cultural trend that I describe in these pages and elsewhere as an *assumption of harmlessness,* in which questions or considerations of harm were largely subordinated to the negative liberty of the autonomous individual (Raymen, 2021). I recall being extremely taken with an early contribution to the deviant leisure blog by Professor Rowland Atkinson. Writing about zones of cultural exception and consumer spaces of extremity in things like video games and pornography, Atkinson wrote of concern regarding a common reaction he would receive when presenting critical accounts of such practices:

> When I have presented on these questions I am increasingly struck by a response that I find more and more alarming and which takes us to the heart of debates about realism in criminology – so what? If I'm taking head shots a thousand times a day, who cares? If I enjoy watching fisting or simulated rape, where is the harm in that?
>
> *Atkinson, 2014*

Here, Atkinson's concerns reflected my own. Nor did this seem limited to the realms of leisure and consumerism. Instead, it appeared to be a pervasive feature of our politics, economy, and culture more broadly that, as it turns out, has a long history. Even before capitalism's total political-economic triumph, numerous philosophers championed the idea of how one vice may check another to unintentionally bring about an overall good, thereby relativising the harms of the original vices in the process, transforming them into the Good itself (Dupuy, 2014; Hirschman, 1977). Adam Smith's 'Invisible Hand' is among the most familiar examples of such thinking, but it was actually preceded in a less systematic way by the likes of Saint Augustine, Vico, Montesquieu, and Bernard Mandeville among others, who spoke of turning 'private vices' into 'publick benefits' (Mandeville, 1988 [1732]). From this emerged the question that was going to be the original basis of this book: How have we arrived at a point in history in which it has become the social, moral, and ideological norm to assert that the vast majority of our economic and consumer practices are, essentially, harmless?

But in exploring this question and continuing my own research on leisure and harm, it soon became apparent that this was only part of the story. Something was nagging me about my own work. I was doing research that intuitively sensed and attempted to demonstrate that various leisure practices and industries within late-capitalism and consumer culture were harmful but were being erroneously asserted to be harmless. But on what basis could I do so? How could I respond to Atkinson's 'so-what' audience member who claimed that harm was all relative and that consumer culture and the leisure practices I was scrutinising were, for most people, just a good bit of harmless fun? That we should all be given the freedom to do as we please as consenting adults, and that to challenge or constrain it too severely would actually be harmful in itself. How could I counter? To what could I appeal that would demonstrate that my analysis and verdict was correct? On what basis could I legitimately claim that these things were harmful in a way that logically defeated my hypothetical opponent's counterargument?

Upon interrogating the concept of social harm with a bit more rigour and criticality, it seemed very vague, fuzzy, and underdeveloped – strange for a concept so widely used in both academia and everyday life. It appeared to lack clear and well-established ontological, epistemological, or ethical underpinnings. Throughout the literature, it was repeatedly claimed that social harm was a more ontologically robust alternative to the socially constructed and subjectivist socio-legal category of 'crime'. Intuitively, this seemed correct, yet nowhere in the literature could I find any firm basis for this claim of harm's ontological superiority. It was a claim that seemed to be asserted rather than adequately demonstrated, and there appeared to be gaping and fatal flaws in all of the attempts to conceptualise social harm and establish some rigour to its application. Moreover, as it was being applied to more and more issues, it seemed to be *losing* its coherence and strength to the extent that things were being denounced as 'social harm' on a basis that seemed just as arbitrary (if not more arbitrary) than the process of criminalisation that zemiologists had railed against. When it came to certain matters, there was a dubious assumption of harm*fulness* that somehow co-existed alongside the assumption of harm*lessness*. Social harm, it seems, was being relativised from all angles. As the title of this book suggests, it is a concept with an enigmatic quality in which, much like pornography or corruption, we claim to intuitively know harm when we see it. The entire project of the deviant leisure perspective felt as though it were resting on very shaky foundations.

Therefore, the bigger issue was that the concept of social harm in contemporary society seemed to be lacking any robust, coherent, or adequate foundations whatsoever. Bizarrely, this did not seem to be of much concern to anyone. I have written numerous journal articles and books and delivered dozens of papers on the harms of this and that at academic conferences. In these academic settings, I have never been asked the crucial question of how we can know and argue with confidence and good reason that what I was talking about could be considered harmful. Not once have I been quizzed on what shared standards or criteria are being employed to arrive at this conclusion. This is simply an observation of the lack of scrutiny around these questions, rather than a criticism of others for failing to question me on these matters. After all, until recently I had scarcely asked this question of myself. As is often the case with other concepts in the social sciences that have become very popular very quickly, social harm increasingly feels like a term to be invoked and asserted rather than a concept with substantial meaning and rigour (see Carrier, 2017; Hayward and Schuilenberg, 2014 for similar trends with other ideas such as moral economy or resistance).

This is somewhat understandable. I am a criminologist by trade, but from personal experience encountering the concept of social harm felt like a liberating breath of fresh air. As the social harm literature demonstrates, some of the most pressing issues facing global society are harms that not only lie beyond the present scope of legal prohibition but are thoroughly normalised and integral to the functioning of liberal-capitalist political economy. Social harm's conceptual toolkit permitted my colleagues and I to roam free. As criminologists, we no longer had to sit on the sidelines and leave such important matters to scholars in other disciplines. We could have our say, and we could do so without having to manufacture some tenuous link back to crime or the criminal justice system in order for it to be deemed 'proper criminology' (White, 2012). Disciplinary boundaries began to feel more porous and less constraining – perhaps even less relevant or necessary. After all, as Canning and Tombs (2021) rightly observe, the concept of social harm is not the exclusive preserve of criminology or zemiology but is used, implicitly or explicitly, in a wide variety of fields. It is a concept that *transcends* disciplinary boundaries, and as a result, social harm research looks and feels more *trans*-disciplinary or even *post*-disciplinary, rather than merely *inter*disciplinary.

But it also feels like the field has gotten a little carried away and put the proverbial cart before the horse. The study of social harm has progressed rapidly without a firm grounding for its foundational concept. Consequently, it is becoming increasingly difficult to anchor the meaning of the concept of social harm in a coherent way, what the likes of Žižek (2006) would describe as the decline of symbolic efficiency. This ambiguity is not only a problem with the concept of social harm. We are arguably experiencing a similar decline of symbolic efficiency around adjacent concepts such as justice. An interesting article by Gangoli et al (2020) explored what justice meant to BAME victims/survivors and how these groups understood justice. In our present era of postmodern pluralism, we no longer bat an eyelid at such studies. On the contrary, it is *assumed* that different people will have different understandings of 'justice' or 'harm' based along the usual lines of identity. It is assumed that this is a natural and unavoidable state of affairs that is entirely unproblematic, and that we should simply accept such pluralisation. But concepts like harm or justice are core concepts and symbolic terms that are essential to our living together harmoniously. Is it really OK that these terms have such pluralistic meanings? Should we not be more alarmed at this state of affairs? As it stands, concepts like social harm and 'justice' are either being thinned-out into irrelevance or pluralised into incoherence to the extent that we are arguably becoming ethically, politically, and culturally unintelligible to one another.

Social harm's epistemological and ontological void is actually acknowledged in social harm texts with relative frequency, but it is rarely dwelled on for long. Within such texts, it has become almost customary to acknowledge this problem, only to casually skirt the issue by stating that dealing with this problem is 'beyond the scope of this book/chapter/article' before carrying on with the rest of the argument. It seems to be treated as a technical matter of little importance that does not get in the way of us doing research and declaring that this or that practice, industry, institution, or systemic structure is harmful. We can simply say and argue that they are harmful, and our data and the personal convictions of both the author and the approving reader decree this to be a self-evident truth. It is arguable that this is partially due to the neoliberalisation of the university and academic research. Academics operating under the pressure of the Research Excellence Framework (REF) and other metrics have to publish frequently in high impact journals, cobble together a port-folio of three and four-star outputs, and deliver impact case studies. Such conditions lend themselves to short-termism and empiricism, and implicitly discourages academic work that engages with these deeper questions which, while important and relevant for our everyday lives, are time-consuming to answer and do not necessar-ily yield immediate 'impact' as measured by things such as the REF.

But irrespective of these issues, surely having clear ontological, epistemological, and ethical principles underpinning the concept of social harm must be a pre-requisite of being able to say with authority that something is harmful? Otherwise, why would any-one listen and take our zemiological claims seriously, particularly those who might be sceptical of our claims? But this does not seem to be the case. In actual fact, as this book intends to demonstrate, the concept of harm seems to be in a gravely underdeveloped state of disorder, and yet a growing mountain of critical criminological and zemiological research continues to expand on these ill-formed and unstable foundations. Harms are relativised by numerous dif-ferent parties and authoritatively asserted by others in an emotivist fashion. I myself continue to write articles talking about the harms of this or that, *as if* I am referring to some shared, impersonal stand-ards or criteria on which we all agree, but which do not seem to exist anywhere in the literature. This is not to say that this growing mountain of work does not have merit or value. But it does leave unanswered questions. Given that social harm is potentially one of the most potent and transformative concepts currently available to the social sciences, this is an issue that has to be rectified.

As a result, the parameters of this book had to expand. It was not only a question of how it had become the norm to assert the harmlessness of various industries and practices, but also a question of why we now find it so difficult to establish any zemiological consensus or adequate principles for the concept of social harm. These questions seem more pertinent than ever. We live in a time of great political, cultural, and zemiological discord, trapped in a series of seemingly interminable deadlocks on a whole host of issues. The harms of 'microaggressions' and free speech versus the harms of no-platforming and cancel culture. The harms of 'opening up' from the Covid-19 pandemic versus the harms of remaining under lockdown or other public health restrictions. Whether or not children wishing to receive medical treatment to undergo gender transition can provide informed consent and receive such treatment without their parents' permission, and the potential harms on both sides of this argument. The list could be endless. These deadlocks can seemingly find no terminus, largely because we seem to be lacking any shared foundations upon which we evaluate both harm and the Good; and what we do collectively agree upon seems to be shrinking rapidly. Rather than acknowledging the absence of these shared foundations and going back to identify where things went wrong and how we can establish or re-establish some consensus, the preference seems to be further fragmentation and a degeneration into emotivist and manipulative slanging matches. Rather than engage in reasoned argumentation, we sling accusations at our opponents, mock them, and endeavour to make them appear as inherently bad or stupid people, thereby rendering any onlooker who agrees with aspects of their argument as equally bad or stupid (MacIntyre, 2011). This amounts to an infantile and Manichean world that is erroneously split into 'goodies' and 'baddies' across a whole host of social and zemiological issues.

The present book, therefore, is concerned with answering these aforementioned questions and explaining how we have arrived at this point. Chapters 1 and 2 are primarily concerned with outlining the shortcomings of the most prominent existing conceptualisations of social harm, demonstrating that the concept is actually in the seriously underdeveloped state of disorder and relativisation that I claim it to be, and consider the consequences of social harm's conceptual poverty along the way. Chapter 3 draws on ideas from theoretical psychoanalysis to consider why there is a consistent tendency to relativise, rationalise, and disavow certain harms. These early foundational chapters are a pre-requisite for the rest of the book's argument, which is primarily concerned with *how* the concept of harm has come to be in this condition. While human societies have always relativised and downplayed certain harms across time, what is different and concerning about our present moment is twofold. Firstly, it is the apparent inability to establish meaningful consensus on what should be legitimately considered harmful at all, let alone how we rank order such harms. Relatedly, it is that the tools necessary for establishing such a consensus are prohibited to us by liberalism's insistence on the sovereignty of the autonomous individual. How have we come to arrive in this position; and how is it even possible that an entire field of social scientific research can be based on a concept with relatively ethereal foundations? These questions – which are really one and the same question – constitute the bedrock of this book. As the argument that follows will hopefully show, answering these questions and understanding the genesis of social harm's precarious conceptual condition also provides us with helpful directions for forming coherent and consistent ontological, epistemological, and ethical foundations for the concept of social harm that will be of benefit to critical criminology and zemiology.

Unearthing the causes of this problem necessitates a very long view of history. The argument I pursue in these pages does not identify a singular or abrupt cause, but rather outlines a lengthy process and transition spanning many centuries. It is a product of trends, developments, and episodes in moral and political philosophy, religion, law, economics and culture, the consequences of which are not fully apparent for many centuries and the relationships between them are highly circuitous and therefore obscured from their original authors and actors. Indeed, the analysis takes us from Greek and Roman antiquity to the birth of Christianity, right up to the present day. But the reader should be warned against the mistake of confusing the present work with that of a history book. In the course of working on this book, I have read the work of numerous academic historians who provide exceptionally detailed analyses, descriptions, and chronological accounts of chosen historical periods or events. I had no intention of attempting to do the same. To try and do so would not only be unnecessary for the purpose of this book, but would actually obscure rather than illuminate its central argument and analysis. Instead, I have taken inspiration from Karl Polanyi's approach to history in his seminal work, *The Great Transformation*, in which he writes that 'we shall feel free to dwell on scenes of the past with the sole object of throwing light on matters of the present; we shall make detailed analyses of critical periods and almost completely disregard the connecting stretches of time' (Polanyi, 2001: 4). I have taken a similar 'helicopter view' of history, flying across thousands of years and dropping down in a few selected places, paying attention to episodes, developments, ideas, and individuals which, based upon my reading and research, seemed most important for understanding the concept of social harm's impoverished condition. Identifying where to 'drop down' and what to pass over has been the most challenging aspect of this book by far. It is inevitable that readers will question the inclusion of certain figures or periods and the exclusion of others. They may feel that some things have been given short shrift and others have been given disproportionate attention. But this is something that I hope can be debated as a means to enhancing the book's argument and correcting it where necessary, rather than as grounds for disqualifying its relevance altogether. This book is intended to be the start of a conversation rather than a final word.

I opened this preface with a reflection on what I perceived to be the inadequacies of my own work and how they became the basis for the rationale of this book, and I have done so for specific reasons. First of all, it is the truth. Secondly, it is my opinion that self-subversion and poking holes in one's own work can always be a productive exercise in generating new lines of enquiry, and I have certainly found that to be the case with this book. But there is a third reason. In the pages that follow I am critical in places of others working under a broad social harm approach. The nature of my argument meant that this was entirely unavoidable. Given the time and effort that academics put into their work, it is always hard not to take such critique personally. But it also feels – and perhaps readers feel this also – that it is increasingly difficult to have calm, civilised, and reasonable intellectual disagreement in contemporary academic and public life. By explaining the origins of this book, I hope it will be clear to the reader that it has emerged from self-critique as much as it has from critique of others, and that any critique of others is done in good faith and in the intellectual spirit of trying to move things forwards with this all-important concept. I am indebted to many of those contemporary academics I critique. Their work has not only established social harm as the foundation of zemiology but also has, in many respects, contributed to the broadening of critical criminology's horizons and scope, without which my research would not exist. Therefore, I hope readers engage with the argument with an open mind and in similar good faith.

A point on style before the book begins in earnest. Some books are written in such a way that the reader can flit back and forth between chapters and read them out of order without it affecting the ability to comprehend or digest the book's wider argument. This is increasingly the case in an era of digital publishing in which readers have the option of purchasing electronic copies of individual chapters instead of the entire monograph, and authors are encouraged to write in such a way that individual chapters can be read independently of the rest of the book and are not reliant on the context of preceding or subsequent chapters in order to make sense on their own. For better or worse that is not the case with this book. The reader is taken through the argument step-by-step in a somewhat linear fashion. The arguments of one chapter will often rely heavily upon the arguments of those that precede it, and the arguments of the early chapters will gradually come into sharper focus upon reading the later ones. As a result, each individual chapter will not always be entirely intelligible on its own terms. Furthermore, as alluded to earlier, the argument deals with events in academic, political, economic, religious, and cultural history which are, for the most part, dealt with chronologically. Together, this chronological element and my own stylistic limitations dictate that the full argument of the book is to be best understood by reading the chapters in order from beginning to end.

References

Atkinson, R. (2014) 'The Draw of the Undertow: Extremity, Otherness and Emergent Harm in Gaming and Pornography'. Available at: https://deviantleisure.com/2014/08/04/the-draw-of-the-undertow-exremity-otherness-and-emergent-harm-in-gaming-and-pornography/.

Canning, V. and Tombs, S. (2021) From Social Harm to Zemiology: A Critical Introduction. Abingdon. Routledge.

Carrier, J. (2017) 'Moral Economy: What's in a Name'. Anthropological Theory. doi: 10.1177/1463499617735259.

Dupuy, J.P. (2014) *Economy and the Future: A Crisis of Faith*. East Lansing, MI. Michigan State University Press.

Gangoli, G., Bates, L. and Hester, M. (2020) 'What Does Justice Mean to Black and Minority Ethnic (BME) Victims/Survivors of Gender-Based Violence'. *Journal of Ethnic and Migration Studies*. 46(15): 3119–3135.

Hall, S., Winlow, S. and Ancrum, C. (2008) *Criminal Identities and Consumer Culture: Crime, Exclusion and the New Culture of Narcissism*. Abingdon. Routledge.

Hayward, K. and Schuilenberg, M. (2014) 'To Resist=To Create?'. *Tijdschrift over Cultuur & Criminaliteit*, 4(1): 22–36

Heath, J. and Potter, A. (2006) *The Rebel Sell*. Chichester. Capstone.

Hirschman, A. (1977) *The Passions and the Interests: Political Arguments for Capitalism before Its Tritumph*. Princeton, NJ. Princeton University Press.

MacIntyre, A. (2011) *After Virtue*. London. Bloomsbury.

Mandeville, B. (1988 [1732]) *The Fable of the Bees or Private Vices, Publick Benefits*. Indianapolis. The Online Library of Liberty.

Miles, S. (1998) *Consumerism As a Way of Life*. London. Sage.

Polanyi, K. (2001) *The Great Transformation: The Political and Economic Origins of Our Time*. Boston, MA. Beacon Press.

Raymen, T. (2018) *Parkour, Deviance and Leisure in the Late-Capitalist City: An Ethnography*. Bingley. Emerald.

Raymen, T. (2021) 'The assumption of harmlessness' in P. Davies. P. Leighton and T. Wyatt (Eds) *The Palgrave Handbook of Social Harm*. Switzerland. Palgrave Macmillan: 59–88.

Raymen, T. and Smith, O. (Eds) (2019) *Deviant Leisure: Criminological Perspectives on Leisure and Harm*. Switzerland. Palgrave Macmillan.

Smith, O. and Raymen, T. (2016) 'Deviant Leisure: A Criminological Perspective'. *Theoretical Criminology*. Available at: http://tcr.sagepub.com/content/early/2016/08/10/1362480616660188.abstract.

White, R. (2012) 'But is it criminology? Faith' in S. Winlow and R. Atkinson (Eds) *New Directions in Crime and Deviancy*. Abingdon. Routledge: 87–99.

Žižek, S. (2006) *How to Read Lacan*. New York, NY. W.W. Norton & Company.

1

A DISQUIETING SUGGESTION FOR CRIMINOLOGY AND ZEMIOLOGY

At the opening of Alasdair MacIntyre's seminal text, *After Virtue*, he poses 'a disquieting suggestion' for the field of moral philosophy and contemporary society more broadly. He imagines a fictitious scientific dystopia in which the natural sciences are held responsible by the general public for a series of environmental disasters and catastrophes. Amidst widespread riots, laboratories are burned to the ground; scientific books, writings, and technical equipment are destroyed; and physicians and biologists are publicly executed for their alleged crimes. Eventually, a 'Know-Nothing' political movement takes power and abolishes science from schools and universities, prohibiting its practice. After a certain passage of time, this society witnesses a countermovement to the successful destruction and abolition of science. Enlightened members of the population seek to try and revive the practice of science, but MacIntyre's imaginary counterinsurgents have, unfortunately, largely forgotten what science was or how it was practised. All they possess are fragments: half-burned books explicating theories which lack the broader context which establishes their significance; incomplete periodic tables; and technical instruments whose original use has long been forgotten. Regardless, these fragments are cobbled together, and 'science' is restored under a set of practices named physics, chemistry, and biology. The new scientists argue about the theory of relativity,

DOI: 10.4324/9781003098546-1

Darwin's theory of evolution, and Newton's law of universal gravitation despite possessing only a partial knowledge of such things. However, in this fictitious scenario, nobody realises that what they are doing is not 'natural science' at all – at least not in the sense that we understand natural science – because 'everything that they do and say conforms to certain canons of consistency and coherence and those contexts which would be needed to make sense of what they are doing have been lost, perhaps irretrievably' (MacIntyre, 2011: 1–2). In this pseudo-scientific culture, its inhabitants would continue to *use* scientific language in a similar way to its prior use. But absent of the beliefs, evidence, and wider underpinning scientific context, such language is in a state of grave disorder. Rival and competing scientific premises would abound. But with no criteria available to arbitrate between them, these arguments would be interminable, and a 'subjectivist' natural science would emerge in which the use of scientific language would appear to be an entirely arbitrary choice that cannot be settled systematically. It is here that the point of such a tale is revealed, as MacIntyre proposes his 'disquieting suggestion':

> The hypothesis which I wish to advance is that in the actual world we inhabit the language of morality is in the same state of grave disorder as the language of natural science in the imaginary world which I described. What we possess, if this view is true, are the fragments of a conceptual scheme, parts which now lack those contexts from which their significance derived. We possess indeed simulacra of morality, we continue to use many of the key expressions. But we have—very largely, if not entirely—lost our comprehension, both theoretical and practical, of morality.
>
> *MacIntyre, 2011*: 2–3

This is a bold claim by MacIntyre. This book will draw heavily upon his work and expand upon his arguments later. For now, it is enough to say that MacIntyre argues that moral precepts and judgements were once uttered within a context of a shared ethical foundation of practical beliefs and a conception of society and the subject in which there were impersonal standards justified by a shared conception of the Good. However, as a result of extremely disruptive changes in the late middle ages and carrying through early modernity and the enlightenment, this shared context has since been lost – and for some deemed an impossibility – thereby demanding that moral rules and injunctions acquire a new justification and authority. What the European philosophers of modernity provided, MacIntyre argues, were rival and incompatible accounts which were conceptually incommensurable, deprived of any shared impersonal standard rooted within a shared conception of the Good. The core premises of rival moral arguments were and continue to be built upon a series of normative or evaluative starting points which may be internally coherent but are entirely opposed to and irreconcilable with one another, 'such that we possess no rational way of weighing the claims of one against the other' (*ibid.* 2011: 8). MacIntyre suggests that in the absence of a *shared* normative concept or moral authority which can arbitrate between them, the respective parties in disagreement argue with one another endlessly by employing their incommensurable normative concepts to establish the legitimacy of their own argument *and* determine the wrongheadedness of their opponents. Logically, such a situation reaches an impasse in which the moral issue in question has become systematically unsettlable. 'From our rival conclusions', MacIntyre writes, 'we can argue back to our rival premises; but when we do arrive at our premises argument ceases and the invocation of one premise against another becomes a matter of pure assertion and counter-assertion' (*ibid.* 2011: 8).

MacIntyre uses a variety of examples such as the issue of taxation, arguments around war, and the debates around abortion to illustrate his point. But we also often see this when it comes to more explicitly criminological or zemiological issues that are perhaps more familiar to those working in these fields. Take the sex work industry as an example. There are those who argue against the sex work industry, claiming that it is inherently harmful to women and gender relations more broadly. The basic starting point for this argument is that the sex work industry is organised around the exploitation and sexual objectification of women, reducing women to sexual commodities to be purchased by men, and consequently perpetuating inequalities and patriarchal relations between men and women along intersecting axes of class, racial, and global inequality. On the other side of this argument are those who advocate for the sex work industry. Their starting point is typically one based around liberty and individual freedom. Who are we to say what women can and cannot do with their bodies? They should be free to do as they please as consenting adults and enter into any form of employment or self-employment they choose. Sex work should be considered as a form of work like any other. Sex workers sell their sexual labour just as labourers on a construction site sell their physical labour or academics sell their intellectual labour. Various offshoots of this argument revolve around the notion that the prohibition of sex work criminalises their customers (or in some countries, sex workers themselves), thereby placing women into increased danger, and each side argues endlessly over whether a legalised and regulated sex work industry is more dangerous and damaging to women than a prohibitionist stance. Other offshoots are that prohibition stigmatises sex work and, by extension, stigmatises and oppresses female sexuality, and that a prohibitionist position is effectively a representation of patriarchal ideas around female sexuality.

The point, MacIntyre argues, is that on their own merits, both of these arguments are internally coherent and valid. The problem is that their starting points are so incommensurable that they logically cannot defeat one another or engage in productive dialogue with one another. One is arguing from a perspective of equality in gender relations. The other is arguing from a starting position organised around individual liberty and freedom of choice. In truth, both sides would likely claim that their respective arguments are made in the name of both equality *and* freedom. This makes things even more confusing because their conceptions of what freedom and equality really mean, what they look like, and how to attain them are so radically different that they are largely incapable of having a meaningful dialogue in such a way that we can rationally weigh the arguments against one another. If we evaluate an opponent's position according to our own standards and starting point, it is inevitable that our opponent's argument will seem absurd. But the same is true when applied in reverse. While we may be convinced of the legitimacy of our own arguments, they are viewed as equally absurd and illogical when evaluated according to the starting premises of our opponent.

To put this in Lacanian terms, what is lacking here is a shared 'quilting point'. For the psychoanalyst Jacques Lacan, terms such as 'freedom', 'equality', and even 'harm' are *floating signifiers*. Their meaning is open and therefore requires an ideological 'quilting point' or 'nodal point' which anchors the term, fixes its meaning, and halts this slippage of meaning (Žižek, 1989). If we quilt the term 'freedom', for instance, through the nodal points of socialism, liberalism, or feminism, it acquires a number of different meanings. A socialist understanding of freedom is freedom from the merciless exploitation of the capitalist system; a feminist understanding of freedom would be freedom from gendered norms generated by the patriarchal system; and a liberal understanding of freedom would be freedom from the state or other forms of custom, tradition, morality, or religion. These quilting points offer up incommensurable meanings, and MacIntyre's point is that in the absence of a shared ethical background or quilting point, arguments on a topic like sex work are *all* made in the name of freedom and equality but in radically different ways. Consequently, these respective arguments are fundamentally incapable of arriving at any terminus.

MacIntyre argues that as a consequence of this state of affairs, two things inevitably occur. Firstly, since the starting premises of the rival arguments are conceptually incommensurable and therefore cannot logically defeat one another, the respective parties in the argument can give no definitive reasons for choosing one set of starting premises over another. Therefore, positions on a whole host of issues and topics are chosen somewhat arbitrarily before we've even entered the field of debate, based upon individual or collective self-interest, friendship, biography, inherited political allegiances, or, as the sentimentalist moral philosophers would have it, by an intuitive 'moral sense' (Eagleton, 2009).

Secondly, MacIntyre suggests that morality and discourse in the social sciences more widely has descended into a culture of *emotivism* in which moral utterances and disagreements have become little more than manipulative expressions of already-held personal preferences, feelings, and ideological beliefs. Since one side cannot triumph over the other due to radically incommensurable starting points, we increasingly resort to highly emotive language to try and win the day. We try and discredit our opponent's character, belittle them, denigrate them, and make them look evil, stupid, or disingenuous. Anyone masochistic enough to hint at a political or moral opinion on Twitter will immediately recognise this interminable pattern. Contemporary debates about all manner of social issues take on an increasingly binary nature to the extent that they become almost Manichean – a battle of absolute good against absolute evil (Nagle, 2017). On social media, users change their profile picture or use hashtags like #FBPE, #BrexitMeansBrexit, #BlackLivesMatter, or #MAGA in their profiles as a means for clearly establishing one's position, and these can be used to quickly spot the 'goodies' and the 'baddies' on a whole host of issues depending on your position. Exchanges are increasingly littered with wild accusations of fascism, racism, misogyny, or some other form of prejudice. Inflammatory and derogatory terms like 'Uncle Tom', 'house negro', 'TERF', and many others that were previously considered taboo are becoming an increasingly familiar part of our collective vernacular, while ostensibly descriptive terms like 'boomer' or 'millennial' are used in an almost exclusively pejorative sense, a clear indicator of a culture of emotivism.

The Covid-19 lockdowns raised similar moral and zemiological quandaries around the harms of remaining in lockdowns or under other public health restrictions versus the harms of 'opening-up' and removing such restrictions, and this issue was indeed looked at and talked about explicitly through the language of harm. Here we had broadly deontological responses which argued that we must not risk the lives of anyone, and that therefore anything that would jeopardise any single life was ethically unjustifiable. These clashed with more utilitarian responses which felt that the majority should not be asked to make significant sacrifices that were detrimental to their employment, financial security, mental well-being, or even personal safety simply to protect a relative minority of people who were highly vulnerable to the most severe consequences of the virus. A third position took an approach which was more reflective around human flourishing. This approach asked questions around what it is to live a good life and to what extent and for how long the issue of quality of life should be subordinated to the mere preservation and endurance of life, what Ellis et al (2021) describe as the 'administration of non-death'.

The radically irreconcilable nature of these various positions meant that arguments about whether to 'open-up' or remain locked down or under public health restrictions became characterised by increasingly emotivist debates. Those in favour of lockdown argued that those who wanted to come out of lockdowns or end mask-wearing were endangering the lives of their loved ones. The death of their parents or grandmother would be on their hands. Lockdown sceptics were badged – sometimes erroneously – as intellectually deficient conspiracy theorists and anti-vaxxers, or as being on the political far-right and therefore not to be listened to or trusted (Ahearne and Freudenthal, 2021). Those in favour of opening-up told 'lockdowners' that they were unnecessarily jeopardising their children's future and their educational and social development, and stealing their childhoods; or that the professional middle classes working comfortably from home were callously disregarding the need for others to earn a living.

How are we supposed to decide between these positions? Indeed, the emotivist debates around how we should respond to the Covid-19 pandemic revealed the extent to which the concept of social harm is in an impoverished and underdeveloped state of disorder, for the concept of harm currently has no answers to these questions. Various topics and issues have often been badged as 'social harm' on the basis that they compromise economic security, health, freedom, and so on. But as we will see in more detail below, these are ideals that are not always compatible, and when they come into conflict, we currently have no good basis on which to rank order them and decide whether in any given situation we should prioritise health, economic security, freedom, or some other value or ideal, or to what extent.

Since there can be no final rational victor in this emotivist culture, moral and zemiological disagreement descends into a manipulative clash of wills in which there is nothing to do but for 'one will to align the attitudes, feelings, preference and choices of another with its own' (MacIntyre, 2011: 28). The argument that wins the day is the one made with more effective emotive power and can garner more support by tapping into feelings such as guilt, anger, shame, fear, and so on. It wins by force, not reason. Interestingly, recent quantitative research which tracks the use of language in millions of books, news articles, and academic sources from 1850 to 2019 found that since the 1980s, there has been a marked decline in the use of words associated with fact-based argumentation and a corresponding sharp increase in emotionally laden language. This has also been accompanied by a parallel shift from collectivist to more individualistic language in this same time period (Scheffer et al, 2021). Therefore, in our contemporary culture of emotivism, the meaning beneath a moral or evaluative judgement equates to 'I approve of this, do so as well', or its negative: 'I disapprove of this, do so as well'. However, MacIntyre's point is that rather than accepting this relativism and the arbitrary 'choosing' of one side over another, such moral or evaluative judgements are still uttered *as if* they refer to some impersonal standard or shared truth. As Lutz

(2012) argues, it is rare to encounter true relativists or emotivists, despite the claim of many to be relativists. Our liberal political order is allegedly accustomed to relativism. It is structured on the basic premise that we are entitled to our own opinions about what is right, good, and what constitutes the best form of life, but that we must not impose this conception upon others (Dews, 2008). Somewhat paradoxically, this demand has its own universalism which inevitably runs into problems, as we are currently witnessing with regard to debates around free speech. But nevertheless, as Lutz writes, no one takes relativism to its logical conclusion:

> When we see gross injustice, we react with confidence, we punish those who harm others, and we do it because we are sure that doing so is right, not just legally right, but morally right – and not just morally right from our own peculiar point of view …. If moral relativism really is the problem underlying contemporary moral and political disputes, it is a very selective kind of moral relativism.
>
> *Lutz, 2012: 81*

In a culture truly committed to relativism, disputes would be far more amicable than they are today, for a true culture of relativism would be one that is *tolerant* of differing opinions. But ours is what has been termed a 'cancel culture', in which individuals from different political, cultural, and moral perspectives no-platform, boycott, mute, block, bully, and abuse one another in order to achieve or preserve political or intellectual orthodoxy (Wight, 2021). They do so not only because they dislike their opposition and find their position repugnant, but also because their arguments are incapable of logically defeating the other. On their own terms, each side of the argument is legitimate and internally coherent. But because the starting premises are irreconcilable whilst also being held to be universally true, there can be no way of breaking the deadlock, hence the shrill tone of contemporary debate. We can therefore understand 'cancel culture' as a product of the culture of emotivism.

Therefore, the primary issue is not relativism. Rather, as we outlined earlier, it is that the starting premises of the opposing positions in these arguments are fundamentally incommensurable and lack a shared ethics and therefore cannot be directly weighed against one another in precisely the way that MacIntyre describes. Consequently, what can be genuinely considered harmful *becomes* relativised and obfuscated. But this relativism is a *symptom* of a deeper causative absence, not a cause in itself. Indeed, it is impossible for relativism to be a cause in and of itself, for relativism can only emerge within a particular type of political, socio-cultural, and moral culture. Namely, one that is lacking in shared ethical foundations and has descended into *symbolic inefficiency* due to the conflict of too many ideals and too many ways of life without any means for deciding between them. Therefore, it is critical that we investigate the genesis and causative processes underlying this loss of a shared ethical background that can arbitrate between these competing claims. In essence, that is the purpose of this book.

It should be said that this emotivist state of affairs often suits those in power or those who perpetrate social harms. For starters, those in power are often those with the loudest voices, the biggest platforms, and the most resources to both get out their message and denigrate their opponents. Secondly, while we may often speak 'truth to power' and challenge their actions, such truth-speaking often has little impact. Arguments go on and on as both sides talk over (or past) each other with the sole purpose of getting the last word. But since each side cannot definitively and rationally defeat the other, what tends to happen is that the disputed social practice remains in place by default, largely unchanged and usually in favour of elite economic, political, or cultural interests. All the while, we quietly content ourselves with the consolation prize that such democratic debate is permitted in our society, despite it having no impact upon the undemocratic continuation of the practices in question.

The Relevance of MacIntyre's Disquieting Suggestion for Social Harm

What is the purpose of recalling MacIntyre's disquieting suggestion above? Firstly, given our disciplinary subject matter, the state of morality in contemporary society undeniably has serious implications for the study of social harm in criminology and zemiology. Despite the unpardonable scarcity of moral philosophical discussion within these fields, we must agree with the basic sentiment expressed by British criminologist Anthony Bottoms (2002: 24) when he remarks, 'if they are true to their calling, all criminologists have to be interested in morality'. Moreover, if MacIntyre is right in his suggestion that the language of morality is in a state of grave disorder – and this book will suggest that he is – then these implications become all the more serious as zemiology grows and critical criminology shifts a greater proportion of its attention beyond the socio-legal category of crime and the criminal justice system, and towards systemic forms of *social harm* (Briggs, 2021; Cooper and Whyte, 2017; Hall and Winlow, 2015, 2018; Hillyard and Tombs, 2004; Pemberton, 2015; Raymen, 2019; Raymen and Smith, 2019; White, 2013, 2019).

Secondly, it is to suggest that the language and concept of harm is in a grave state of disorder that is similar – albeit slightly different – to MacIntyre's verdict on the language and conceptual coherence of morality. On the surface of things, the study of social harm would appear to be in robust health. Since the late 1990s, the study of legal-but-harmful social, cultural, environmental, and political-economic practices has exploded. In both academic and everyday life, we regularly *use* the language of harm to shed light on some of the most important social problems facing liberal capitalist societies which are beset by crises on almost all fronts. In recent years, academics have discussed the harms of contemporary work and employment practices (Lloyd, 2018); the systemic harms of austerity and neoliberalism (Cooper and Whyte, 2017); the harms of a speculative and privatised housing market (Atkinson and Blandy, 2017; Madden and Marcuse, 2016); the interpersonal, environmental, and socially corrosive harms of leisure and consumer culture (Smith and Raymen, 2016); the harms of prejudiced microaggressions; the human and environmental harms of climate change in the capitalist Anthropocene (Brisman and South, 2014; White, 2019); and the harms of indebtedness and the financial industry (Horsley, 2015); and the list goes on. Indeed, Canning and Tombs (2021: 53) claim that while there may be divergences in ranking the seriousness of harms or how non-criminal harms stack up against criminal harms in terms of their severity, there is a remarkable level of agreement on what should and should not be considered as harmful. I will return to and contest this point to a certain extent later. Nevertheless, such confident and frequent use of the concept and language of harm would suggest that there exists some shared impersonal standards or criteria upon which we agree regarding what can and cannot be described as socially harmful.

But in fact, when we begin to probe and penetrate deeper, there remains a remarkable paucity of coherence or consensus around the conceptualisation and content of social harm. Beyond the odd tokenistic reference, the overwhelming majority of books and articles that address some form of social harm make little if any reference to the shared criteria they have employed to determine that the issue being addressed is harmful. Perhaps, as Canning and Tombs (2021) suggest, this is because the issue under question appears to the researchers and their readers as so obviously and undeniably harmful that it doesn't need to be explained as to why or on what basis this has been determined? But if such scholars were to be pressed for an explanation as to why the issue being addressed should be understood as an instance of social harm, what resources would they have at their disposal?

In *Beyond Criminology*, published in 2004, it was conceded in a chapter by two of the editors that there remained 'an awful lot of work to be done in terms of defining precisely what is meant by social harm' (Hillyard and Tombs, 2004: 19). Given the philosophically complex nature of the problem and the fact that zemiology was still in its infancy, this was perfectly understandable at the time. But at the time of writing, we are 18 years on from the publication of *Beyond Criminology*, and despite the quite astounding growth of research which takes a harm-oriented approach, we do not seem to have made many meaningful strides towards this end. One of the foremost defenders and advocates of the concept of social harm recently acknowledged the conspicuous absence of any clear agreement regarding the ontological, ethical, or epistemological basis upon which we determine whether a particular phenomenon should be characterised as a form of 'social harm' (Tombs, 2018). Typologies of harm have abounded since Hillyard and Tombs' (2004) initial typology in *Beyond Criminology* (see for example Canning and Tombs, 2021; Pemberton, 2015; Smith and Raymen, 2016). But as Hall et al (2020) argue, such typologies offer us little in terms of establishing ontological, ethical, and epistemological principles which can ground the concept, rendering them somewhat premature. We can talk of harms and endlessly group them into various categories and sub-categories, but unless we're clear on what basis we are calling something harmful, simple typologies amount to little more than a list-making and categorisation exercise.

Pemberton (2015), on the other hand, offers an even more concerning but insightful observation that what is perhaps most remarkable about the study of social harm is the relative scarcity of genuine attempts to define social harm within the criminological and zemiological literature. It is true that within the pages of theoretical books and articles on the concept of social harm, it has become commonplace to fall back on the disclaimer that working towards a clear ontology of harm is 'beyond the scope' of the present text. This job, it seems, is perpetually left to other scholars who are yet to be identified, but who we are sure will take up this task at some unspecified point in the future.

Among those attempts to conceptualise social harm that do exist, there remains deep disagreement over the ontological and ethical basis of social harm, and palpable concern and uncertainty over its conceptual parameters and the breadth of its application. In *Beyond Criminology*, Hillyard and Tombs (2004) argued that harm was to be defined by its operationalisation. That is to say, harm is partially defined according to how it is applied and what the individual interprets, feels, and experiences as harmful. This basic position was reiterated by Canning and Tombs (2021), in which they question whether it is necessary to establish an ontology of harm at all:

> [I]n our view, we can reflect very fruitfully on the question of what makes harm harmful and how we recognise harm without setting out an ontology of harm *per se*. This may be a provisional state of affairs – beyond the scope of this text but something to be determined or achieved subsequently. Or, it may be that interrogating the question rather than reaching an answer is the key here: it might be a productive process without endpoint, *so that what is experienced as harm, recognised as harm and approximates some of the criteria[1] discussed in this chapter to date, therefore counts as harm in an empirical sense*, perhaps always subject to challenge, contest, confirmation and in the absence of any epistemological or ontological certainties?
>
> *Canning and Tombs, 2021: 102, emphasis added*

There is plenty here to unpack and discuss. For starters, this echoes a basically pluralist position, one arguably inherited from criminological theory's tendency towards a postmodern liberal pluralism in which numerous approaches are welcome to take their place in the plurality of ontological or epistemological positions on offer, but there is not and cannot be any one position of authority from which harm can be judged or that should be taken too seriously (Hall, 2012). The overall atmosphere of social harm studies should be like that of a supremely successful academic seminar. Plenty of lively discussion and thought-provoking debate, but without any firm conclusions or actions at the end of it, barring the pledge to organise another seminar. Canning and Tombs are absolutely right that discussion on what constitutes social harm should never be fully closed and should instead be carefully revised, debated, and updated in accordance with developments in reality. But when it comes to the arenas of crime, harm, law, and policy – areas which, if we get wrong, can have quite severe impacts on people's lives – it is questionable as to whether such scepticism towards our ability to establish some authoritative basis for discerning harm is satisfactory.

On the one hand, this debate and discussion without endpoint can appear quite open-minded, democratic, and geared around an aversion to any form of zemiological hegemony or orthodoxy. Various perspectives sit horizontally next to one another, more or less equal in merit. Thought about more closely, however, the claim that understandings of harm must be essentially plural rather than founded on ontologically grounded universal values quickly assumes the position of a hegemonic orthodoxy itself. It becomes 'a power that has the power to pretend it's not a power; but a legitimate consensual authority' (Hall, 2012: 73). Any attempt to claim that there is a definitive set of ontological, epistemological, or ethical principles upon which we reliably base the concept of social harm is pre-emptively dismissed as far too authoritarian and imposing, perhaps even with claims or insinuations that they exhibit a sinister and oppressive normativity. In the consequent vacuum opened up by this state of affairs, the individual's feelings, experiences, and interpretations of harm are given significant primacy. The individual's 'personal truth' can trump, or at least be considered on a par with, any set of ontologically grounded values.

However, it is obvious that basing the concept of harm upon whatever the individual interprets or empirically experiences as harmful is a seriously inadequate foundation for a number of reasons. For starters, at various points in the life course, there are many things that an individual may erroneously interpret or empirically experience as harmful to themselves, which, in reality, are perhaps harmless or even beneficial. More importantly, such an approach cannot take account of that which is in fact harmful but is never empirically experienced or interpreted as such and is instead often experienced as positive and beneficial. For a long time, burning fossil fuels was not experienced or interpreted as harmful, despite it now being perhaps the gravest and most serious harm facing humanity. Similarly, technological devices such as laptops, smartphones, and tablets have been overwhelmingly experienced as beneficial, convenient, and positive developments in our lives. When technology does come under critique – such as commentary which discusses how it is used to manipulate consumers and voters or the toxicity of social media – the message is very much focused on the social application and use of technology. It is considered a neutral and inert tool in itself. Little attention is given to those harms which perhaps lurk beneath the empirical realm of social experience. As the likes of Carr (2010) observe, the increasing use of these devices is, in many respects, damaging our cognitive abilities and transforming our neurological make-up in ways that hamper our capacity to remember, concentrate, and do things like read for extended periods of time and become deeply immersed in particular activities. Given that these processes lie in the deep recesses of the brain's neurological structure, they are scarcely noticed or empirically experienced as harmful and consequently escape our attention. Canning and Tombs' (2021) approach, therefore, is a starkly empiricist one. It functions by endeavouring to close the gap between *seems* and *is*, to the extent that there can be little contrast between '*seems to me*' and '*is in fact*'.

Furthermore, such an approach does not offer us a path to zemiological agreement or a means for resolving zemiological disagreement. Instead, it just returns us to the emotivist deadlock described above. Suppose a scenario in which one person, group, or community claims that they empirically experience something as harmful and that it should be prohibited, either formally through law or through more informal means of social control. An opposing side counters that to prohibit, outlaw, or cast any kind of moral approbation on this would be empirically experienced as harmful to them. In the absence of any ontological and epistemological certainties beyond our respective empirical experiences that can intervene and adjudicate the matter, how is this deadlock to be resolved? We are drawn back into a manipulative set of social relations, in which each side competes to display that the issue will be empirically experienced as more harmful for one side than another, without any possibility for a logical conclusion other than, to quote the same line from MacIntyre again, for 'one will to align the attitudes, feelings, preference and choices of another with its own' (MacIntyre, 2011: 28). In fact, in spite of Canning and Tombs' professed antiliberalism, their approach is redolent of liberalism's emphasis on the autonomous sovereignty of the individual. This is particularly problematic, given that a significant part of the rationale for the systematic study of social harm is that it offers a more ontologically robust alternative to the socially constructed and subjectivist socio-legal category of crime.

There is a further issue at stake here that is related to the point above. Conflating harm with whatever the individual experiences or interprets to be harmful also opens up the possibility of overturning the presumption of innocence, a key principle of Western European civilisations since canon lawyers of the Catholic Church rediscovered Roman Law in the 12th century (Siedentop, 2014). While we are of course talking about harm and not 'law' *per se,* allegations of harm in various forms often have serious legal, professional, and personal consequences. A good example of this occurred in the summer of 2018 at Smith College in the United States, in an incident that was reported on at length by the *New York Times* (see Powell, 2021 for the full story). In this incident, a female BAME student who was working on campus was found eating lunch in the cafeteria lounge of a dormitory that had been closed for the summer, with only a few dormitories left open for a summer camp taking place on campus. Numerous members of staff had mentioned this to the student in question, and a member of campus security approached her and, recognising her as a student, had a brief and polite conversation (which the student recorded). After these interactions, the student authored a social media post accusing the various staff members of racial harassment, posting their photographs and names. In her post, the student reflected on the harm she felt and experienced. 'All I did was be Black', she wrote on social media. Her feeling was that in being approached by these staff members, her presence on the campus of an elite liberal arts college was being questioned because of the colour of her skin. This was part of 'a pattern of discrimination toward [her] as a black woman that has spanned throughout [her] year here from non-black staff and students at the college'.

The story quickly gained traction on social media and was picked up by several national news outlets. Various campus groups came to the student's support, demanding that more be done about racism on campus, and the American Civil Liberties Union (ACLU) took the student's case, stating that she was profiled for 'eating while Black'. The president of Smith College promptly apologised for the incident having taken place, stating that the student's encounter with campus staff was part of a wider pattern of 'living while Black' harassment cases occurring nationwide. One of the members of staff was immediately placed on paid leave without any discussion, while others were subject to online abuse, which prompted one staff member to leave their job and another to check into hospital with existing health issues that were exacerbated by the stress and anxiety of the publicity surrounding the incident.

A law firm specialising in discrimination cases was subsequently hired to thoroughly investigate the incident to determine whether any college employees had violated the college's affirmative action policy covering race relations on campus. After several months of investigation, the law firm published a 35-page report[2] concluding that there was no sufficient evidence of discrimination or harassment on the part of any of the employees with whom the student interacted, nor was there any evidence for the student's allegation that this was part of a wider pattern of racialised harassment that she had personally experienced on campus. The student was approached because there was a summer camp for teenagers taking place on campus. Given that the camp-goers were minors, all involved with the camp were required to have background checks and certain sections of campus were reserved for camp attendees and staff, including the dormitory cafeteria in which the student was approached. Student workers who were on campus in the summer were explicitly told not to use these buildings. What is most remarkable, however, was the college president's response to the report. Despite the report's conclusive findings that there was no evidence of discrimination or harassment, the college president nevertheless claimed that the report 'validated the student's lived experience', and that it was 'impossible to rule out the potential role of implicit racial bias' (Powell, 2021). Despite the facts of the case, the student's personal experience and interpretation of events could not be determined to be a false interpretation of reality.

The case is interesting for the present discussion for a number of reasons. Firstly, it shows the dangers of having subjective empirical experience and personal interpretation as a legitimate basis for the concept of social harm. For the student in question, her interpretation of interactions with campus staff as an incident of racially motivated suspicion and harassment was a deeply held personal truth. This was her empirical experience of events, and she was absolutely certain that this was the reason behind her being approached by campus staff. On the other hand, the testimony of the accused staff and the facts surrounding their conduct and interactions with the student reveal a truth that is diametrically opposed to her own. How are we to decide between these respective truths when using personal experience as a universal barometer for harm? This speaks to McGowan's (2018) point that all universals are, paradoxically, predicated upon what is absent. When we try and understand the universal as that which is *present,* this always entails an exclusion. It is always a particularity masquerading as a universal, and therefore we articulate the true universal in terms of what gets left out. For example, who are we *not* referring to when espousing the need to promote universal principles of equality, inclusivity, and diversity? To whom do we not imagine that these terms apply? Similarly, when trying to establish personal experience as a universal basis for harm, we must ask: whose personal experience and interpretation counts most, whose counts less, and, in certain situations, whose does not count at all, and why? The universal of personal experience either leads us back to a deadlock in which everyone's personal experience and interpretation counts equally, or if we privilege one individual's personal experience over another, it leads us to a particularity masquerading as a universal.

The response of the college president is another reason for this case being of interest to our present discussion. In concluding that it is impossible to rule out the potential role of implicit racial bias, the college president effectively rules out the possibility of innocence in cases such as these. Since such implicit bias is often unconscious, making the perpetrator unaware of its influence, it becomes impossible to prove or disprove whether the decision of staff members to approach the student was racially motivated, irrespective of factual accounts of their actual conduct and decision-making processes. The primacy of personal experience and interpretation results in a dangerous situation where the presumption of innocence in such cases is replaced by the impossibility of innocence and in which guilt is assumed even when it cannot be proven. We therefore remain trapped within the emotivist deadlock described above. Nor is this an isolated case. There are others which more explicitly challenge the principle of the presumption of innocence based upon personal interpretation that they are unsafe. One such case is that of David Miller, a professor of political sociology who was dismissed by the University of Bristol over allegedly anti-Semitic comments made during lectures. During the investigation prior to his dismissal, the Union of Jewish Students (UJS) denounced the university for continuing to allow Professor Miller to teach while under investigation. This decision, the UJS write in their letter, '*assumes his innocence* in a very serious case of antisemitic conduct'[3] (emphasis added). In Weberian terms, it seems we are reverting away from 'formal rationality' (law based on facts that take precedence over substantive principles) and 'substantive rationality' (rules that reflect moral principles), towards a 'substantive irrationality' in which decisions are made in a more arbitrary way based on conscience, intuition, and emotional evaluations (Weber, 1954).

So if this is not a suitable basis for the concept of social harm, we might choose to adopt Hall's (2012) notion of a core-periphery model of harm, in which a set of universally agreed upon core harms co-exists alongside a more subjective and relativised periphery. Hall is no doubt correct that such a core-periphery model must eventually come into being. However, as he readily acknowledges, there appears to be little consensus on which harms should be placed in which category, or how and where the line between core and periphery should be drawn. Some in academia have followed liberal criminology's fetishistic attachment to hard-line social constructionism by declaring that '[l]ike crime, [social] harm is clearly a social construction' (Millie, 2016: 5), with no ontological reality whatsoever. Of course, claims that harm has no ontological reality would be dismissed out-of-hand by those individuals and families experiencing, for example, the concrete reality of desperation and perpetual anxiety that stems from being indebted to legal yet hyper-exploitative high-interest moneylenders, or the debilitating effects of gambling addictions upon the individual's mental, financial, and familial well-being. Therefore, it would seem that social harm certainly has at least 'one foot in reality' (Hall and Winlow,

2015) and for this reason is distinct from and more ontologically robust than the socio-legal category of 'crime'.

Along these lines, Pemberton (2015), among others, has offered an ontological approach which argues that social harm constitutes the compromising of human flourishing through the systematic denial of access to basic human needs like healthcare, education, safe working practices, and so on (Doyal and Gough, 1984, 1991). Pemberton's approach, however, is a fundamentally *ethical* one, a point exposed by Lasslett (2010). However, the central role played by ethics in Pemberton's account is not necessarily a subjective flaw that corrupts the otherwise 'objective' concept of social harm. On the contrary, ethics is an unavoidable and indispensable facet of the concept of harm. The problem with Pemberton's approach is that ethics has not been given sufficient attention, and the ethical models underpinning this work have instead been an unacknowledged, inherited, and therefore under-scrutinised element of Pemberton's approach to the conceptualisation of social harm. Indeed, what is most problematic about Pemberton's approach is not that he roots social harm within a fundamentally ethical notion of human flourishing. It is that he fails to elaborate on the content of what constitutes human flourishing, thereby leaving it relatively open-ended and failing to emphasise the necessity of a collective and *positive* notion of liberty and human flourishing which pushes past liberalism's negative ideological attachment to sovereign individualism. Pemberton himself, in addition to other thinkers such as Hillyard and Tombs (2017), has claimed that a human needs approach to the concept of social harm does indeed work from this position of positive liberty and actively addresses the problems with liberal individualism's negative ideology. But such an argument is specious. It fails to understand that such a conception of positive liberty, reminiscent of the liberal philosopher Isaiah Berlin (2002), buttresses the individual's negative liberty, rather than directly challenging it. While theories of human need claim to espouse a notion of *positive* liberty (Doyal and Gough, 1984, 1991; Pemberton, 2015), what this really amounts to is a slightly more ambitious, welfare-oriented, and socialistic brand of negative liberty with a different name. It extends the traditional negative liberties of the right to life; freedom from torture and freedom of expression and so on to include 'human needs' of equal access to physical and mental health services; education and personal development; and employment, among others.

However, this does not constitute a substantive departure from the philosophy of liberal individualism. This is because the term 'human flourishing', which is positioned in this literature as the ontological and 'ethical' foundations of the concept of social harm, is employed in such a way as to deprive it of its original meaning and remove it from its context as part of a wider conceptual scheme which made the term functional. Human flourishing is originally an Aristotelian term which presupposes human beings possess a collectively understood *telos*: a purpose and perfected state of being or end towards which we are constantly striving. But within this social harm literature, there is no discussion of what constitutes 'human flourishing'. The criteria for human flourishing are very much left open for the individual to decide, allowing the term to work within the confines of liberal individualism quite comfortably. Under this framework, therefore, positive liberty is defined as the provider of basic material needs and services for individuals to enact their individual freedom to behave according to their sovereign view of 'human flourishing'. To thrust a particular conception of human flourishing, a particular type of life which is deemed 'good' upon the individual is, within the liberal universe, to 'sin against the truth of … man' (Berlin, 2002) and begin down the slippery slope to totalitarian horror. Positive and negative liberty thus collapse into one another, and Pemberton's needs-based 'human flourishing' approach is left in its individualised and pluralistic form. This opens up questions regarding the limits to these pluralised notions of human flourishing. What happens when one individual's flourishing conflicts with and potentially harms another's, and in the event of such a conflict, whose human flourishing is privileged and why? This returns us once more to the situation described by MacIntyre above in which moral discussions around what constitutes social harm become a manipulative clash of wills.

Pemberton's approach encounters a further problem related to the above. The human needs that are listed as pre-requisites for human flourishing – and whose denial or jeopardisation is argued to constitute a form of social harm – often embody certain ideals which are incommensurable. Two of these, for example, are that of freedom and security, and Pemberton often refers to the latter in an economic sense. These are two ideals that simply cannot be judged from the same standpoint and can often come into conflict with one another. The issue of border policy, migration, and the impact upon workers' wages is an example. The ethical ideal of freedom would suggest that people should be able to move across borders freely and with ease, relocating across the world as they see fit. According to this ethical ideal, it would be wrong to constrain their free movement and put prohibitive barriers in place. However, free movement of labour has also been shown to have a detrimental impact upon wages in nations receiving an influx of migrants, particularly in low-wage precarious forms of work (Vargas-Silva et al, 2016). Access to a wider pool of labour without a proportionate increase in available jobs affords capital the opportunity to drive wages down, which is precisely why free movement was a favoured policy of neo-liberal thinkers who believed it would force the market to innovate and become more efficient (Hayek, 1948 [1939]; Slobodian, 2018). Consequently, free movement of labour across borders compromises the economic security of the low-wage working class in the host nation, not to mention damaging the economies of nations losing large numbers of migrants, with research indicating that those most adversely affected are often migrant workers themselves (Vargas-Silva et al, 2016; Vickers et al, 2016).

This returns us to the problem outlined by MacIntyre (2011) at the beginning of this chapter. In the absence of a shared ethical background, how are we to decide between these competing ideals? How are we to rank order them and arbitrate between them when they come into conflict? Unfortunately, Pemberton's model has no answer for these dilemmas, and in practice what has occurred once again is an interminable debate that is incapable of resolving itself and which consequently takes on an increasingly emotivist character. Advocates of free movement try to deny or downplay the impact upon wages and economic security and dismiss their opponents as xenophobes, racists, or far-right nationalists rather than as low-wage workers concerned about their financial and employment security. Advocates of tougher controls on migration and economic protectionism denounce their opponents pejoratively as 'woke', 'PC', and disingenuous, concerned more about having access to cheaper goods and services than about the fate of migrants. Indeed, this was one of the key battlegrounds of the Brexit debate – perhaps the best recent example of the culture of emotivism.

In an effort to avoid these muddy waters and prevent the concept of social harm from becoming too nebulous, others such as Lasslett (2010) have argued for a much more rigid ontological approach to conceptualising social harm. This line of thought suggests that the concept of social harm should be detached from the question of ethics entirely, limiting its application to those processes, structures, and relations which disrupt or fail to preserve the organic and inorganic reproduction of human beings and their environment. Such an approach, it is alleged, allows criminologists and social harm scholars to remain more strictly focused upon the most truly serious forms of harmful practice which threaten the organic and inorganic reproduction of human life: exposure to toxic chemicals; the creation of food, water, or vital resource scarcity; or the denial of access to vital medicines which help to preserve and reproduce the vital organic properties of the human body, and so on.

While this approach certainly addresses and provides some ontological grounding to certain core harms, there nevertheless remains a much broader range of social practices and industries which, while perhaps more peripheral, we nevertheless do and arguably should call harmful. It is becoming widely acknowledged, for example, that the intensely comparative and envy-inducing culture of contemporary social media is cultivating widespread forms of depression, anxiety, and body dysmorphia among many individuals within society—particularly young people. Similarly, consumerism's competitive-individualist and ever-changing sign-value system, which connects personal self-worth and identity to lifestyle and consumption habits, are contributing to destructive levels of personal debt, existential angst, and other financial and mental health issues (Horsley, 2015; James, 2010; Raymen and Smith, 2017). Can we deny that these practices are immensely harmful and detrimental to the human condition and the social more generally, despite not *necessarily* threatening the organic and inorganic reproduction of all human persons? Can we only call such things harmful when they culminate in suicide or self-harm? Therefore, while Lasslett's (2010) approach should be commended for trying to establish an idea of the core harms upon which criminologists and zemiologists should focus, it remains conceptually inadequate as it severely constricts the broader conceptual application of social harm and negates its deeper critical potential. Moreover, as will be argued in the following chapter, the question of social harm can never be detached from ethics.

Majid Yar's (2012) approach, perhaps one of the most novel in the literature, grounds human needs, human flourishing, and social harm within Honneth's (1996) Hegelian theory of recognition. Here, Yar draws on Hegel's master-slave relation, in which a dominant subject (the master) enjoys ostensibly unrestricted freedom from the other (the slave), and in which the slave exists to serve the desires of the master and confirm their status as master. Of course, the master is in fact not autonomous. His status as the master is dependent upon the recognition of the slave. This leads Yar to argue that we are not autonomous self-subsistent entities as presented in standard liberal discourse. Rather, he argues that our identities are always socially interdependent and reliant upon their real and symbolic recognition by the other. This recognition is a fundamental need for human well-being. As he writes:

> The individual comes to know himself, to recognise himself as a being with particular attributes or properties, through the acknowledgement conferred by an 'other'. An individual's sense of worth remains mere 'subjective self-certainty', and hence uncertain of itself, unless that sense of worth (or 'idea-of-self') is affirmed by others.
>
> *Yar, 2012: 57*

Yar, therefore, establishes a series of elemental forms of recognition which he argues, 'establish at a fundamental anthropological level the "basic needs" that comprise the conditions of human integrity and well-being (what Aristotelians call "flourishing")' (Yar, 2012: 59). These forms of recognition are love, rights, and esteem. 'Each', Yar argues, 'corresponds to a basic element that is required to secure the subject's integrity in its relation to self and others .... From this viewpoint, social harms can be understood to comprise nothing other than *the inter-subjective experience of being refused recognition with respect to any or all of these dimensions of need*' (Yar, 2012: 59). One of the strong points of this approach, as Lloyd (2018) emphasises, is that it is multi-axial. It can link a number of complex zemiological phenomena together, without 'flattening' meaning or eradicating nuance. Another is that it attempts to establish a founding ethical concept to link together the somewhat heterogeneous set of harms studied by academics in this field.

Yar's approach has nevertheless encountered several criticisms. Pemberton (2015) has offered a legitimate empirical objection, arguing that notions of 'love', 'rights', and 'self-esteem' are far too vague and subjective to provide any stable foundation for the concept of harm. Hall's (2012) critique, on the other hand, is more substantive. Hall argues that such an approach fails to recognise the severed class relation within neoliberal capitalism, which renders the Hegelian master-slave relation redundant. In a previous era of more localised economic relations, the master (capital) needed the slave (mass labour). But today, through mass deindustrialisation, automation, the rise of finance capitalism, the mobility of capital, and the free movement of persons and labour, which provides capital with access to the entire world's labour force, the elite masters of neoliberal capitalism no longer depend on the recognition of the slaves. A significant proportion of global capital accumulation does not rely on labour whatsoever, and that which does has an enormous reserve army of labour at its disposal which significantly reduces the need for capital to concede recognition to labour. The master-slave relation, argues Hall, has been totally decoupled, to the extent that the elite never even come into contact with much of the global populace (Atkinson, 2016), let alone depend on them. Perhaps the strongest evidence for Hall's claim can be found in the aftermath of the Covid-19 pandemic. A common statement in the early days of the pandemic was that the lockdowns revealed upon whom we are truly reliant, namely, the working class. While the super-rich and professional middle classes were working comfortably from home during lockdown safely isolated from the virus, it was the couriers, lorry drivers, supermarket workers, warehouse employees, and shelf-stackers that kept everything turning. However, from April 2020 to July 2020, it was the world's billionaires who increased their wealth by 27.5% (Neate, 2020), and while there was temporarily a lot of sentimental and rhetorical recognition of the indispensability of 'keyworkers', this has not manifested itself into a particularly strong political will to bring an end to zero-hour contracts, raise the minimum wage, or make substantial improvements on workers' rights.

However, while Hall is absolutely correct, his critique arguably does not go far enough. In contemporary society, one could contend that the master-slave relation has not just been severed by today's elites and their financial power. The situation is far more severe. Postmodern-liberal capitalism's culture of competitive and cynical individualism has made many people in contemporary society extremely hostile to traditional social roles and 'mass' forms of collective identity, which are treated as archaic and restrictive 'dead weights' on our unique individuality (Winlow and Hall, 2012). This is a culture that has been cultivated by liberal capitalism's masters who have achieved that transcendent position of special liberty in which they no longer need to recognise the 'slave' or any other ethical customs or mores. This desire has arguably metastasised throughout the social body to the extent that it is not only that the slave's position is no longer recognised by the master, but that it is pre-emptively rejected and no longer recognised by the slave themselves. The contemporary subject, existing within an inefficient symbolic order, enters what Lacan describes as the Imaginary – a realm of misidentifications with images in the external world – viewing themselves not as the 'slave' but as a master-in-waiting. Is this not the desire of many individuals chasing fame on reality television shows, or entrepreneurs and social media personalities seeking followers in their drive to become 'influencers'? Indeed, this is largely a consequence of changes in the labour market in the late 20th and early 21st centuries, which has made it increasingly difficult for the subject to find value in the poorly paid, precarious, and emotionally degrading forms of service work that now dominate the Western labour market (Lloyd, 2018), particularly when there is no prospect of recognition or concession from late capitalism's masters. Therefore, the master-slave relation is not just severed by capitalism's elites but has been dissolved entirely from both sides, thereby making its reformation – as Yar advocates – impossible.

This dearth of conceptual coherence contradicts the confidence with which the language of harm is *used*. It suggests that the idea of harm currently possesses no such agreed upon criteria or standard that is effective, and that it is a concept that is employed somewhat intuitively and, therefore, arbitrarily. Harm is quickly reduced to pluralistic and individualised definitions of whether a behaviour or social practice is 'harmful' or not, thereby robbing it of its crucial ontological robustness. This is the precise view expressed by the likes of Millie (2016: 5) when he writes 'what I consider harmful behaviour may be quite different from what you call harmful, and it may change depending on context [...] there may be differences in what we perceive as harmless wrongdoing as well as wrong-less harm'. This is a plainly *emotivist* position applied to the concept of social harm.

There are also other issues with the contemporary study of social harm beyond this core problem, namely, the role of the individual within social harm studies and the somewhat overzealous disdain for a focus on the individual. Zemiology's reluctance to look at individuals stems from its core argument with criminology. Criminology, zemiologists argue, has been far too focused upon the individual at the expense of looking at wider systems, structures, and social processes which are harmful in and of themselves – irrespective of whether crime occurs or not – and often cause and generate the problematic socio-economic and cultural contexts in which crime probabilistically tends to occur. Relatedly, zemiology has taken issue with criminology's *legal* individualism. Why look at individual acts of crime which consist of minor and petty events when the scale and severity of such individual acts pale in comparison to the harms generated by the state, the corporation, and the dominant political, economic, and socio-cultural structures of our society?

While this legitimate call to move from looking exclusively individual acts to looking at the harms of systemic structures has been one of zemiology's most important and welcome interventions, zemiology has arguably been too keen to turn its eyes away from the individual. There needs to be some account of how such systems and structures come into being and reproduce themselves, for there are no systems without agents. Structures and systems do not operate autonomously of the actions and energies of individuals operating within them, and as certain critical scholars point out, we are not ideological dupes doing things without knowing it (Hall and Winlow, 2015; Žižek, 1989, 2000, 2008). In fact, we are the precise opposite. We *know* of the harms of climate change, yet we continue to take far-flung holidays abroad and use more and more non-essential carbon-intensive electronic devices and systems. We know of the low wages, poor conditions, and human rights conditions in which our clothes and commodities are produced, yet we continue to buy new clothes and keep up with the fashion. We know of these harms but perpetually disavow them from our conscious minds or engage in interpassive 'ethical consumption' which we know, deep down, is entirely ineffective (Pfaller, 2014; Smith and Brisman, 2021; Žižek, 2009). Nor are we the entirely oppressed 'reluctant subjects' of our present political-economic system, either. Such a position cannot account for the success and

longevity of a political-economic system that increasingly benefits a few at the expense of the many. Lloyd (2018) is perhaps an
exception to this trend of conveniently banishing the individual
from the zemiological stage. Applying ultra-realist criminological theory to the study of social harm, he observes that where
zemiologists see harm as a result of various inequalities and power
dynamics, ultra-realism sees those inequalities and power dynamics as stemming from a willingness to positively inflict harm on
others or negatively harm others through willing participation in
the systems that produce such harms (Lloyd, 2018: 24).

Therefore, the disquieting suggestion of this book is that concept of social harm appears to be in a seriously underdeveloped
state of disorder. Nevertheless, the systematic study of social harm
carries on undeterred, disavowing this knowledge. We find ourselves in the strange position of frenetically producing countless
empirical studies which document and describe myriad forms of
social harm whilst ignoring the proverbial elephant in the room
that there is a striking lack of social and academic consensus
regarding the parameters and ontological and ethical basis of a
concept which is the foundational starting point of zemiology and
an increasingly central concept for criminology as well. Perhaps
this is due to what is arguably a significant political and ethical
homogeneity among scholars in this field, whose application of
the concept to certain issues seems entirely self-legitimising, and
consequently not requiring much forensic re-examination of the
robustness of social harm's conceptual foundation. However, there
is a significant degree of discord in society more widely about
what is and is not harmful. Moreover, given that the concept of
social harm is proliferating and being applied to an ever-wider
array of issues, it is not unreasonable to foresee a time in the near
future where the absence of adequate conceptual foundations for
the concept of social harm and the absence of a shared and robust
ethical background begins to generate discord *within* this field as
well, as scholars begin to question with greater urgency the legitimacy of its application to certain topics and issues. Therefore,
the aforementioned proverbial elephant can be ignored no longer.
In order to work towards the establishment of some coherence
around the concept of social harm, we must begin from the beginning again and rethink the concept of social harm by returning to
some epistemological and ontological first principles.

Notes

1 The criteria to which they are referring is another typology of harm which expands upon and updates Hillyard and Tombs' (2004) original typology to reflect the synergistic and relational nature of harms along spatial, temporal, and gendered and racial lines. In this typology, Canning and Tombs refer to spatial and temporal harms, gendered and racialised harms, and humanocentric and environmental harms. However, to describe this updated typology as a set of 'criteria' for determining harm is somewhat generous. The typology itself offers no 'criteria' to address the concept of social harm's ontological and epistemological deficit; it simply lists and orders different types of harm. This much is indicated by the content of Canning and Tombs' quote.

2 A full copy of the report is freely available online at https://www.smith. edu/sites/default/files/media/Documents/President/investigative-report.pdf

3 It should be made clear that I am not speculating as to whether or not Miller was guilty of anti-Semitism in this instance. Whether he was guilty or not is irrelevant to the point being made here, which is simply that the UJS challenged the principle of the assumption of innocence before a full investigation and verdict had been completed. See the following link for the full letter: https://twitter.com/UJS_UK/status/1425730831528734723

References

Ahearne, G. and Freudenthal, R. (2021) 'The Health/Power/Criminality Nexus in the State of Exception'. *Journal of Contemporary Crime, Harm, and Ethics*. 1(1): 108–115.

Atkinson, R. (2016) 'Limited Exposure: Social Concealment, Mobility and Engagement with Public Space by the Super-Rich in London'. *Environment and Planning A: Economy and Space*. 48(7): 1302–1317. doi: 10.1177/0308518X15598323.

Atkinson, R. and Blandy, S. (2017) *Domestic Fortress: Fear and the New Home Front*. Manchester. Manchester University Press.

Berlin, I. (2002) *Liberty*. Oxford. Oxford University Press.

Bottoms, A. (2002) 'Morality, crime, compliance and public policy' in A. Bottoms and M. Tonry (Eds) *Ideology, Crime, and Criminal Justice: A Symposium in Honour of Sir Leon Radzinowicz*. Cullompton. Willan: 20–53.

Briggs, D. (2021) *Climate Changed: Refugee Border Stories and the Business of Misery*. Abingdon. Routledge.

Brisman, A. and South, N. (2014) *Green Cultural Criminology: Constructions of Environmental Harm, Consumerism and Resistance to Ecocide*. Abingdon. Routledge.

Canning, V. and Tombs, S. (2021) *From Social Harm to Zemiology: A Critical Introduction*. Abingdon. Routledge.

Carr, N. (2010) *The Shallows: How the Internet Is Changing the Way We Think, Read, and Remember*. New York, NY. W.W. Norton & Company.

Cooper, V. and Whyte, D. (Eds) (2017) *The Violence of Austerity*. London. Pluto Press.

Dews, P. (2008) *The Idea of Evil*. Oxford. Wiley.

Doyal, L. and Gough, I. (1984) 'A Theory of Human Needs'. *Critical Social Policy*. 4(10): 6–38.

Doyal, L. and Gough, I. (1991) *A Theory of Human Need*. Basingstoke. Palgrave Macmillan.

Eagleton, T. (2009) *Trouble with Strangers: A Study of Ethics*. Oxford. Blackwell.

Ellis, A., Telford, L., Lloyd, A. and Briggs, D. (2021) 'For the Greater Good: Sacrificial Violence and the Coronavirus Pandemic'. *Journal of Contemporary Crime, Harm, and Ethics*. 1(1): 1–22.

Hall, S. (2012) *Theorising Crime and Deviance: A New Perspective*. London. Sage.

Hall, S. and Winlow, S. (2015) *Revitalising Criminological Theory: Towards a New Ultra-Realism*. Abingdon. Routledge.

Hall, S. and Winlow, S. (2018) 'Big trouble or little evils: The ideological struggle over the concept of harm' in A. Boukli and J. Kotzé (Eds) *Zemiology: Reconnecting Crime and Social Harm*. Cham. Palgrave Macmillan.

Hall, S., Kuldova, T. and Horsley, M. (Eds) (2020) *Crime, Harm, and Consumerism*. Abingdon. Routledge.

Hayek, F.A. (1948 [1939]) 'The economic conditions of interstate federalism' reprinted in *Individualism and Economic Order*. Chicago, IL. University of Chicago Press.

Hillyard, P. and Tombs, S. (2004) 'Beyond criminology?' in P. Hillyard, C. Pantazis, S. Tombs and D. Gordon (Eds) *Beyond Criminology: Taking Harm Seriously*. London. Pluto Press: 10–29.

Hillyard, P. and Tombs, S. (2017) 'Social harm and zemiology' in A. Liebling, S. Maruna and L. McAra (Eds) *The Oxford Handbook of Criminology* (6th edition). Oxford. Oxford University Press: 284–305.

Honneth, A. (1996) *The Struggle for Recognition: The Moral Grammar of Social Conflicts*. Cambridge, MA. MIT Press.

Horsley, M. (2015) *The Dark Side of Prosperity: Late Capitalism's Culture of Indebtedness*. London. Ashgate.

James, O. (2010) *Britain on the Couch: How Keeping up with the Joneses Has Depressed Us Since 1950*. New York, NY. Random House.

Lasslett, K. (2010) 'Crime or Social Harm: A Dialectical Perspective'. *Crime, Law and Social Change*. 54: 1–19.

Lloyd, A. (2018) *The Harms of Work: An Ultra-Realist Account of the Service Economy*. Bristol. Policy Press.

Lutz, C.S. (2012) *Reading Alasdair MacIntyre's after Virtue*. London. Continuum Publishing Group.

MacIntyre, A. (2011) *After Virtue*. London. Bloomsbury.

Madden, D. and Marcuse, P. (2016) *In Defense of Housing*. London. Verso.

McGowan, T. (2018) 'The Absent Universal: From the Master Signifier to the Missing Signifier'. *Problemi International*. 2(2): 195–214.

Millie, A. (2016) *Philosophical Criminology*. Bristol. Policy Press.

Nagle, A. (2017) *Kill All Normies: Online Culture Wars from 4Chan and Tumblr to Trump and the Alt-Right.* London. Zero Books.

Neate, R. (2020) 'Billionaires Wealth Rises to $10.2 Trillion amid Covid Crisis'. *The Guardian.* 7th October 2020. Available at: https://www.theguardian.com/business/2020/oct/07/covid-19-crisis-boosts-the-fortunes-of-worlds-billionaires.

Pemberton, S. (2015) *Harmful Societies: Understanding Social Harm.* Bristol. Policy Press.

Pfaller, R. (2014) *Interpassivity: The Aesthetics of Delegated Enjoyment.* Edinburgh. Edinburgh University Press.

Powell, M. (2021) 'Inside a Battle Over Race, Class and Power at Smith College'. *The New York Times.* 24th February 2021. Available at: https://www.nytimes.com/2021/02/24/us/smith-college-race.html.

Raymen, T. (2019) 'The Enigma of Social Harm and the Barrier of Liberalism: Why Zemiology Needs a Theory of the Good'. *Justice, Power, and Resistance.* 3(1): 134–163.

Raymen, T. and Smith, O. (2017) 'Lifestyle Gambling, Indebtedness and Anxiety: A Deviant Leisure Perspective'. *Journal of Consumer Culture.* Retrieved from https://DOI.org/10.1177/1469540517736559.

Raymen, T. and Smith, O. (Eds) (2019) *Deviant Leisure: Criminological Perspectives on Leisure and Harm.* Switzerland. Palgrave Macmillan.

Scheffer, M., van de Leemput, I., Weinans, E. and Bollen, J. (2021) 'The Rise and Fall of Rationality in Language'. *Psychological and Cognitive Sciences.* https://doi.org/10.1073/pnas.2107848118.

Siedentop, L. (2014) *Inventing the Individual: The Origins of Western Liberalism.* Cambridge, MA. Harvard University Press.

Slobodian, Q. (2018) *Globalists: The End of Empire and the Birth of Neoliberalism.* Cambridge, MA. Harvard University Press.

Smith, O. and Raymen, T. (2016) 'Deviant Leisure: A Criminological Perspective'. *Theoretical Criminology.* Available at: http://tcr.sagepub.com/content/early/2016/08/10/1362480616660188.abstract.

Smith, O. and Brisman, A. (2021) 'Plastic Waste and the Environmental Crisis Industry'. *Critical Criminology.* 29: 289–309. https://doi.org/10.1007/s10612-021-09562-4.

Tombs, S. (2018) 'For pragmatism and politics: Crime, social harm, and zemiology' in A. Boukli and J. Kotzé (Eds) *Zemiology: Reconnecting Crime and Social Harm.* Cham. Palgrave Macmillan: 11–32.

Vargas-Silva, C., Markaky, Y. and Sumption, M. (2016) *The Impacts of International Migration on Poverty in the UK.* Joseph Rowntree Foundation. Available online: https://www.jrf.org.uk/report/impacts-international-migration-poverty-uk#:~:text=Significant%20effects%20of%20migration%20on,income%2C%20UK%2Dborn%20people.

Vickers, T., Clayton, J., Davison, H., Hudson, L., Cañadas, M.A., Biddle, P., Lilley, S., Fletcher, G. and Chantkowski, M. (2016) *'New Migrants' in the Northeast Workforce: Final Report.* Nottingham. Nottingham Trent University.

Weber, M. (1954) *Law in Economy and Society.* Cambridge, MA. Harvard University Press.

White, R. (2013) *Environmental Harm: An Eco-Justice Perspective.* Bristol. Policy Press.

White, R. (2019) 'Loving the planet to death: Tourism and ecocide' in T. Raymen and O. Smith (Eds) *Deviant Leisure: Criminological Perspectives on Leisure and Harm.* Cham. Palgrave: 285–304.

Wight, C. (2021) 'Critical Dogmatism: Academic Freedom Confronts Moral and Epistemological Certainty'. *Political Studies Review.* 19(3): 435–449. doi: 10.1177/1478929920942069.

Winlow, S. and Hall, S. (2012) 'What Is an 'Ethics Committee'? Academic Governance in an Epoch of Belief and Incredulity'. *The British Journal of Criminology.* 52(2): 400–416. https://doi.org/10.1093/bjc/azr082.

Yar, M. (2012) 'Critical criminology, critical theory and social harm' in S. Hall and S. Winlow (Eds) *New Directions in Criminological Theory.* Abingdon: Routledge.

Žižek, S. (1989) *The Sublime Object of Ideology.* London. Verso.

Žižek, S. (2000) *The Ticklish Subject: The Absent Centre of Political Ontology.* New York, NY. Verso Books.

Žižek, S. (2008) *Violence: Six Sideways Reflections.* London. Verso.

Žižek, S. (2009) *First as Tragedy, Then as Farce.* London. Verso.

2

SOCIAL HARM IN AN ERA OF LIBERAL CYNICISM AND ITS CONSEQUENCES

When scholars have embarked on an attempt to conceptualise social harm, the question which often seems to inform their efforts is: 'What *is* social harm?' Pemberton (2015) uses this precise language when reviewing the various attempts at defining social harm and attempting to provide a definition or conceptual framework of his own, acknowledging that 'up to this point, it remains difficult to discern what "social harm" actually *is*' (Pemberton, 2015: 18; emphasis added). Similarly, Canning and Tombs (2021: 51) employ this question – what *is* social harm? – as the subheading of a section in their book which attempts to wrestle social harm into some conceptual coherence. While beginning with such a question would seem to be an obvious starting point, I would argue that it is a false one that confuses subsequent thinking around the concept, for the phrasing of the question itself embeds within it an important but flawed assumption. When we ask, 'what *is* social harm?', the question seems to speak of the concept of social harm in the *abstract*, suggesting that it possesses a pure, objective, *a priori* ontological reality that is independent of whatever is being evaluated as the object or subject of harm. It is spoken of as if the objective *essence* of harm exists somewhere 'out there' in Plato's realm of Ideal Forms (Hall et al, 2020), waiting to be grasped and articulated into an elegant, indisputable, and timeless definition that captures harm's pure ontological reality and subsequently resolves all of our uncertainty.

DOI: 10.4324/9781003098546-2

This is not to say that social harm is purely a social construction that has no ontological reality. It is simply to acknowledge that social harm is an *evaluative* term; one that only makes sense when it is placed in relation to some object or subject. On its own, the question 'what is social harm?' is completely unintelligible. If we posed the question 'what is social harm?' in normal everyday conversation, the most likely response would be 'in relation to what?' Perhaps this explains why there is such a tendency to create typologies when attempting to conceptualise social harm. In the struggle to conceive an abstract answer to the unintelligible question 'what *is* social harm?', academics naturally drift towards the formation of typologies because it situates harm in a specific context and places it in relation to something. But as we have established, creating typologies of harm is putting the cart before the horse and they do little in helping us to establish a clear ontological, epistemological, and ethical basis for the concept of harm. Arguably, the abstract question 'what is social harm?' reflects changes in moral language and philosophy that attempted to establish abstract moral principles that were entirely divorced from the human *telos* and the shared goods and ends of social roles, practices, and political communities (MacIntyre, 2011); a process that occurred across several centuries that we will encounter in more depth later.

Therefore, it would seem we need a better starting question. I would argue that the better starting question – and one that should be the starting point for any harm-oriented research – is an epistemological one. Namely, how can we *know*, with confidence and good reason, that someone or something is being harmed and that someone or something is harmful? This question is the gaping epistemological void at the core of social harm research, and it is a question that, as the previous chapter endeavoured to demonstrate, is yet to be adequately addressed. Starting with this question forces us to go back and consider what it is we need to know about things – human beings, communities, institutions, the environment, and so on – in order to ascertain whether or not they have been seriously harmed.

A Return to First Principles

To begin, we must acknowledge a basic tenet of critical realism that we need to understand ontology before we can understand epistemology (Bhaskar, 1997; Hall and Winlow, 2015). Put simply, we can talk about this or that being harmed and this structure or that process as being harmful, but unless we have some inkling of what human beings and our natural and social worlds actually *are*, at an ontological level, then we are continually drawn back into the doldrums of assertive and manipulative emotivism. We must have some notion of the nature and the *telos* of human beings, social roles, institutions, and the environment before we can determine whether someone or something is being harmed.

When one thinks about the concept of social harm a little deeper, this much is perfectly clear. As stated above, social harm is an evaluative concept, and therefore can only function as part of a historical sequence. It is only intelligible and fully functional when it follows on the back of established criteria that are shared by the general population and by which we evaluate a given social role, practice, process, or form of behaviour (Raymen, 2021). To say that someone, something, or some group has been harmed is really to say that something has gone *wrong* with that person, thing, or group of people. But in order to establish that something has gone wrong, there must, by necessity, be a shared and agreed upon *goal,* purpose, nature, or ideal state of things that the person, institution, or social practice is trying to realise or maintain. For example, we can now claim with confidence that our global climate, environment, and various animal populations and eco-systems are being harmed because we have a clear ontological understanding of their nature. We know how these things are supposed to behave, develop, and interact under ideal conditions, and therefore we can tell when they are flourishing and when they are not. That is to say, we have a clear understanding of the *telos* of the global climate, eco-systems, and animal populations and a clear understanding of when they are flourishing. When we speak of children, we know broadly by what age they ought to have attained certain standards of language, movement, and motor skills, and capacity for cooperative social activity, among other things. Similarly, in order for the statement that contemporary academia is being *harmed* by the neoliberalisation of the university to be at all intelligible, there must first be some collective idea of the virtues, purpose, and *telos* of the university that is being damaged or is in decline.

This is the first step. The second step is being able to identify *why* the climate, child, or university is failing to move towards its *telos*. These reasons might have nothing to do with individual human or social processes, or they might only *appear* not to. For example, particular diseases among animals or humans that upon closer inspection are linked to human-generated pollution, developments in technology, toxic substances in consumer products, or political-economic and cultural changes. The Covid-19 pandemic, for instance, is now widely held to have resulted from the transmission of the SARS-CoV-2 virus from animals to humans, something which would seem to be an unfortunate occurrence of nature that has nothing to do with *social* harm. But as Malm (2020) has argued, this kind of 'zoonotic spillover' has been rising in recent decades due to increased human encroachment upon the natural environment and humans coming into closer contact with a wider range of wild animal species – something undoubtedly related to capitalist political economy and issues around deforestation. Similarly, when we say that academia is being harmed by the neoliberalisation of the university, we must be able to demonstrate with good evidence and argumentation that it is the processes of neoliberalism that are primarily responsible for the harm being caused and consider whether or not there are additional forces and influences at play. This second step is immensely important, and it is imperative that we remain open to all manner of diverse explanations and causes. But for the purposes of the present argument, I want to remain focused on this first step of understanding the nature of something. That is to say, its *telos*.

MacIntyre (2016) observes that we are entirely comfortable with this notion of the *telos* when talking about non-human things like eco-systems, dolphins, or gorillas. It is uncontroversial for scientists who study these things to speak of their 'nature', and when we say that this species or that eco-system is doing well or doing badly, 'our judgment is not expressive of our feelings, attitudes, or other psychological states. Its truth or falsity is determined by appeal to standards that are independent of the observer' (MacIntyre, 2016: 25). However, when applied to human beings, their social roles, and the various institutions and practices that make up our shared social, political, cultural, and economic life we move onto a teleological terrain with which the contemporary social sciences are often uncomfortable, instead preferring an emphasis on pluralism and autonomous individual choice. Some might disagree and counter this claim with the argument that the likes of Pemberton (2015) and others have framed social harm within the teleological language of 'human flourishing'. But as we touched upon in the previous chapter, if we examine things more closely, this is not really the case and Pemberton's conceptualisation of social harm could not be described as teleological in any meaningful sense.[1] Pemberton's (2015) approach is based on Doyal and Gough's (1984, 1991) theory of human needs, which is based on the liberal philosopher Rawls' *Theory of Justice*. Like Rawls (1971), Pemberton outlines a set of prerequisites, tools, resources, and protections required for human flourishing – what Rawls describes as a 'thin theory' of the Good – without offering a vision of what human flourishing actually looks like, of what it is to live a Good life, and to what ends these tools, resources, and protections should be directed. When it comes to the ends of life – of what 'human flourishing' actually entails and what one should do in order to achieve it – the autonomous choice of the individual is sovereign, and the *telos* is not just absent but prohibited. But in the absence of the *telos* and with 'human flourishing' left in an entirely individualised and therefore pluralised form, it becomes immensely difficult to develop a consistent notion of social harm within Pemberton's model. If we deprive ourselves of a shared vision of what constitutes human flourishing, how are we to evaluate whether or not this flourishing is being compromised or whether someone or something is being harmed?

Take the contemporary environment of social media as an example. On the one hand, commentators have argued that it is a toxic space that is detrimental to people of all sorts of biographies, but particularly young people and females. Moving past obvious examples of bullying, trolling, and hate speech, critics of social media have argued convincingly that it is a space that normalises comparison and unrealistic body-image ideals, fostering an online culture of pseudo-pacified competition as friends and influencers endeavour to induce envy in their followers through the display of one's exciting lifestyle, beauty, and consumer competence (Smith and Raymen, 2016). Facebook's own internal research shows that it is aware that platforms such as Instagram have a detrimental impact upon young women and girls (Wells et al, 2021). For such critics, social media is a harmful space that cultivates lack, anxiety, and dissatisfaction among its users, not to mention deeply narcissistic subjectivities. However, the counterargument is that for some people this very same cultural and digital space is extremely important to their own sense of human flourishing. It is a space that provides them with inspiration, motivation, and information; it is an indispensable platform for them to establish and maintain friendships with others, particularly as they transition to new places; and it is a deeply self-affirming digital-cultural space that constitutes a key part of their sense of identity and is an important source of self-esteem and being in the world (Slater et al, 2017; Thomas et al, 2017). It is a space that satisfies a number of the important human needs outlined by Doyal and Gough (1991), and its removal from their lives would be experienced as harmful to their own personal sense of human flourishing.

Now, a more robust Neo-Aristotelian conception of human flourishing asks what it is to live well. It asks questions as to what our energies and efforts should be directed towards, and what a good and meaningful life is for human persons in a diverse array of situations. Moreover, it asks these questions not in a pluralist and liberal-individualistic manner but in a way that seeks an objective answer, such that the initially subjective 'what is the good for me?' also becomes entangled with the broader question of 'what is the good for humankind more generally?' Pemberton's approach, on the other hand, does not venture into these waters. There are only certain prerequisites for human flourishing, the content of which is up to the sovereign individual to decide. This reticence to speculate as to what human flourishing actually involves and the preference to leave human flourishing in a more individualised form creates a problem for Pemberton's approach when it comes to examples such as the one above. The absence of a more robust conception of what constitutes human flourishing means that we are deprived of the means for telling the one group that they are mistaken in their belief that social media is instrumental to their own human flourishing, that it is not contributing towards their true good, and that such digital spaces are actually compromising their ability to truly flourish, and they should therefore direct their attentions and energies to other pursuits. Within the present context of liberal modernity which staunchly defends an autonomous sovereign individualism, such a stance would be seen as unbearably paternalistic. Consequently, we are left in a situation in which the very same cultural space is experienced as deeply detrimental to the human flourishing of one set of people and deeply instrumental for the human flourishing of another, with no available means for deciding between them and determining definitively as to whether social media is harmful or not. We are simply left with the rather unsatisfactory conclusion that it is harmful to some people and not to others. The added kick in the teeth is that those who do experience such spaces as harmful are left to wonder whether there is something wrong with them which makes them incapable of functioning well within such digital spaces.

This same problem reproduces itself in any situation or social activity that involves the choices and preferences of the individual. The absence of a more comprehensive account of human flourishing – an account of what it is to live well, of what it is to live a meaningful life, and what our energies should be directed towards – means that it becomes extremely difficult to determine that certain industries or practices are harmful *as such*. All we are capable of saying is that they *can* cause harm to *certain* individuals in *certain* situations. With reference to gambling, for instance, all we can say is how in some cases gambling can compromise the individual's economic security or mental health in harmful ways. But we cannot say any more than this. We have no grounds of saying that this is something that people should not be doing more generally, and that to truly flourish and live good lives they should avoid such activities and direct their energies elsewhere. Consequently, as long as such extreme cases remain in a relative minority, and so long as such industries and participants can craft ultimately false narratives which depict such practices as contributing to various individuals' own privatised notion of human flourishing, such harmful practices and industries can remain in place almost by default.

Indeed, my own ethnographic research into gambling encountered this very issue. We were investigating how the convergence of consumer culture and the technological developments of smart phones and betting apps were creating the emergence of what we termed 'lifestyle gambling'. Such a convergence, we argued, had allowed sports betting to slip its traditional moorings of the betting shop and become a fully socialised form of gambling that was embedded within wider networks of leisure, consumption, identity, and friendship, consequently becoming an increasingly integral part of the wider masculine weekend leisure experience. This is something that was being encouraged and capitalised upon by the gambling industry (Raymen and Smith, 2017), and we found such a convergence to have a significantly harmful impact upon many of our participants as indebtedness, mental health issues, and the breakdown of romantic and family relationships became an all-too-familiar part of their daily lives. While many of these individuals came to recognise the harmful nature of such gambling, others who were new to sports betting and had their gambling under a modicum of control found such lifestyle gambling to be an important part of their lives. It provided them with valued experiences of excitement and enjoyment in what they perceived to be otherwise mundane lives, and willingness to enter into such markets was part and parcel of their access to friendship and networks of socialisation. When we challenged our participants on the legitimacy of the gambling industry and whether or not it was harmful, the response was painfully predictable. Sure, they argued, certain people experienced harms related to this kind of gambling. But far more did not. Who were we to decide what they should do with their time? Who were we to decide what a truly good life entailed? In their opinion, such hedonistic enjoyment was part of the good life. Such liberal–individualistic responses are vindicated by statistics which show that only 0.5% of the population are considered to be problem gamblers, and industry-sponsored research which shows that such socialised forms of gambling actually *promote* responsible gambling (Parke et al, 2012). We will return to this point later when we discuss what I describe as the assumption of harmlessness that is prevalent in contemporary economic and cultural life.

Therefore, as suggested in the previous chapter, we must be careful not to forget about the individual. Systems, structures, industries, corporations, and institutions must be studied through the lens of social harm. But it is consumers who give such harmful industries both the ethical permission and the market demand to continue selling their harmful products, and in the absence of a more comprehensive account of human flourishing we have no grounds to stop them. This is something of a blind sport for social harm studies. Any Rawlsian approach to social harm – which at its core Pemberton's is – will struggle with this very issue, since Rawls' liberalism precludes any coherent or shared notion of the Good. For Rawls (1971: 192), virtues and ethics are not that which allow individuals to achieve their true end; but are rather a set of dispositions that incline people to follow the basic rules of justice. 'It is true', Rawls writes, 'that men, to live together, must agree on something; but they must not agree on fundamentals, or things they think in some religious sense most important, if by this one means the *one* proper form of life for a reasonable man to adopt' (Rawls cited in Forrester, 2019: 18).

As Forrester (2019) observes, the prominent neoliberal thinker Friedrich Hayek wrote that he had 'no basic quarrel' with Rawls. Consistent with his intellectual lineage, Rawls fundamentally rejects any notion of the telos. This rejection means that, for Rawls, the principles of justice should ensure the basic rules of how people are to interact in order to live harmoniously with each other and the basic needs and goods they should be assured of and afforded. When it comes to what *ends* should be pursued, Rawls maintains that the individual must remain entirely sovereign, free from any social, ethical, or theological guidance.

But as the likes of Milbank and Pabst (2016) and Žižek (2012) observe, this quite quickly produces a rather chaotic state of affairs. In the absence of the *telos* and with only basic rules to govern how people are to interact with one another, any judgment whatsoever is easily reframed as a form of 'discrimination', 'harassment', or 'stigmatisation' of the individual, contributing to the rapid expansion of legal rules and moral injunctions which attempt to guard against any form of normative judgment whatsoever. This results in a perverse situation in which the attempt to tackle harms become repositioned as harmful in and of themselves. Anti-obesity campaigns promoting healthy eating and fitness become accused of stigmatising and invalidating the self-worth of obese people (Johnstone and Grant, 2019; ITV, 2020). As Žižek (2012: np) queries, 'If there are no shared mores in place to influence the law, just the bare facts of subjects "harassing" other subjects, then who – in the absence of such mores – will decide what counts as "harassment"?' Once everything can be positioned as harmful or 'problematic' – to use a favoured term of cultural politics' contemporary parlance – then nothing is.

Furthermore, Pemberton's approach only really applies to individual human beings in an abstract sense. For example, it is difficult to ascertain how we would transfer Pemberton's model to understand how systemic social processes harm not just individuals but also specific institutions, social roles, life-stages, communities, or social practices. Again, given the Rawlsian underpinnings of Pemberton's approach via the work of Doyal and Gough (1984, 1991), this shortcoming is entirely unsurprising. Rawls (1971) defined justice in terms of the individual in an abstract sense, rather than within the context of a political community or a community of roles and practices. Rawls attempts to discern the principles of justice by imagining someone who, prior to their entry into society, is behind a 'veil of ignorance' and is completely unaware of what his or her position in that society would be in terms of their natural ability, wealth, class position, cultural capital, and so on. Rawls' wager is that someone in this position would choose the principles of justice he outlines. But by beginning his conception of justice by imagining someone about to enter into society behind a 'veil of ignorance', Rawls entirely severs the individual from that society. Like Hobbes' (2017 [1642]) 'mushroom people', this is an individual without any natural relationships or entrance into particular traditions, communities, or shared social roles, institutions, and practices. They are simply individuals pondering their best interests as *individuals* rather than as members of these more collective political and social communities. This thought exercise is designed to develop a notion of the right that is independent of any particular notion of the Good. It thereby prohibits from the outset any notion of shared goods, and justice simply helps to define and protect the individual's position *against* the community and the interests of other individuals.

This is not a minor point. Social institutions, social roles, and social practices offer rich contributions to our shared social life which we do not want to see damaged or jeopardised, and the absence or decline of which would be experienced socially, culturally, and individually as a deep loss. We can have economic security, high levels of education, safety at work, political freedoms, low levels of pollution and high life expectancy. But without healthy social institutions, social roles, and social and cultural practices, life would be very drab indeed and it would be extremely difficult to achieve 'human flourishing' in its traditional sense. Few would likely quibble with the conclusion that various social practices and institutions such as the university, journalism, politics, and the arts have been damaged or transformed in ways that are not only harmful to us as individuals, but harmful to our collective social, cultural, and political lives. But on what basis can we make this claim? As it stands, none of the existing approaches to social harm are equipped with a conceptual framework or criteria for determining whether or not these institutions, roles, or practices have been harmed, be it Lasslett's narrowly ontological approach, Pemberton's 'human flourishing' approach, Yar's recognition-based approach, or the various typologies that have been formulated. Given the term '*social* harm[2]', it is significant that the most sophisticated conceptualisations of social harm to-date seem to exclude vast swathes of 'the social' from their evaluative frameworks. This is not to say that in both everyday discourse and academic life people and scholars have not talked about these harms. It is simply to observe that the most prominent conceptualisations of social harm fail to provide a framework for determining on what basis we can say that this is the case.

For example, the late cultural theorist Mark Fisher (2014) has argued that 21st century culture is marked by an inertia that he refers to — following Berardi (2011) — as 'the slow cancellation of the future'. As Fisher is at pains to stress, his argument is not simply the case of a middle-aged man failing to come to terms with the contemporary cultural trends and tastes of the young, and asserting the nostalgic claim that things were better back in his day. His critique is more severe, claiming that 'it is just this picture — with its assumption that the young are automatically at the leading edge of cultural change —that is now entirely out of date' (Fisher, 2013: 7). In the contemporary context of capitalist realism, culture is struggling to produce anything that is truly *new*, and that the distinction between past and present has broken down and entirely blurred into one another. To make this point, he engages in a thought experiment around music:

> Rather than the old recoiling from the 'new' in fear and incomprehension, those whose expectations were formed in an earlier era are more likely to be startled by the sheer persistence of recognisable forms. It was through the mutations of popular music that many of those of us who grew up in the 1960s, 70s and 80s learned to measure the passage of cultural time. But faced with 21st century music, it is the very sense of future shock which has disappeared … Imagine any record released in the past couple of years being beamed back in time to, say, 1995 and played on the radio. It's hard to think that it will produce any jolt in the listeners. On the contrary, what would be likely to shock our 1995 audience would be the very recognisability of the sounds: would music really have changed so little in the next 17 years? Contrast this with the rapid turnover of styles between the 1960s and the 90s: play a jungle record from 1993 to someone in 1989 and it would have sounded like something so new that it would have challenged them to rethink what music was, or could be.
>
> *(Fisher, 2014: 7–8)*

Fisher goes on to recount other examples, such as his conviction upon first seeing an Arctic Monkey's music video in the mid-2000s that they were an obscure band from the 1980s that had only recently been unearthed. His explanation of the harm experienced by the social practice of music is rooted in the processes of neoliberal capitalism. The evisceration of the post-war welfare state, which previously provided young artists with an indirect source of funding (and therefore time), has deprived would-be musicians with some crucial resources for cultural experimentation. Combined with the relentless process of marketisation and its demand to produce records at an ever-faster pace, and there is in a tendency to turn out increasingly generic music based upon a model of what has already been successful, thereby reproducing what already exists.

But it is not just music. Numerous scholars have talked of the harmful decline of the university, as its traditional grand ideals and *raison d'être* have faded into ghostly traces amidst processes of marketisation and the commercialisation of knowledge, which encourages factionalism, careerism, and careful homogeneity with prevailing academic orthodoxy rather than a commitment to truth and the expansion of knowledge. Wedel (2014) has documented how transnational governance today is performed through informality, flexibility, and a blurring of roles and interests. She documents the emergence of what she describes as 'flexian' actors who, over the course of their careers, move seamlessly across sectors such as politics, finance, business, media, academia, and lobbying, often holding multiple roles across these sectors simultaneously. For example, the political representative who holds shares or sits on the board of a major corporation and is permitted to initiate parliamentary proceedings or sit on select committees in areas related to their outside interests (Green and Homroy, 2020). The journalist who ostensibly offers neutral and objective reporting, despite being employed by a PR firm who represent a particular political figure. The academic who offers expert medical or scientific analysis while also working for a think tank that is directly funded by a major pharmaceutical company. This blending and blurring of roles means that when these actors offer opinion or advice, it is unclear which hat they're wearing or in whose interests they're speaking and acting, such that we can never be sure if these 'flexian' individuals are serving the goods internal to their social roles. This degrades trust in major institutions and the health of democracy as a whole, reflected in the widespread cynicism towards politicians, distrust of public health advice, and disengagement with mainstream media. These vital social institutions have undoubtedly been harmed. But within the existing literature, there is currently no conceptualisation of social harm which can provide a basis upon which we can say so.

All of these examples speak implicitly or explicitly in the language of the *telos* of social institutions, social roles, and social practices. They speak in terms of how this *telos* has been corrupted or compromised. This is because social practices, as a complex form of cooperative human activity, have goods and standards *internal* to their practice that are distinct from the goods *external* to social practices, such as money, power, prestige, recognition, and so on (MacIntyre, 2011). We realise the *telos* of social practices when we pursue their internal goods and the virtues, qualities and excellences required for their attainment. This is what allows us to speak in functional terms of a 'good' university or academic, a 'good' politician, or a 'good' teacher. As MacIntyre points out, the philosopher David Hume was entirely incorrect with his 'is-ought' problem that a normative judgment of what one *ought* to do can never follow from a statement of what *is*. This, MacIntyre claims, has become a general principle of modern ethics, but it is quite easily debunked. If we accept the notion that social roles, practices, and institutions have a *telos*, then from the starting observation that 'She is a doctor', it is perfectly valid to utter the following judgment that 'she ought to do whatever a doctor ought to do'. The telos of these social practices demands that we accept the authority of shared standards of excellence required to judge them, but it also provides indicators as to when these practices are being harmed or are perhaps inflicting harm; such that they have diverged from their *telos* or that individuals, institutions, or communities are being systematically prevented from realising the *telos* of their social roles and practices. Social harm research has overwhelmingly focused on when social institutions, roles, and practices are *perpetrators* of harm. Given what I have argued to be the Rawlsian underpinnings of certain zemiological research and that Rawls' philosophy looks at institutions almost exclusively in terms of what they owe to individuals according to the principles of justice, it should be expected that zemiological research should wind up doing the same. But it is equally important that our conceptualisations of social harm can also provide a basis for determining when social institutions and practices are *being harmed* by certain structures, processes, and individuals. It may often be the case that a social institution is being harmful because it has already been harmed and drawn away from its telos in precisely the same way that criminologists often try to understand and explain the harmful actions of individual criminal actors in terms of the harms they have experienced throughout the course of their lives.

This is not to say that the teleological foundations of social harm that I am proposing render it a static and unchanging concept. Quite the contrary, social harm is a concept that must evolve and be carefully revised alongside changes in social reality. Research and deliberation must take place on what constitutes 'good' governance, 'good' policing, and so on. When considering these questions, we must consider the ends and purposes of practices, institutions, and social roles as part of a wider social and political community, but we should also consider of what conflicts are wrapped up within these practices, institutions, and roles. For it is through consideration of these conflicts that we can often come to realise our *telos* in these circumstances (see Anderson in MacIntyre, 2011: 191).

Climate change, for example, forces us to reconsider the goods internal to a variety of social practices. The practice of food production and distribution is one example. Under these environmental conditions, being a 'good' food producer and distributor involves producing nutritious food in a sustainable and environmentally friendly fashion, with greater emphasis placed upon growing, distributing, and consuming affordable food locally rather than the global importation and exportation of food with all of its environmental consequences. In contradistinction to Millie (2016: 6), who describes criminology and zemiology as a sort of 'bad-ology' – 'the study of bad stuff that happens' – this transforms social harm into a fundamentally positive concept which, in attempting to identify what is wrong with the world, is simultaneously involved in envisioning a better society and 'constructing an imagination for the type of lives we want to lead, the society we want to live in, and the subjectivities we want to cultivate' (Raymen, 2019: 150). But what is most important is that social harm retains, at its core, a coherent and *collectively shared* notion of the Good or the *telos* which can act as a benchmark against which we can evaluate various social practices and behaviours to make claims of 'harm' socially intelligible. As Pemberton has acknowledged, 'we gain an understanding of harm exactly because it represents the converse reality of an imagined desirable state' (Pemberton, 2015: 32).

However, as a society long guided by the principles of liberalism and has privileged individual choice and pluralism over shared goals and ends, this is precisely the vision that we lack. We lack a common conception of the human and social good, a clear and rational basis for determining what that common good might be, or a grounded understanding of ethics that extends beyond negativistic rights-based ethics in order to determine what can be genuinely conceived of as social harm (MacIntyre, 2011). The ultimate good is that of *negative liberty*: an open-ended, pluralistic, and criterionless notion of 'freedom' which is simply the absence of constraint other than law and *private* conscience. For the concept of harm, which includes but is not limited to the legal sphere and is an inherently social concept which necessitates wider public coherence than is demanded of private conscience, this is not a viable foundation. It is clear that we live in a time of deep discord in which discussion about our shared ends and goals – our *telos* – is more imperative than ever. But such deliberations are antithetical to postmodern liberalism's fundamental principles. In lieu of such deliberations and in order to avoid any excessive infringements upon the individual's economic or cultural sovereignty, political liberalism has put in place procedural rules and legalistic standards – such as human rights – to firmly establish the allegedly neutral 'ground rules' for 'fair play' between a plurality of individual freedoms in open competition with one another in the economic and cultural arenas (Rawls, 1971). These are a set of *a priori* 'evils' which effectively eliminate harm's inherently dialectical nature and, in doing so, compromise the concept's robustness and intelligibility. Alain Badiou (2001) argues that in liberal societies, 'evil is that from which the Good is derived', and that the good is understood as the mere *absence* of these a priori evils. But in a society of widening divisions and inequalities in which there is a growing sense of decline, decay, and a belief that life is and will continue to be worse than it was before, such claims are struggling to hold water. Moreover, in establishing such *a priori* evils, political liberalism has largely prohibited any fundamental rethinking of these procedural rules. As Adrian Pabst (2019: 111) has written: 'In the name of neutrality that only liberal ground rules can secure, debates about the common human good and the shared ends of human flourishing have been banished from the court of public political discussion'. In an age in which there is desperate need for real mutuality and the establishment of shared social ends and goals, discussion of shared social purpose has been replaced by adherence to procedure. Discussion of the collective Good has been replaced by legal rights and pessimistic economic contract, and we are told (and tell one another) that in such a diverse society, when it comes to matters of values and ethics, we can only agree to disagree and be satisfied to allow everyone the privilege of their individual choice. Consistent with its latent pessimism, liberalism has shed its originally hopeful and utopian clothes in favour of a garb more appropriate to its true nature as the 'realm of lesser evil' (Milbank and Pabst, 2016; Winlow, 2012). In our liberal society, there is no shared good, for this is always perceived as a mere front for despotic power (Fawcett, 2014). Therefore, as I have argued elsewhere, it is not merely that a consensus on what we consider to constitute harm is difficult to come by, but that the cynical individualism of postmodernist liberal capitalism *fundamentally precludes any such consensus being reached* (Raymen, 2019).

The reader should note that I speak of liberalism more generally here. I point this out because social harm scholars have been eager to discuss the ills of *neoliberalism* as a political-economic doctrine, but they have scarcely discussed liberalism more generally. A quick word search for 'liberalism' in these books and articles will return countless hits of *neo*liberalism, but rarely any substantive discussion of liberalism more widely. However, as Milbank and Pabst (2016) argue that the past 50 years of contemporary capitalism have been the story of an unspoken collusion of two liberalisms. At a basic philosophical level, the economic liberalism of the neoliberal-right and the socio-cultural liberalism of the liberal-left are essentially mirror images of each other. The classical liberals and contemporary neoliberals of the right have espoused principles of liberty in their efforts to curtail the scope of government's intervention in private property rights or the imposition of regulations upon business. Simultaneously, the socio-cultural liberalism of the left has advocated individual rights and freedom of self-expression in fields such as identity, consumer culture, and sexuality and permit government intervention insofar as it protects those basic liberties and ensures the avoidance of any mistreatment of the individual. This is the fundamental principle behind 'negative liberty' or John Stuart Mill's (2003) 'harm principle'. Of course, while they have been depicted as bitter enemies, these two liberalisms have long been in a tacit alliance that has served the interests of a post-industrial consumer capitalism grounded in notions of 'freedom' and 'choice' (Lasch, 1985).

The result has been the establishment of 'a new, scarcely questionable consensus masquerading as a pragmatic centrism that concealed its ideological commitment to limitless liberations and mindless modernization' (Milbank and Pabst, 2016: 13).

This is neither a caricature of liberalism, nor a denial of the significant differences between these wings of liberal thought. Rather, this is an attempt to penetrate the core *domain assumptions* and common characteristics shared by positions across the broad liberal spectrum, which have developed as the foundational basis of modern moral philosophy, politics, and perspectives on social harm (Raymen, 2019). All liberalisms across this spectrum concentrate liberty and moral authority within an individual that achieved sovereignty by rebelling against traditional collective institutions of moral theological, or political, authority (Berlin, 2002). They express a marked distrust of tradition, custom, and collective identities and associated responsibilities that are experienced not as sources of nourishment but as an oppressive weight upon the individual's creative freedoms. Even the natural world and human biology are seen as arbitrary impediments to the expression of individual freedom that must be dominated, mastered, and submitted to individual choice and desire. And they all reject the classical notion of human beings and their social roles and practices as possessing some natural teleological purpose and conceive of the human subject as a fully constituted and autonomous individual who freely chooses to enter into a society constituted only by floating and contractual social relationships that are always subject to renegotiation and potential exit (Deneen, 2018). For liberalism in all its various guises, freedom is the right to autonomously pursue one's privately defined notion of the Good life unimpeded by intrusive moral or political authorities (Winlow and Hall, 2013).

The Assumption of Harmlessness

As a consequence, our long-standing attachment to the negative freedom of liberal individualism and the cynical hostility towards a *positive* universal ethics has provided the ideal conditions for the preservation and flourishing of what I describe as liberal capitalism's *assumption of harmlessness*. There is also, I will argue, an equally erroneous assumption of harm*fulness* that is problematic in different ways and is related to the assumption of harmlessness, but I will deal with that at a later point. For now, I wish to stay focused on liberal capitalism's political economic assumption of harm*lessness*.

The assumption of harmlessness is not new. On the contrary, it was central to 17th century political arguments advocating for the expansion and embrace of nascent capitalist markets developing at the time (Hirschman, 1977). These were societies in the throes of the process of what Jean-Pierre Dupuy calls 'desacralisation', 'riven by civil strife and foreign wars, unable to look outside itself for the moral authority it once found in religion' (Dupuy, 2014: 9). The historian Albert Hirschman's influential book, *The Passions and the Interests*, returns to the work of the likes of Montesquieu, Bernard Mandeville, Frances Hutcheson, James Steuart, and David Hume, among others, to survey the intellectual climate of the time and explore the political arguments being made for capitalism before its total triumph. Hirschman discovered that, at the time, the predominant intellectual and political opinion among these leading intellectual figures was that economic self-interest and the individualised pursuit of private gain was perceived as the most effective antidote in restraining the violent passions. The atomisation of individuals, the creation of mutual indifference, and the cultivation of calculating subjectivities geared towards a selfish and individualistic preoccupation with personal affairs – what Frances Hutcheson described as the 'calm desire for wealth' – were embraced as a means of putting an end to the violent 'passions' for power, fame, and grandeur which had characterised the civil strife between feudal lords, religious groups, and the foreign wars of monarchs. In comparison to the 'passions', individualistic profiteering was seen as harmless and innocuous, captured by Samuel Johnson's famous remark that 'There are few ways in which a man can be more innocently employed than in getting money' (Boswell, 1933: 567). Hirschman notes that as peculiar as this argument may seem in the present context, 'Capitalism was supposed to accomplish what was soon to be denounced as its worst feature' (Hirschman, 1977: 132; see also Bloom, 2017). In the minds of these intellectuals, the impoverishment of social life and the violence of capitalist economy were to be put in service of the good as a means of *containing* 'real' physical violence. Dupuy[3] (2014), building on Hirschman's historical research, argues that the capitalist economy therefore *contains* violence in both senses of the word. The economy has a certain violence within itself – the aggressive, individualistic, morally ambivalent, and at times destructive pursuit of capital accumulation and socio-symbolic competition. Through a process of self-exteriorisation, this original violence also 'contains' violence in the other sense of keeping real physical conflict at bay (Dupuy, 2014; see also Hall, 2012a on the pseudo-pacification process). This violence, in containing itself, is put in service of the Good, and is thus transformed into the good itself.

With all of our hindsight on the ills of liberal capitalism, we may look back astonished as to how we could have ever taken seriously the claim that capitalism could contain violence or despotism. To do so, however, would display a lack of critical self-reflection on our current political-economic and cultural context. In the cynical and fatalistic era of 'capitalist realism' (Fisher, 2009) in which liberal capitalism is positioned as the least worst of all political-economic systems and all alternatives are dismissed as doomed to economic catastrophe and totalitarian disaster, it is not unreasonable to argue that this assumption of harmlessness is as clearly identifiable and functional as ever, albeit in a slightly different way. At this stage, readers might object that such a claim is obviously invalid. How can there be an assumption of harmlessness in contemporary society? After all, do we not constantly read and hear stories about the impending ecological consequences of our travel and consumption habits? Are we not witnessing calls for more careful scrutiny of the advertising practices of the gambling industry or the legitimacy of fixed-odds betting terminals (FOBTs)? Do we not see documentaries on TV exposing the hyper-exploitative employment practices of popular retailers who produce our clothes and ship our online purchases? However, it is this acknowledgment that is a central prerequisite to the contemporary assumption of harmlessness; an assumption which is established, quite paradoxically, upon an initial acknowledgment of the harm experienced by others that is to be *fetishistically disavowed* later on down the line (Žižek, 2008; see also Kuldova, 2019).

Indeed, we are permitted – even encouraged – to express a sentimentalist woe at the worst excesses of our political-economic system. We can make calls for a more humanist commercialism that truly *cares* about the planet, and champion awareness-raising about world hunger, gender equality, and so on (Eagleton, 2009; Žižek, 2009). This is the default setting of many contemporary celebrities, politicians, and business elites who are among capitalism's greatest beneficiaries. At the level of thought and speech, we can openly acknowledge that we are not true believers in capitalism (Žižek, 1989). But at the level of action, such thoughts and concerns must never intrude too far upon economic competition and the negative freedom of the sovereign individual to the extent that they demand transformative political-economic action, meaningful prohibition, or inspire genuine collective consideration of the ends of life. The freedom of the sovereign individual must not be threatened or constrained, and the obscene real of liberal-capitalism's competitive individualism must be tempered but not suffocated. As an economic system, capitalism cannot function under the extreme poles of anarchic individualism or genuine political or ethical pacification (Hall, 2012a). Therefore, the initial acknowledgement of harm described above is followed quickly by a series of defensive caveats. The assumption of harmlessness functions by first daring harm to be named and acknowledged, only to incite one of the interminable zemiological disagreements mentioned in the previous chapter which dismiss claims to the inherent harmfulness of a given practice or activity.

To use one example discussed above, if one were to demand the abolishment of the gambling industry and the prohibition of gambling due to rises in addiction, indebtedness, suicide, and other problems, one would be likely to immediately encounter rebuttals such as: 'Well not *all* people become problem gamblers, so why should everyone – including myself – be prohibited from gambling?' 'It's their individual choice, nobody is forcing them to gamble.' Or, even better, 'People will gamble regardless. Is it not better that the practice is regulated? After all, the gambling industry contributes huge benefits to the economy and employs lots of people. They give huge sums of money to various charities and donate money to help those with gambling addiction'. As a perfect example of Fisher's (2009) notion of *capitalist realism*, the reduction of the maximum stake on FOBTs from £100 to £2 was delayed by then-Chancellor of the Exchequer Phillip Hammond, citing the need to mitigate the loss of up to 21,000 jobs estimated by a report written on behalf of the gambling industry by accountancy firm KPMG. Similarly, when suggesting radical political-economic reforms and behavioural change to try and address climate change or attempting to institute a job guarantee programme to address poverty, the questions that often arise are not whether this is the right thing to do but 'can the economy afford it?' Is it too great an impingement upon people's individual liberty? Can governments afford to institute a job guarantee programme or a Green New Deal (Mitchell and Fazi, 2017;

Tcherneva, 2020)? Can we absorb the loss of the fossil fuel industry? What will happen to those nations and cities in the global South who are so heavily reliant upon our tourism? In attempting to reduce carbon emissions by scaling back global tourism, are we not condemning these already-deprived nations to further economic peril?

Consequently, the philosopher Slavoj Žižek (2009) observes that, within our current moment of 'cultural capitalism', this assumption of harmlessness has become embedded deeper than ever to the extent that it is almost universalised and has become significantly advanced in its techniques. Rather than simply accumulating capital and then giving to charity, in today's mode of 'cultural capitalism' our anti-consumerist duty to do something for the greater good is included *within the very act of consumption itself.* As Dupuy would put it, the harmful act of consumption *contains* the harms it produces in a self-exteriorising fashion, in both senses of the word. Žižek (2009: 53) cites a Starbucks advert which appeared in *USA Today* which is illustrative of this logic:

> When you buy Starbucks, whether you realize it or not, you're buying into something bigger than a cup of coffee. You're buying into a coffee ethic. Through our Starbucks Shared Planet program, we purchase more Fair-Trade coffee than any company in the world, ensuring that the farmers who grow the beans receive a fair price for their hard work. And, we invest in and improve coffee-growing practices and communities around the globe. It's good coffee karma ... Oh, and a little bit of the price of a cup of Starbucks coffee helps furnish the place with comfy chairs, good music, and the right atmosphere to dream, work and chat in. We all need places like that these days ... When you choose Starbucks, you are buying a cup of coffee from a company that cares. No wonder it tastes so good.

The ideological assumption of harmlessness, therefore, denotes the way in which contemporary liberal consumer capitalism 'contains' harm in both senses of the word in precisely the same way that Hirschman and Dupuy describe. It is acknowledged that there is a certain degree of harm within various social and economic practices, and even within the political economic system more generally. But this harm, it is claimed, is the 'price of freedom'. It is deemed necessary and put in service of the good. It develops the economy, it generates jobs, and keeps people fed, and it develops wealth which facilitates charitable organisations. It keeps at bay the greater harms of economic collapse, of intensified global poverty, or the power of the state or other authorities to have a say on how we live our lives or enjoy our leisure time. It is a harm that, put in service of the 'good', is transformed and rendered harmless – thereby relativising the concept of harm more generally. This goes a step further than Žižek's (2008) notion of 'systemic violence'. For Žižek (2008), the systemic violence (or harm) of late-capitalism is the 'zero-level' of the normal peaceful state of things, and we perceive 'subjective violence' – the conventional understanding of violence as performed by an identifiable agent against an identifiable victim through acts of crime or terror – as the perturbation of this 'peaceful' norm. Consequently, it serves to disguise the violence inherent to the normal state of things. But this arguably does not go far enough. It is not only that this systemic violence (or harm) provides the 'zero-level' against which we develop our conventional understanding of violence. More disturbingly, the perpetuation of the systemic violence of late-capitalism provides the foundations upon which our current liberal-individualist and pluralistic ideas of a 'good' life and a 'good' society are built. Our current individualised notion of the good is *dependent* upon a certain level of harm. This brings added meaning to Badiou's (2001) comment that in liberal capitalist societies, 'evil is that from which the good is derived'. Badiou, of course, meant that liberal societies imagine the Good as the *absence* of a set of a priori evils. However, reading Badiou through Dupuy, we can suggest that our idea of the Good is equally derived from the *presence* and acceptance of other 'lesser' but necessary harms or evils. It *contains* 'evil' (or harm) in both senses of the word. Consequently, this completely hamstrings our ability to denounce certain practices as harmful with confidence. There is a constant urge to let them off the hook as a 'necessary evil'.

Theoretical psychoanalysis is also instructive when looking at the assumption of harmlessness and the extent to which such an assumption exists in contemporary society, particularly Jacques Lacan's return to Freud and his conception of the superego. The common understanding of Freud's superego at its most basic is that it is the site of ethical regulation and prohibition. It exists in opposition to the raw instinctual drives, hedonism, and excesses of the id which are unmediated by social pressure or custom. It attempts to keep them in check through community laws, ethics, and customs which are internalised by the subject and function as a chief internal regulatory mechanism through inflicting a psychic guilt on the subject. This conception of the id and the superego are commonly represented in popular culture in cartoons, when 'angel' and 'devil' figures appear on the opposite shoulders of a subject caught in a dilemma. The devil figure represents the id, while the angel figure represents the superego, as they bicker between each other whispering conflicting messages in the ear of the subject who stands bewildered between them. Lacan's argument, however, is that this image of the superego as the site of ethical regulation is too simplistic. On the contrary, Lacan argues, the superego bombards us with *conflicting* messages. In order to fit in with the laws and customs of our community, we might have to act in deeply unethical ways. For instance, we might be caught between messages to live a good and ethical life, while experiencing the pressure to achieve wealth and fame which involve taking actions which are fundamentally contradictory to those messages. No matter what we do, we find ourselves experiencing a perpetual sense of guilt, unable to satisfy the demands of the superego. If we return to our cartoon analogy through Lacan's analytical lens, the devil and the angel figures do not represent the opposed forces of the id and the superego. Instead, they are both the representatives of the superego and its contradictory messages. Žižek (2002) takes this critique of the idea of the superego as an austere, ethical, and almost Protestant site of prohibition and regulation a step further. He argues that in contemporary society and culture, there has been a reorientation of the cultural superego towards a cultural injunction to *enjoy*. The contemporary superego commands us to enjoy and indulge, to pursue our desires, to transgress traditional symbolic laws and customs. Nowadays, Žižek argues, the superego is more likely to inflict guilt on the subject for *failing* to indulge our desires, capitalise on an opportunity, or foregoing certain experiences and pleasures because we have succumbed to other ethical injunctions or responsibilities. We are perfectly aware of this reorientation in contemporary society. It is demonstrated by widespread use of the popular acronym 'FOMO' (fear of missing out) to describe experiences of guilt at the prospect of failing to indulge in some consumer experience; and this sense of fear and guilt has been empirically evidenced in a number of different ethnographies on consumerism, leisure, and crime (Briggs and Ellis, 2016; Hall et al, 2008; Raymen and Smith, 2017; Smith, 2014; Tudor, 2018; Winlow and Hall, 2006).

Therefore, in some respects, we can position the assumption of harmlessness as a primary manifestation of reoriented nature of the contemporary superego towards an injunction to enjoy. The assumption of harmlessness has become embedded within our everyday language and subjectivities. We hear it in commonplace assertions such as 'well, there's no harm in that', or in rhetorical questions such as 'what's the harm?', or 'why shouldn't I do that?' This is because the ideological assumption of harmlessness has a dual-purpose. It serves not only to justify the existence of harmful industries or government practices and shield them from intense scrutiny. It also serves to protect *ourselves* from the traumatic realities of harm upon which our most mundane social practices and normalised consumer pleasures are based and produced. As mentioned above, social harm is not merely perpetrated by abstract global forces of political-economic structures, governments, and big businesses, independent of human facilitation. Social harms are undeniably symptoms of widening economic, cultural, and environmental inequalities that are systemic to capitalism. But as ultra-realist criminologists have reminded us (Hall, 2012a; Lloyd, 2018), such inequalities are created by individual actors living in liberal capitalist societies who have developed the kind of competitive-individualistic and narcissistic subjectivities that are willing to reject social and political solidarity in favour of an instrumental individualism that is willing to engage, directly or indirectly, in the perpetuation and tacit acceptance of these inequalities and harms.

Central to understanding this process is what Žižek (1989) revealed as late-modern capitalism's reversal of ideology. Traditionally, as Marx claimed, ideology was a process of *doing it without knowing it*. However, as mentioned above, Žižek argues that late-modern capitalism reproduces itself by doing the precise opposite. Within late-modern liberal capitalism, ideology functions at the level of *action* rather than *thought*. As mentioned above, we are invited to acknowledge the harmful nature of many of our economic and consumptive practices, so long as we continue to engage with them. We *know* that we are contributing to climate change and violently transforming local communities and the environment when we travel abroad on holiday to far-flung tourist destinations. We know that many of the consumer commodities we buy in shops or via online retailers are produced through the suffering of workers experiencing highly questionable employment practices at several points in the production and supply chain (Lloyd, 2018). We know that our enjoyment of a new sanitised leisure district within the post-industrial city is founded on the gentrification, spatial destruction, and dispersal of working-class communities. We are encouraged to decry the vulgarity of our consumer culture, so long as we continue to consume and engage in such leisure practices. As Žižek (2009) points out, it is at the precise moment in which we believe we have 'escaped' ideology that we are most deeply immersed within ideology. We tell ourselves that we have not been duped by the siren call of consumerism. We *know* deep down that the commodities we covet and fetishise have no real immanent magical quality. This surplus of meaning inscribed into the object is simply the workings of the clever advertising industries. At the level of thought, capitalism allows dissent and encourages us to declare ourselves as not among its true believers. This is what allows an immensely oppressive and destructive system such as capitalism to continue. It does not ask us to *truly* believe, but to only act *as if* we believe by continuing to work, shop, travel abroad, and so forth. As Winlow (2019) so pithily puts it: 'The archetypal capitalist subject these days articulates anti-capitalist rhetoric while lost in the [consumerist] pursuit of transcendental purity and awareness'.

It is important to note, however, that in most cases such 'knowledge' has little impact upon our enjoyment of the commodity, the gentrified space, or the tourist destination (Kuldova, 2019). We *know* that the shirt or the dress we have just bought has no immanent or magical qualities. They are simply clothes made of basic materials which are farmed in environmentally harmful ways, produced by borderline slave labour in some far-flung corner of some far-flung country. We *know* that Starbucks is not really an ethical company or that their beans are any 'better' than other high street chains. But irrespective of this knowledge, we still enjoy them. The structure of the ideological assumption of harmlessness – working in conjunction with liberal-postmodernism and capitalist realism's cynical rejection of all alternatives – grants us the means to act *as if we did not know* and thereby enjoy these products and lifestyles relatively free of guilt. Consequently, when confronted with questions about the legitimacy of a particular practice or action, the assumption of harmlessness inspires rhetorical questions which are the quintessential examples of liberalism's negative politics: 'why *shouldn't* children have smartphones?' 'Why *shouldn't* I go on three luxury holidays a year?' 'Why *shouldn't* gambling be an accepted leisure industry?' 'What's the harm?' This is not simply a semiotic coincidence. It is a habit of language that is a product of the assumption of harmlessness and liber-alism's negative ideology. When such questions are formulated in the obverse positive way – why *should* children have smartphones? Why *should* people go on three luxury holidays a year? Why *should* gam-bling be an accepted leisure industry? – we begin to move into the more teleological realm of considering the proper goals and ends of life, social roles, and social practices, and what it is to live a Good life. The assumption of harmlessness is designed to pre-emptively prohibit these kinds of questions and deliberations, instead favouring a nega-tive, open-ended and criterionless notion of individual freedom and moral sovereignty that has little consideration of the wider social body beyond the interests of the self. As such, it is immensely beneficial for capitalism's continued expansion and the opening-up of new markets.

In the absence of the *telos* and genuine deliberation about shared goods and ends, this stage of liberal capitalism's ideological assump-tion of harmlessness functions similarly to Popper's falsification prin-ciple. One need only find an example to contradict the statement that a particular practice or industry is inherently harmful in order to falsify it entirely, irrespective of the vast swathes of evidence to suggest that the statement is true. Both the ideological assumption of harmlessness and Popper's falsification principle are symptoms of our contemporary society's culture of pervasive cynicism towards all truth claims. While it is acknowledged that certain harms do occur, these are deemed to be individually and circumstantially specific, rather than systemic to the practice or institution itself. Or, if they are recognised as systemic, they are outweighed on-balance by the 'good' deeds performed by the industry. At its essence whatever social practice is under scrutiny is declared essentially harmless and remains in place almost by default. To return to gambling as an example, we simply require piecemeal reform, better regulation around the adver-tising of gambling, technological constraints upon games and gaming machines, more awareness campaigns around the risks of gambling, and so on. In fact, those who wish to abolish the gambling industry might risk the moralising accusations of stigmatising those who enjoy gambling. There are, we point out, individuals and organisations out there who are ironing-out the harms and the kinks in the system. There is no need to press for wholesale political-economic change. No need to challenge the destructiveness and validity of liberalism's primacy upon negative individual freedom. No need to confront the obscene real of capitalism too closely or deliberate too deeply over what should be the proper shared goals and ends of life. We just need to develop better tools to identify those who are vulnerable and at risk and develop strategies that can mitigate the worst excesses of their problems. Rather than being recognised as symptoms of deep social problems that are to be resolved by ambitious theoretical work that attempts to re-imagine a different ethical, political, and economic basis for society, social harms have become transformed into risks to be managed (Beck, 1992).

Subsequently, the assumption of harmlessness inspires a post-political fetishisation of piecemeal harm-reduction and harm-minimisation. The use of the term 'fetish' here is deliberate and important. In psychoanalytic theory, the fetish always covers over a lack and sustains a fantasy. In this scenario, the fetish of piece-meal harm-reduction covers over the lack of an alternative political-economic or ethical vision for the transformation of the way things are and sustains the fantasy of an active and socially progressive society trying to improve the lives and well-being of its citizens, despite the fact that piecemeal harm-reduction really amounts to a 'stodgy conservatism' and preservation of the status quo (Badiou, 2001). It is an example of a post-political *interpassivity* described by the likes of Žižek (1997) and Dean (2005). As Dean explains, when we are interpassive, something else – the fetishised object – is active on our behalf. We *think* and convince ourselves that we are being active, when in reality, by allowing the frantic activity of the fetish to act in our stead, we are being passive. Academics will be familiar with this feeling when downloading articles, buying books, or printing papers that we know, deep down, we are not going to have the time to read for a long time. However, in the act of downloading the articles and storing them in well-organised folders on our laptops or putting the books up on our cluttered shelves, we interpassively *feel* that we are productively engaging in the academic literature as if the laptop or bookshelf has read them for us, on our behalf. The assumption of harmlessness similarly instigates the frantic and interpassive production of descriptions of harm and harm-reduction studies which serves to *foreclose* what is necessary: deep ethical, philosophical, and political thinking which can provide the foundations for imagining and reconstructing a society on such a basis that these harms would be impossible.

Under these conditions, it is no surprise that so much academic focus and research funding within the social sciences is geared towards demonstrating 'impact' and developing 'pragmatic' and 'realistic' policy-oriented work to achieve piecemeal harm-reduction which transgresses neither the negative freedoms of liberal subjects nor the economic needs of capital too brusquely. Liberal catastrophists tell us that pursuing a new ethical and political basis for society is hopelessly idealistic and will only lead to new forms of inequality and oppression. It is a waste of time, the privilege of academics with the time, money, and material comfort to pontificate on such matters. It is better to try and make a difference by addressing and trying to manage people's immediate struggles and problems – the post-political administration of everyday life (Žižek, 2008). However, as Winlow (2017: 181) has argued, given the scale of the problems we currently face, such a stance is nonsensical. The true idealism is to believe that what exists can be rehabilitated, that technological fixes will emerge from corporate capital, and that the bad people and bad businesses will stop doing the bad things if we simply speak 'truth to power', raise more awareness, and show them the horrors of liberal-capitalism's worst excesses. It is to believe in the assumption of harmlessness and the fantasy that the harmful practices of capitalism are capable, through their self-exteriorisation, of containing themselves.

★★★

As Hall (2020) has written, history is a series of continuities and discontinuities. However, it is the contention of this book that the assumption of harmlessness constitutes a significant historical continuity which has been vital to the establishment and reproduction of capitalism throughout modernity up to the present day. In the following chapters, we begin a journey to understand how and why we have arrived at a point in history in which the concept of harm has become so relativised and incoherent that it has become a social, moral, and ideological norm to assert that the vast majority of our economic and consumer practices are, essentially, harmless.

Answers to this kind of question will usually lay blame at the door of some structural formation, political philosophy, or political-economic system. Conservatives decry liberalism's individualism, secularism, and disregard for cultural-ethical mores, customs, and traditions for creating a pluralistic and morally incoherent world. Liberals respond in kind by denouncing conservatism's attachment to regressive traditions, customs, and religions, and how such attachments force its adherents to turn a blind eye to obvious harms and prejudices, thereby relativising them. Marxist thinkers locate the problem within the current political-economic system of capitalism, whose incessant drive to accumulate surplus capital and open up new markets relies upon the exploitation of human nature, natural resources, and the relativisation of human, social, and environmental harms. Feminists might blame patriarchal social structures and notions of masculinity, while others might concoct analyses which combine a variety of these positions and others not mentioned here. These arguments have merit. We certainly cannot hope to answer the question which is the bedrock of this book without such analyses, and elements of them have already been on display in this chapter. The question necessitates a cultural history, looking at deep historical and cultural change in areas such as political economy, law, religion, political and moral philosophy, and their corresponding impact on economic realities, cultural, and ethical mores, and the language and concept of harm.

However, while being necessary, such analyses also seem to be insufficient on their own. As standalone explanations, they depict these structural processes and changes as simply happening, abstracted from the realities, desires, anxieties, and insecurities of individual men and women, who are positioned in a desubjectivising way as dupes – the passive and ignorant victims of history – who play no agentic role in the perpetuation, reproduction, and acceptance of the processes that have contributed to harm's relativisation or obfuscation. In fact, as is now well-established, we are subjects with quite a bit of knowledge of these processes and are agentic in their perpetuation than such analyses can allow (Hall, 2012b; Hall and Winlow, 2015). As emphasised earlier, one of the key contributions of ultra-realist criminology is the recognition that such processes and changes are not just products of abstract forces which operate independently of human facilitation and take place without wider support (Hall and Winlow, 2015; Raymen and Kuldova, 2021). Consequently, such analyses fail to explain at a deeper level why human populations ever allowed the perpetuation of certain harmful practices and the obfuscation of harm and related concepts to take place. The wager of the following chapter, which is a central aspect of the argument of this book, is that there is something within the nature of human subjectivity – our drives, the structure of the psyche, the nature of human desire, and the way we relate to the external world – that can help us to answer this question. Consequently, the following chapter approaches the concept of social harm through the lens of theoretical psychoanalysis. These lessons will then be deployed in the chapters that come after and situated within shifting historical, religious, political, cultural, and economic contexts.

Notes

1 It is worth observing that there is no mention of Aristotle or Aristotelian ethics anywhere in Pemberton's *Understanding Harmful Societies* book.
2 I am aware that in Pemberton's work the 'social' in social harm is meant to describe those harms which are caused and mediated by systemic social structures and processes. But nevertheless, the point remains. It is a shortcoming if the 'social' in social harm refers only to those social structures and processes doing the harming and not also those social institutions, formations, roles, and practices that are being harmed as a result of these processes.
3 It should be noted that Dupuy (2013, 2014) makes a larger argument about how this resembles the religious ritual of violent sacrifice. The original violence of sacrificing an innocent victim is performed to 'contain' violence in the sense of appeasing the wrath of Gods. In the case of Christianity, Christ, the son of God, is sacrificed on the cross and later realised to be innocent of his alleged crimes, encouraging humanity to follow his teachings of peace and to 'love thy neighbour as thyself' and thereby 'contain' future human violence. The original violence of the sacrifice is self-exteriorised and put in the service of the Good, is transformed into the sacred and therefore the good itself.

References

Badiou, A. (2001) *Ethics: An Essay on the Understanding of Evil.* London. Verso.

Beck, U. (1992) *Risk Society: Towards a New Modernity.* London. Sage.

Berardi, F. (2011) *After the Future.* Edinburgh. AK Press.

Berlin, I. (2002) *Liberty.* Oxford. Oxford University Press.

Bhaskar, R. (1997 [1975]) *A Realist Theory of Science.* London. Verso.

Bloom, P. (2017) *The Ethics of Neoliberalism: The Business of Making Capitalism Moral.* Abingdon. Routledge.

Boswell, J. (1933) *The Life of Samuel Johnson, LL.D. Volume 1.* New York: Oxford University Press.

Briggs, D. and Ellis, A. (2016) 'The Last Night of Freedom: Consumerism, Deviance and the Stag Party'. *Deviant Behaviour.* DOI: 10.1080/01639625.2016.1197678.

Canning, V. and Tombs, S. (2021) *From Social Harm to Zemiology: A Critical Introduction.* Abingdon. Routledge.

Dean, J. (2005) 'Communicative Capitalism: Circulation and the Foreclosure of Politics'. *Cultural Politics.* 1(1): 51–74.

Deneen, P. (2018) *Why Liberalism Failed.* New Haven. Yale University Press.

Doyal, L. and Gough, I. (1984) 'A Theory of Human Needs'. *Critical Social Policy.* 4(10): 6–38.

Doyal, L. and Gough, I. (1991) *A Theory of Human Need.* Basingstoke. Palgrave Macmillan.

Dupuy, J.P. (2013) *The Mark of the Sacred.* Redwood City. Stanford University Press.

Dupuy, J.P. (2014) *Economy and the Future: A Crisis of Faith.* East Lansing. Michigan State University Press.

Eagleton, T. (2009) *Trouble with Strangers: A Study of Ethics.* Oxford. Blackwell.

Fawcett, E. (2014) *Liberalism: The Life of an Idea.* Princeton. Princeton University Press.

Fisher, M. (2009) *Capitalist Realism: Is There No Alternative?* Winchester. Zero Books.

Fisher, M. (2013) 'Exiting the Vampire Castle'. *Open Democracy UK.* 24th November 2013. Available at: https://www.opendemocracy.net/en/opendemocracyuk/exiting-vampire-castle/.

Fisher, M. (2014) *Ghosts of My Life: Writings on Depression, Hauntology and Lost Futures.* London. Zero.

Forrester, K. (2019) *In the Shadow of Justice: Postwar Liberalism and the Remaking of Political Philosophy.* Princeton. Princeton University Press.

Green, C. and Homroy, S. (2020) *Bringing Connections Onboard: The Value of Political Influence.* IZA Institute of Labor Economics. Available at: https://ftp.iza.org/dp13392.pdf.

Hall, S. (2012a) *Theorising Crime and Deviance: A New Perspective.* London. Sage.

Hall, S. (2012b) 'The Solicitation of the Trap: On Transcendence and Transcendental Materialism in Advanced Consumer-Capitalism'. *Human Studies.* 35(3): 365–381.

Hall, S. (2020) 'Consumer Culture and English History's Lost Object' in S. Hall, T. Kuldova and M. Horsley (Eds) *Crime, Harm and Consumerism.* Abingdon. Routledge: 21–38.

Hall, S., Kuldova, T. and Horsley, M. (2020) 'Introduction' in S. Hall, T. Kuldova, and M. Horsley (Eds) *Crime, Harm and Consumerism.* Abingdon. Routledge: 1–18.

Hall, S. and Winlow, S. (2015) *Revitalising Criminological Theory: Towards a New Ultra-Realism.* Abingdon. Routledge.

Hall, S., Winlow, S. and Ancrum, C. (2008) *Criminal Identities and Consumer Culture: Crime, Exclusion and the New Culture of Narcissism.* Abingdon. Routledge.

Hirschman, A. (1977) *The Passions and the Interests: Political Arguments for Capitalism before Its Triumph.* Princeton. Princeton University Press.

Hobbes, T. (2017 [1642]) 'De Cive' in D. Baumgold (Ed) *Three Text Edition of Thomas Hobbes' Political Theory: The Elements of Law, De Cive, and Leviathan.* Cambridge. Cambridge University Press.

ITV (2020) 'Obesity Campaign Branded "Stigmatising" by Eating Disorder Specialists'. Available at: https://www.itv.com/news/2020-07-27/obesity-campaign-branded-stigmatising-by-eating-disorder-specialists.

Johnstone, G. and Grant, S. (2019) 'Weight Stigmatisation in Anti-Obesity Campaigns: The Role of Images'. *Health Promotion Journal of Australia.* 30(1): 37–46.

Kuldova, T. (2019) 'Fetishism and the Problem of Disavowal'. *Qualitative Market Research: An International Journal.* 22(5): 766–780.

Lasch, C. (1985) *The Minimal Self: Psychic Survival in Troubled Times.* New York. Norton.

Lloyd, A. (2018) *The Harms of Work: An Ultra-Realist Account of the Service Economy.* Bristol. Policy Press.

MacIntyre, A. (2011) *After Virtue.* London. Bloomsbury.

MacIntyre, A. (2016) *Ethics in the Conflicts of Modernity.* Cambridge. Cambridge University Press.

Malm, A. (2020) *Corona, Climate, Chronic Emergency: War Communism in the Twenty-First Century.* London. Verso.

Milbank, J. and Pabst, A. (2016) *The Politics of Virtue: Post-Liberalism and the Human Future.* London. Rowman and Littlefield.

Mill, J.S. (2003) *On Liberty.* New Haven. Yale University Press.

Millie, A. (2016) *Philosophical Criminology.* Bristol. Policy Press.

Mitchell, W. and Fazi, T. (2017) *Reclaiming the State: A Progressive Vision of Sovereignty for a Post-Neoliberal World.* London. Pluto Press.

Pabst, A. (2019) *The Demons of Liberal Democracy.* Cambridge. Polity Press.

Parke, J., Wardle, H. and Rigbye, J., et al. (2012) *Exploring Social Gambling: Scoping, Classification and Evidence Review.* Gambling Commission. Viewed. 24/03/2017. Available at: http://eprints.lincoln.ac.uk/16412/.

Pemberton, S. (2015) *Harmful Societies: Understanding Social Harm.* Bristol. Policy Press.

Rawls, J. (1971) *A Theory of Justice.* Cambridge. Harvard University Press.

Raymen, T. (2019) 'The Enigma of Social Harm and the Barrier of Liberalism: Why Zemiology Needs a Theory of the Good'. *Justice, Power, and Resistance.* 3(1): 134–163.

Raymen, T. (2021) 'The Assumption of Harmlessness' in P. Davies, P. Leighton and T. Wyatt (Eds) *The Palgrave Handbook of Social Harm.* Cham. Palgrave Macmillan: 59–88.

Raymen, T. and Kuldova, T. (2021) 'Clarifying Ultra-Realism: A Response to Wood Et. Al'. *Continental Thought & Theory.* 3(2): 242–263.

Raymen, T. and Smith, O. (2017) 'Lifestyle Gambling, Indebtedness and Anxiety: A Deviant Leisure Perspective'. *Journal of Consumer Culture.* Retrieved from https://doi.org/10.1177/1469540517736559.

Slater, A., Varsani, V. and Diedrichs, P.C. (2017) '#fistpo or #loveyourself? The Impact of Fitspiration and Self-Compassion Instagram Images on Women's Body Image, Self-Compassion, and Mood'. *Body Image.* 22: 87–96.

Smith, O. (2014) *Contemporary Adulthood and the Night-Time Economy*. London. Palgrave.

Smith, O. and Raymen, T. (2016) 'Deviant Leisure: A Criminological Perspective'. *Theoretical Criminology*. Available at: http://tcr.sagepub.com/content/early/2016/08/10/1362480616660188.abstract.

Tcherneva, P. (2020) *The Case for a Job Guarantee*. Cambridge. Polity.

Thomas, L., Briggs, P., Hart, A. and Kerrigan, F. (2017) 'Understanding Social Media and Identity Work in Young People Transitioning to University'. *Computers in Human Behaviour*. 76: 541–553.

Tudor, K. (2018) 'Toxic Sovereignty: Understanding Fraud as the Expression of Special Liberty within Late Capitalism'. *Journal of Extreme Anthropology*. 2(2): 7–21. https://doi.org/10.5617/jea.6476.

Wedel, J. (2014) *Unaccountable: How Elite Power Brokers Corrupt Our Finances, Freedom, and Security*. New York. Pegasus.

Wells, G., Horwitz, J. and Seetharaman, D. (2021) 'Facebook Knows Instagram Is Toxic for Teen Girls, Company Documents Show'. *The Wall Street Journal*. 14th September 2021. Available at: https://www.wsj.com/articles/facebook-knows-instagram-is-toxic-for-teen-girls-company-documents-show-11631620739.

Winlow, S. (2012) 'Is It OK to Talk about Capitalism Again? Or, Why Criminology Must Take a Leap of Faith' in S. Winlow and R. Atkinson (Eds) *New Directions in Crime and Deviancy*. Abingdon. Routledge: 21–40.

Winlow, S. (2017) 'The Uses of Catastrophism' in R. Atkinson, L. McKenzie and S. Winlow (Eds) *Building Better Societies: Promoting Social Justice in a World Falling Apart*. Bristol. Policy Press: 179–192.

Winlow, S. (2019) 'What Lies Beneath? Some Notes on Ultra-Realism and the Intellectual Foundations of the "Deviant Leisure" Perspective' in T. Raymen and O. Smith (Eds) *Deviant Leisure: Criminological Perspectives on Leisure and Harm*. Cham. Palgrave: 45–66.

Winlow, S. and Hall, S. (2006) *Violent Night: Urban Leisure and Contemporary Culture*. Oxford. Berg.

Winlow, S. and Hall, S. (2013) *Rethinking Social Exclusion: The End of the Social?* London. Sage.

Žižek, S. (1989) *The Sublime Object of Ideology*. London. Verso.

Žižek, S. (1997) *The Plague of Fantasies*. London. Verso.

Žižek, S. (2002) *For They Know Not What They Do: Enjoyment as a Political Factor*. London. Verso.

Žižek, S. (2008) *Violence: Six Sideways Reflections*. London. Verso.

Žižek, S. (2009) *First as Tragedy, Then as Farce*. London. Verso.

Žižek, S. (2012) 'Liberalism and Its Discontents'. *ABC Religion & Ethics*. 26th October 2012. Available at: https://www.abc.net.au/religion/liberalism-and-its-discontents/10100220.

3

SOCIAL HARM AND ITS RELATIONSHIP TO HUMAN SUBJECTIVITY

It goes without saying that we cannot hope to produce a metatheory of the relativisation of social harm without an analysis of how various religious, cultural, political-economic, and moral philosophical developments have coalesced to contribute to the practical and conceptual obfuscation of social harm. While these types of analysis are indispensable, nor can we look at these processes in a way that abstracts them from the drives, desires, and anxieties of human subjects. As with anything, the structural processes and changes that have contributed to harm's relativisation have not occurred independently of individual human subjects or without their energy, investment, and contextually constrained agency. Unless we adopt unrealistic and desubjectivising accounts which suggest that the vast majority of human beings have been ignorant dupes passively observing these processes and playing no agentic role in their reproduction, we must accept that the processes which have been most prominent in the relativisation and obfuscation of harm have been tacitly accepted, embraced, and perpetuated by individual men and women to varying degrees. This much is echoed by Dews (2008), when he writes:

> Unless we believe that social processes operate entirely above the heads or behind the backs of human agents, are we not bound to conclude that it is – at least in part – *we* who must

DOI: 10.4324/9781003098546-3

accept the blame? Where else are we supposed to put responsibility? Is there no sense in which we are 'what's wrong
with the world'– even though we are so frequently at odds
with ourselves, struggling to act in conformity with what
Korsgaard argues is the *core* of who we are: our 'humanity',
our 'moral identity'?

(Dews, 2008: 213)

The question, of course, is why? The previous chapter argued that
the concept of social harm must be connected to some idea of the
Good and the *telos* of human life and social practices. Both that
chapter and future chapters of this book argue that the loss of this
shared ethical background is deeply implicated in the ontological
and epistemological uncertainty surrounding the conceptualisation
of social harm, contributing to the emergence of an *emotivist* culture which makes relativistic zemiological statements *as if* they are
referring to some shared, impersonal criteria. This chapter pursues
a related, but slightly different line of enquiry. One which considers the possibility that in practice, at a deeper psychic level, the
concept of social harm is fundamentally rooted within particular
human drives, anxieties, and the structure of human desire, and that
this contributes to the tendency for the concept of social harm to
become relativised.

Given the current intellectual climate of the social sciences, such
an argument will inevitably raise eyebrows and inspire a certain
level of scepticism before it has even commenced. Many readers
will be tempted to pre-emptively dismiss it as far too 'reductionist'
or 'deterministic' to be taken seriously. This is a product of the
widespread and often unconscious commitment to liberal philosophy in the social sciences, which expresses a dogged belief in
the autonomous sovereign individual's ability to withstand natural
drives and forces, and instead prefers to skip past the thorny issue
of biology, the existence of multifarious drives, and the influence
of the unconscious on human behaviour, out of fears of patholo-
gising which have an undeniably dark history (Hall and Winlow,
2015; Raymen and Kuldova, 2021). However, we cannot just wish
these things away and disavow their existence and influence. Fields
such as world history, cultural anthropology, neuroscience, psychoanalysis, and emerging developments within criminology continually remind us that these things are real and have profound impacts

on human and social behaviour and development (Damasio, 2000; Ehrenreich, 1997; Ellis, 2016; Harari, 2015; Johnston and Malabou, 2013; Winlow, 2014). As such, rather than treat them as something to be shunned and avoided, they should be treated as potentially valuable intellectual resources which if utilised appropriately can be integrated into, and complemented by, historical, cultural, political-economic, and sociological analysis.

Recent criminological commentators have embraced such an approach, recommending that criminology curtails its tendency to cynically dismiss these aspects of human ontology (Wakeman, 2018). Wakeman, alongside ultra-realist criminologists, draws inspiration from the continental philosophy of transcendental materialism, which argues that we are first and foremost organic 'things' and that biological impulses and primal drives are far from mere social constructs (Johnston, 2008). Rather, human subjectivity – i.e. selfhood and consciousness – inevitably references bodily experiences, drives and unconscious desires. Symbolic processes have emerged to interpret these experiences, and mental processes have emerged to control and direct our thoughts, feelings, and actions as we engage with the world around us (Damasio, 2000). Adrian Johnston (2008) describes this as a 'more-than-material' subjectivity. Our subjectivity develops and emerges from corporeal experience, and while we cannot be exclusively 'reduced' to these original biological impulses, drives, or the structure of our psyche at the expense of studying the realm of culture, ideology, politics, economics, and so on, nor can we adequately explain human behaviour and the social world without some recourse to this 'anterior corporeal ground' (Johnston, 2008: xxiv).

Nevertheless, Winlow (2019) has argued that criminology and the social sciences more broadly have been largely content to adopt theoretical approaches which sidestep these issues and simplify the true complexity of human subjectivity; thereby leaving them unable to identify the fundamental forces that drive individuals and societies to engage in behaviours which harm others, the environment, or even sabotage their own interests. Consequently, scholars interested in the concept of social harm – including myself (Raymen, 2019) – have yet to consider the possibility that the way we practically conceptualise and relativise social harm might be partially rooted within certain base human drives and desires operating in particular historical socio-cultural and political-economic contexts.

But in overlooking these questions, the existing literature on social harm has arguably missed out on key insights into the nature of the concept of social harm, how it is deployed and conceived in practice, and its relationship to the ontology of human subjectivity.

What Are We Doing?

The previous chapter argued that rather than ask, 'what *is* social harm?', our fundamental starting point should be an epistemological question: how we can *know*, with confidence and good reason, that someone or something is being harmed and that someone or something is harmful? In simplified terms, the tentative answer given in that chapter was that we must first know the *nature* of things – their *telos* – before we can know whether they are flourishing or being harmed, and that we must be able to identify the generative processes that are causing them to fail to flourish or realise their *telos*. It was also argued that in our present society – which is overwhelmingly dominated by liberal thought – we are entirely averse to speaking in such terms, preferring instead negative liberty and autonomous individualism.

This chapter asks a related but significantly different question: in practice, what are everyday people actually doing and trying to accomplish when identifying social harm? Together these two questions, when situated within particular historical, socio-cultural, religious, and political-economic contexts, are crucial in understanding the tendency for the concept of social harm to become obfuscated and relativised. The former question identifies what we are lacking and what is necessary to establish some coherence around the concept of harm. The latter question, which is the subject of this chapter, will by the end of this book help us to identify how and why we have arrived at a point in which we lack the necessary shared foundations to establish zemiological coherence and consensus.

So what are everyday people actually doing when identifying social harm? For the time being, we should set aside all of the different theoretical and philosophical approaches to social harm and their underlying ontological, ethical, and political philosophical frameworks. If we strip the concept down to its most basic level, we are arguably always doing at least one of four things when identifying social harms. Firstly, we are attempting to identify and ward off the most immediate mortal and existential threats of death, pain, and suffering, whether that be to our individual person, our community, our environment, our entire species, or some other non-human species. Secondly, we are often protecting the self and one's sense of identity, meaning, and place in the world. Thirdly, and related to the two above, we are imagining and desiring some ultimate 'good' in the future – an ideal state of things for ourselves, our society, our community and families, our class, race, or gender, the planet, and so on – and identifying the behaviours, structures, and processes which actively corrode, undermine, or act as a barrier to this ideal. It should be noted that the latter is logically dependent upon the former. There can be no substantive vision of the Good without the preservation of life, the securitisation of the future, and the sense that our lives have purpose, value, and meaning worth pursuing. This leads us onto the fourth thing we are doing, which is ultimately seeking a condition of homeostasis. As Hall (2012b: 366) recognises, we yearn to 'defeat life's bothersome stirrings and seek comfort, calm, and safety'. It is why political systems and social orders often persist long after most people have recognised that they are no longer functional and are actively harmful and damaging to the well-being and life chances of the majority. It is equally why people may stay in stale and unhappy relationships or jobs that dissatisfy them, even in those instances where realistic alternatives are available. Upheaval, insecurity, and uncertainty in all of its various guises are not a condition that the majority of people enjoy (Young, 2007).

There is plenty of empirical evidence for this claim that we can come on to as the chapter progress. But in truth, we do not really need to look any further than the existing approaches to social harm in criminology and zemiology. At least one of these features, but often more, is present in all of the most substantive and influential attempts to conceptualise social harm (Gibney and Wyatt, 2020; Hall, 2012a; Hillyard and Tombs, 2004; Lasslett, 2010; Pemberton, 2015; Raymen, 2019; Yar, 2012). Hillyard and Tombs' (2004) typology of socially harmful practices begins at this most basic level of attempting to ward off imminent threats of death, pain, and suffering.[1] They begin with physical harms such as preventable deaths, injuries, and diseases caused by social structures, processes, and individual, corporate, and state actors. They then progress onto financial and economic harms which inflict poverty and generate socioeconomic marginalisation, before broadening out to incorporate more symbolic and interpersonal forms of harm such as emotional and psychological harms and cultural safety. Even the ordering of their typology indicates a progression from a basic set of 'core' harms organised around the denial of death and an aversion to material insecurity, toward a more complex and aspirational imagination of a future 'good' society. Hall (2012a) advocates the establishment of what he describes as a 'core-periphery' model to social harm. Here, we establish a set of consensual 'core' harms based upon universal ontological and ethical principles, which co-exist alongside a more relativistic set of peripheral harms related to ideas around the human good. The task of criminologists becomes that of establishing the basis on which we designate various processes, practices, and behaviours into the 'core' and 'peripheral' categories and determining where the line between core and periphery should be drawn and on what basis.

Lasslett's (2010) strict ontological approach is perhaps the clearest example of the drive to ward off threats of death and pain. As we briefly discussed in an earlier chapter, Lasslett argues that the concept of social harm should be detached from the question of ethics entirely, limiting its application to those processes, structures, and relations which disrupt or fail to preserve the organic and inorganic reproduction of human beings and their environment. For Lasslett, scholars of harm should remain focused on warding off death, scanning both the present and the horizon for any threats to life. By the same token, Gibney and Wyatt (2020) adopt a similar stance, albeit it within the language of ethics. Utilising an evolutionary perspective, they extend something akin to Lasslett's approach to all life, human and non-human alike. For Gibney and Wyatt, the 'highest good', the *summum bonum* of life, is the 'survival of [all] life', which leads to a revised definition of harm as *'that which makes the survival of life more fragile'* (Gibney and Wyatt, 2020: 12).

Yar's approach (2012), rooted in three basic forms of recognition – love, rights, and esteem – arguably reflects the individual's desire to protect their sense of self, their identity, and achieve some basic recognition in the world. For Yar, denial of recognition in any of these areas – and by extension the denial of human flourishing – constitutes a form of social harm. Similarly, the primacy given in the present moment to the individual's personal experience and interpretation of various forms of bigotry and prejudice – reflected in Canning and Tombs' (2021) argument that what is experienced as harm should be respected and count empirically as harm – is reflective of this desire to protect the individual's always fragile sense of self.

Other more expansive approaches to social harm demonstrate that the concept is equally derived from some future vision of an idealised 'good'. As we established in the previous chapters, despite its shortcomings Pemberton's approach similarly understands social harm as the compromising of 'human flourishing' through interpersonal or systemic denial of access to basic human needs like healthcare, education, economic security, freedoms of speech and belief, and so on. As quoted in the previous chapter, Pemberton (2015: 32) argues that 'we gain an understanding of harm exactly because it represents the converse reality of an imagined desirable state'. Gibney and Wyatt (2020) also root the concept of social harm within some vision of the Good, although theirs is a more negative conception reminiscent of Badiou's (2001) observation that in liberal societies evil is that from which the Good is derived, in which the Good is the mere absence of *a priori* harms. Likewise, in both this book and elsewhere, I have argued for the concept of harm to be rooted within a theory of the Good, albeit from a different philosophical perspective rooted in a neo-Aristotelian understanding of social practices which eschews the pluralistic individualism espoused by liberalism (Raymen, 2019).

The approaches to the concept of social harm listed above are certainly more complex than I have presented them here. Nor do I wish to impose an overstated and artificial unity on their approaches to social harm. All of them certainly attempt to tackle the question of social harm from vastly different and, in many respects, incongruent ontological, political, and moral philosophical positions. However, the important thing to take away is that despite these differences, the practice of identifying social harms nevertheless seem to continually circle around these four core elements: the preservation of life (understood in terms of both actual and symbolic life which I will expand upon below); the protection of one's sense of self and identity; the pursuit of some future ideal state or 'good' which seems to remain perpetually out of reach and in an unending state of arrival; and the establishment of a homeostatic state of calm, stability, and security. These features of the concept social harm reflect and correspond with certain fundamental human drives and aspects of theoretical psychoanalysis. Namely, the drive to deny death and avoid confronting the reality human finitude (Becker, 1973, 1975); and what psychoanalyst Jacques Lacan describes as the *objet petit a*, otherwise described as the 'lost object' or the 'object-cause of desire'. It is worthwhile to take a moment to explain these ideas and concepts in order to consider how they converge to relate to the concept of social harm and its relativisation.

The Denial of Death

As Gibney and Wyatt (2020) emphasise, the personal and collective social effort to avoid harm and death is truly ancient. Gibney and Wyatt cite the ten commandments as evidence for this, but we could go back even further. Living in the Anthropocene, contemporary human beings are certainly the species which exert the greatest influence on the earth's climate, environment, and its various eco-systems. We consume vast amounts of natural resources and have transformed the natural landscape to suit our lifestyles and endeavours. We hunt a surplus of animals for human consumption as food, fashion, sport, and trophies (Smith, 2019). Indeed, the image that many people have of archaic *Homo sapiens* is that of the hunter. However, as world historians and cultural anthropologists emphasise, this would be a mistake that would erase the vast majority of our nearly 2.5-million-year existence as a species (Harari, 2015). Early humans were an animal of marginal significance who sat squarely in the middle of the food chain. In comparison to other predators, humans' physical attributes have always been rather mediocre – smaller, slower, less physically powerful, and without the teeth and claws of other animals. Moreover, predators in this period would have far outnumbered humans, and while the various species of humans had extraordinarily large brains compared to other mammals, this tool had yet to pay significant dividends (ibid., 2015). Indeed, as research by both Ehrenreich (1997) and Harari (2015) indicate, early humans were likely to have been a potential source of prey, operating as hunters of smaller animals and as opportunistic scavengers, feeding off the kills of larger predators. These larger predators would have functioned as life-giving and life-taking animals – providing food to human scavengers through their kills, whilst also taking life through their predation on humans. They were a source of 'life power', and this, Ehrenreich (1997) argues, partially explains the practice of the sacrificial killing of animals or humans as offerings to a particular god or gods in different human societies and cultures throughout history. Ehrenreich shows that, across a diverse array of archaic societies and cultures, the gods carried a number of recurring characteristics. It was common, for example, for human societies to worship deities who took the form of animals or animal-human hybrids. But it is the ritual of sacrifice which uncovers the almost universal attribute of these gods. Namely, that they are carnivores that humans must feed with meat and blood if humans are to remain in their favour and avoid disaster. This pronounced desire to 'cheat death' and demonstrate a mastery over nature is, Ehrenreich argues, a manifestation of a deep-seated anxiety 'rooted in a primordial experience that we have managed, as a species, to almost entirely repress. And this is the experience, not of hunting, but of being preyed on by animals that were initially far more skilful hunters than ourselves' (Ehrenreich, 1997: 22). It is an anxiety of predation which, once a mastery over nature was established, would extend to other humans through war, conflict, and economy (Becker, 1975; Dupuy, 2014).

For millennia, however, human beings have lived in a state of comparative safety and security to earlier hominids and *H. sapiens*. Yet still, 'the idea of death, the fear of it, haunts the human animal like nothing else' (Becker, 1973: ix). Why? Ernest Becker dedicates himself to this question in *The Denial of Death* (1973) and *Escape from Evil* (1975), and the way in which this most base human fear continues to motivate and shape individual and collective human behaviour. The following quote summarises his opening contention, one that drives the rest of his thought. It is the idea that 'man [*sic*] is cursed with a burden no animal has to bear: he is conscious that his own end is inevitable, that his stomach will die' (Becker, 1975: 3). The obvious objection to be made here is that it is a plain falsehood that human beings are the only animals aware of their own mortality. But Becker is not merely referring to material death, but *symbolic* death. As Damasio (2000) argues, of all the creatures on Earth, human beings display the most advanced form of what he describes as *extended consciousness*, which provides the individual with an elaborate sense of self, identity, and biography, and which makes human beings extremely cognisant, almost painfully so, of their own position within the vast tracts of historical time. As Becker (1975: 4) argues, 'what man [*sic*] really fears is not so much extinction, but extinction *with insignificance*'. This awareness that we will not only die physically, but will also die a 'second' symbolic death in which we are forgotten or marginalised in the sweep of history makes the knowledge of our own finitude a particularly painful truth that is to be repressed or, better, transcended:

> [M]an [*sic*] wants what all organisms want: continuing experience, self-perpetuation as a living being. But we also saw that man…had a consciousness that his life had come to an end here on earth; and so he had to devise another way to continue his self-perpetuation, a way of transcending the world of flesh and blood…This he did by fixing on a world which was not perishable, by devising an 'invisible-project' that would assure his immortality […] We can see that what people want in any epoch is a way of transcending their physical fate, they want to guarantee some kind of indefinite duration, and culture provides them with the necessary immortality symbols or ideologies; societies can be seen as structures of immortality power.
>
> *(Becker, 1975: 63)*

Read through Becker, the arts, religion, the building of towering structures and monuments, culture, scientific breakthroughs, and political struggles are all, in part, projects in the pursuit of symbolic immortality and the drive to cheat death. Reflecting on the Romans and what drove them to their achievements, Saint Augustine wrote, 'What else were they to love, then, but glory, by which they sought to find even after death a kind of life in the mouths of those who praised them?' (Augustine, 1998: 215). One similarly hears politicians, athletes, entrepreneurs, artists, and scholars fret over their 'legacy' and how and for what they will be remembered. The most globally recognisable environmental activist movement has this most base human fear enshrined within its name – *Extinction* Rebellion. Such groups attempt to create an urgency of action around climate change by harnessing this fear and other powerful emotions like guilt by asking those in power to imagine the world they are leaving for their children – their living legacy – to inhabit. The 'culture wars' that have been fought for decades, and are reaching new levels of toxicity at the time of writing (Nagle, 2017), arguably derive their intensity from this drive to attain or retain symbolic immortality. On one side, historically marginalised groups strive to have their voices heard; their struggles, experiences, and traumas recognised; their intellectuals, poets, and novelists read; and demand greater representation in all aspects of public life. Their political opponents, particularly those from the white working class, push back by expressing the sense that they have already been left on the scrapheap of history in socio-economic terms, and the feeling that they are now being materially and symbolically demonised, blamed, and erased altogether by what they perceive as attacks on the traditions, customs, and symbols that represent them and their culture (Winlow et al, 2017). The very name of the movement 'Black Lives *Matter*', and its counter-hashtags #AllLivesMatter or #WhiteLivesMatter, tap into this drive to deny physical and symbolic death, the desire for recognition, and the fear of material and symbolic displacement and erasure.

What Becker argues that we must acknowledge, however, is the relative consistency with which the drive to deny death has propelled people to identify with what he describes as 'sources of life power' (Becker, 1975: 31). Religious belief in the supernatural power of an omnipotent God or Gods, for example, is perhaps the most prominent example of an 'immortality power structure', one that is ever-present in a diverse range of human societies and cultures across vast tracts of time. Notwithstanding a few exceptions, the vast majority of religions maintain some notion of an afterlife, be that through eternal existence in another realm such as in Christianity or Islam, or through reincarnation in Hinduism, Buddhism, and Sikhism. One could even argue that the assumption of harmlessness discussed in the previous chapter has its roots in religion. We have already alluded to the practice of sacrificial killings and offerings in archaic societies as a means of identifying with and maintaining the favours and protections of the gods (Ehrenreich, 1997; Siedentop, 2014: 10–11). As Dupuy (2014) observes, the original violence of sacrificing an innocent victim is performed to 'contain' the much greater violence of the wrath of the gods and ensure that it is directed elsewhere. The original harm of the murderous sacrifice is self-exteriorised and put in the service of the Good, and thereby transformed into the sacred and the good itself. Indeed, the etymological roots of the word 'sacrifice' have their roots in the Latin word *sacer* which means 'sacred' or 'holy' (Dupuy, 2014). They were, as Becker (1975: 6) puts it, 'techniques for sustaining life', and, at a more basic level, an identification with a source of 'life power'.

In archaic societies, leaders of tribes or clans would display tokens and trophies from their exploits of hunting and war (Harari, 2015). The teeth of a great predator were 'the essence [of its] vitality and murderousness' (Becker, 1975: 30) and displaying them positioned the individual as a 'big power man' particularly adept at defying death. As Becker writes, '[i]f you identified with these persons and followed them, then you got the same immunities' (ibid., 1975: 43). Various legends and origin myths are littered with stories of heroes who triumphed over beasts that threatened the security of the community or nation. Perseus over the Gorgon, Theseus over the Minotaur, St. George over the Dragon, David over Goliath (Ehrenreich, 1997). In more recent times, political and military leaders who have triumphed over larger-than-life enemies have been elevated to the status of popular Hero and physically etched into eternity with statues and monuments. Wainwright and Mann (2018) correctly characterise the looming environmental crisis as a Leviathan, which itself is a mythical and gargantuan sea serpent which features in several books of the Hebrew Bible. Climate change, therefore, is experienced as the return of a monstrous and absolute authority in the proper sense of the term, ready to exert its force over us and expose our frailties in the face of its indiscriminate power. Contemporary political, economic, or cultural leaders who can craft a narrative that promises economic and cultural security and sovereignty to the majority can rapidly gain almost cult-like followings. 'People', Becker writes, 'take…their own fears and desires and project them in the form of intense *mana* onto certain figures to which they then defer. They follow these figures with passion and with a trembling heart' (Becker, 1975: 50).

Indeed, some have argued that this partly accounts for the admiration, reverence, and dedicated support of those political figures who are openly – almost comically – corrupt, transgressive, provocative, outright criminal, and certainly harmful in their conduct. For some politicians, these gaffes are a political and electoral death sentence. Others seem to come away without a scratch despite significant press coverage and outrage from their opponents. For figures such as Donald Trump in the US, Putin in Russia, Modi in India, Boris Johnson in the UK, or Andrej Babiš in the Czech Republic, controversial public comments or revelations about their luxurious corruption seems to *enhance* their reputations and their 'power mystique' in the eyes of their supporters. As the likes of Kuldova

(2021) and Vaishnav (2017) have observed, these figures appear to be supported not in *spite* of their corruption, criminality, and their disregard for political custom and convention, but precisely *because* of these characteristics. Not dissimilarly to Becker's 'big power man' or Hall's (2012a) figure of 'special liberty', '[t]heir corruption and their lavish lifestyles are read as a sign that they can deliver, act, and do not shy away from breaking the rules to achieve their objectives' (Kuldova, 2021: 553). In doing so, their followers can participate vicariously in their power and indirectly perceive themselves as experiencing the benefits and protections of its afterglow.

It is no coincidence that such figures are typically populist politicians espousing messages of sovereignty, dignity, and cultural and economic security and have gained followings among many of the most socio-economically marginalised populations who feel they have long suffered profound indignities and whose most treasured cultural traditions, customs, and values are the targets for cultural obliteration from both external and internal forces. For the likes of Trump, every politically incorrect soundbite, every revelation of his misconduct or exemplar of corruption did not inspire his most ardent followers to question their commitment but, for a long time, strengthened it (Littler, 2019). As Trump himself said in 2016, 'I could stand in the middle of Fifth Avenue and shoot somebody, and I wouldn't lose any voters, OK? It's, like, incredible'.[2] At the time, his statement was arguably not entirely inaccurate. The louder his opponents yelled, mocked, and expressed their outrage, the greater his appeal and the more fervently his supporters rushed to his aide in the public arena. This was particularly the case given that the Anglo-American political left are perceived by many as disconnected, urban-based, middle-class cosmopolitan globalists who have abandoned the working class and relegated the importance of their economic concerns in favour of ordering the world around an intersecting hierarchy of race, gender, and sexuality, all the while holding a sneering contempt for the working class and their traditional tendency towards a cultural conservatism (Embery, 2021; Winlow and Hall, 2018). This was captured perfectly by Hilary Clinton's infamous description of Trump supporters as a 'basket of deplorables'. Trump – a New York billionaire – perversely managed to harness a public image as a voice for the provincial masses and a means for this 'basket of deplorables' to express their mutual contempt. Through the slogan 'Make America Great Again', Trump promised security, cultural protection, sovereignty, and a promise to reclaim the lost object of an imaginary American golden age, and his transgressions could not only be overlooked and relativised but enthusiastically embraced as an indicator of his invulnerability to the opinion of the professional political class, an invulnerability that his supporters believed would provide them greater protection and dignity.

Similarly, for a period during the early lockdowns of the COVID-19 pandemic, Amazon – a company often reviled for issues around their employment practices, tax evasion, and detrimental impact upon small businesses – was being heralded as saviours and described in some quarters as the 'new red cross' (Lee and Nilsson, 2020) for their role in the distribution of essential goods and keeping people entertained with various consumer items during lockdown. This is despite the fact that Amazon's CEO and major shareholder, Jeff Bezos – already the world's richest person – was amassing unprecedented wealth[3] at a time of significant economic hardship for millions. Similarly, corporations such as Alphabet and Apple were drafted into help with plans for the development of contact tracing apps. In times of crisis, these corporations, with their masses of wealth and resources, are treated as a source of 'life power'. They are a necessary evil to steer us through the darkest hours; much in the same way Fordist corporations like General Motors and Ford were heralded for their assistance with the war effort in World War II (Herman, 2012). Contemporary corporations and nation states are positioning themselves in similar roles as they make technological innovations, reorient markets, draft policy and engage in geopolitical jockeying which they claim will save humanity from the worst consequences of climate change and position their nation and their people as the beneficiaries of the new global economy in the post-COVID era (Raymen and Smith, 2021; Schwab and Malleret, 2020).

Psychoanalytic Theory and Its Relevance to Social Harm

The remaining three things, I argue, we are often doing when identifying social harms are as follows: firstly, protecting one's sense of self-meaning and identity; secondly, imagining and pursuing an ultimate notion of the 'Good' in the future; and thirdly, seeking a condition of homeostasis. What follows will attempt to demonstrate that Lacanian psychoanalytic theory provides a useful analytical toolkit for making sense of these features and how they can contribute to the tendency to relativise harm under different political, economic, and socio-cultural conditions. Therefore, I will provide a brief exposition of Lacan's conception of the subject and how subjectivity comes into being for those unfamiliar with Lacanian psychoanalysis, and then endeavour to display their relevance to the three remaining aforementioned things we are doing when identifying social harms.

Lacanian psychoanalytic theory's opening gambit is that human subjectivity and desire is driven by a raw sense of *anxiety* and *lack*. As human subjects we spend our lives searching for things to fill in this sense of absence and lack, the sense that something is missing from our lives; be that through loving relationships, faith in God, politics, personal achievements, lifestyle changes, sexual and leisure experiences, money, material commodities, and so on. For the likes of Lacan and Žižek, who build on the work of Freud, this is because we are born into a state Lacan describes as the 'Real'. This is not, it should be clarified, what we collectively experience as reality. Rather, it is a state of nature, a state of *before* culture in which we are simply alive in the world besieged by internal and external stimuli and deprived of any symbolic meanings, customs, or codes of socialisation which can help make our corporeal experiences intelligible. However, for continental psychoanalytic thinkers, this absence of symbolic meaning, a state without culture in which we exist from birth, is not a site of original freedom as it is presented in standard liberal discourse, but a profoundly traumatic experience (Žižek, 2000). Desperate to escape the 'terror of the Real' and establish some sense of homeostasis, this original lack and anxiety drives the subject outwards to actively solicit the coherence of the symbolic order's relatively rigid ideological systems and sets of symbols, customs, and codes, which pre-exist the subject and can 'fill up' the void of subjectivity by providing a frame of reference with which the subject can identify, orient itself, and make coherent sense of its life (Hall, 2012b).

A second related reason is, Lacan acknowledges, that in comparison to most other mammals we are born extremely prematurely. This has roots in physical anthropology, and our aforementioned hominid ancestor's status as a source of prey (Ehrenreich, 1997).

This status, it has been argued by various world historians and biological anthropologists, is one of the reasons why early hominids originally 'stood up' and became bipedal. Standing taller made it easier to scan the landscape for sources of danger and food, while freeing up hands for carrying food, signalling, and making weapons (Harari, 2015). But this also had a profound evolutionary knock-on effect on the development of human psychology and subjectivity. Standing upright narrowed the pelvis, which in turn narrowed the birth canal. Deaths in childbirth were common, and natural selection therefore favoured earlier births when the infant's body is smaller and more supple (Harari, 2015). Consequently, human beings live in a prolonged period of prematurational helplessness at the beginning of life in which we are dependent upon a parent or carer for absolutely everything: food, movement, personal cleanliness, clothing and warmth, comfort, security, and so on for years after birth. As small infants, therefore, we are essentially needy narcissists, the centre of the universe (Homer, 2005). The others around the infant simply exist to cater to their needs and whims with little conception of the other as a subject of its own, with its own needs and desires.

This stage is what Lacan describes as the Imaginary, which reigns supreme in the first eighteen months of life and is the site of his famous notion of the 'mirror stage'. In the Imaginary, the human infant seeks a sense of completeness by identifying with images outside of itself (Hall et al, 2008). The child begins to recognise themselves in the mirror image, be it an actual mirror or any source of reflection which responds to their needs and demands for recognition, usually a parent or significant other. They attempt to play with the image, controlling and governing its movements and actions, deriving a sense of pleasure from both the unity and completeness of the mirror image and their mastery over it, something that is in complete contrast to the infant's experience of their own bodies as fragmented, incomplete, and not entirely under their control. For Lacan, the infant misidentifies with this mirror image. It is a stage of primary narcissism and perfect unity with the image, in which there is no boundary or differentiation between the self and the image, but rather that both are one and the same. The image *is* the self. There is no genuine otherness and, as such, they are the only self in the world. But as Homer (2005) acknowledges, the image is also fundamentally alienating, in that it takes the place of the self.

The sense of completeness and wholeness is attained at the cost of the fact that this unified identity is that of an other – the mirror image. As Hall et al (2008: 177–178) write, 'from the very beginning, the human psyche is trapped in a delusional treadmill, oscillating between the alienating external image, in which it sees itself recognised and reflected as something other than its real self, and a sense of its fragmented internal body'.

This is the Lacanian Imaginary, a realm of misidentifications with illusory images and fantasies that provide a false sense of completeness, wholeness, and unity that is otherwise absent. Even as the subject matures and enters the social world, Hall et al (2008) argue, there is nevertheless an urge to regress to this prior stage of primary narcissism that can be felt at any time during the life course. This is no doubt aided today by a liberal-individualist culture which makes the whims and desires of the autonomous individual sovereign, and a consumer culture that offers up fantasy images of the self that become the imaginary essence of complete identity. Real and symbolic differences are obliterated in the Lacanian Imaginary, and Terry Eagleton captures the amorphous and ambiguous nature of the Imaginary perfectly in the following passage:

> In this peculiar configuration of psychic space, where there is as yet no clearly organised ego or centre of consciousness, there can be no genuine otherness. My interiority is somehow 'out there', as one phenomenon among others, while whatever is out there is on intimate terms with me, part of my inner stuff. Yet I also feel my inner life as alien and estranged, as though a piece of my selfhood has been captivated by an image and reified by it. This image seems able to exert a power over me which both does and does not spring from myself. In the domain of the imaginary, then, it is not apparent whether I am myself or another, inside or outside myself, behind or before a mirror.
>
> *(Eagleton, 2009: 3)*

In order to progress beyond the mirror stage and its primary narcissism, the child must grow out of this transitivism that Eagleton describes. They must be pried apart from their delusional unity and misidentifications with the *imago* and begin to recognise true otherness, taking up a place within the symbolic order – a defined system of roles, relations, customs, laws, and prohibitions 'in which you are an exchangeable function rather than a unique, irreplaceable, living, and breathing animal' (ibid.: 6). It is effectively the painful recognition that the child is not the only self in the world, that they are not the sole object of the other's desire, and that the other's desire is often directed elsewhere towards other subjects and objects. The fledgling subject must come to understand themselves and their place in the world within this pre-existing symbolic order through submission to and recognition from the Big Other, the set of institutions, customs, relations, and codes that are the politico-cultural and ethical embodiment of the Symbolic Order. For example, my status and identity as an academic with a certain level of expertise is contingent upon it being recognised by the Big Other. Therefore, I must submit to the Other's standards of what is required to be recognised as an academic. I must complete a PhD that is examined and passed by other experts in the field and awarded by an established university. I must publish academic research in reputable peer-reviewed journals and so on. In short, I must be recognised as an academic by the Big Other before I can legitimately claim to be one. Otherwise, my claim to be an academic would be hollow, a mere expression of personal feeling or desire that lacks any wider significance or recognition. This is the meaning behind Lacan's quip that language speaks us more than we speak language. Therefore, it is the Symbolic Order's complex system of signs, laws, traditions, and relations that allow the subject to escape the pre-symbolic terror of the Real – in which any sense of meaning or symbolisation is impossible – and progress beyond the unstable and narcissistic misidentifications and fantasies of the Imaginary. Provided that there is a healthy functioning Symbolic Order in place, it provides the subject with a relatively fixed, secure, and stable means to understand and orient themselves to the world around them, and it provides basic standards for what things mean.

It should be noted that the Symbolic Order and the Big Other are not 'real' in any objective or material sense. Rather, they are a form of collective fiction and shared ideological illusion generated by a particular set of social and ethical principles and values which reflect our vision of the Good life for individuals and society. As such, the Symbolic Order and Big Other can only exist and perform their function of ordering social life for as long as we act *as if they exist*. Therefore, the meaningful substance of the Symbolic Order is always an artifice and extremely fragile. Collective agreement and commitment to these shared fictions is imperative if we are to maintain a well-ordered, comprehensible, and liveable social space. This is what Žižek terms *symbolic efficiency*. Living under this framework, the subject is always a subject of ideology. Žižek rejects the common understanding of ideology as a 'false consciousness' which distorts reality and prevents us from grasping it as such. This is a common mistake perpetrated by social scientists and social harm scholars who view ideology as fundamentally oppressive and backwards, and view utopia as non-ideological (Copson, 2016). Rather, it is the collective belief and submission to the ideology of the Symbolic Order and the Big Other – be it utopian or regressive – that allows us to structure reality. Without the shared ideological illusion of the Symbolic Order – embodied by the Big Other's network of institutions – we are left without any meaningful substance through which to construct reality and confront the trauma of the Real or avoid regressions into the individualistic narcissism of the Imaginary.

In the contemporary context of an era of liberal postmodernism, this is significant in terms of the second thing we are doing when identifying social harms: protecting our sense of self-meaning and identity. As we explored briefly in the previous chapter, liberal postmodernism's faithless cynicism towards all forms of normativity, collective identity, authority, tradition, or belief has effectively been an all-out attack on the symbolic order itself (Milbank and Pabst, 2016; Winlow and Hall, 2012, 2013; Žižek, 2000). Reflexive critique of the symbolic order is healthy. But liberal postmodernism's error has been to conflate all forms of power with domination and systematically deconstruct the existing symbolic order without constructing a new one to take its place. Instead, every form of normativity, universal ethics, and collective identity is viewed as an unbearable oppression upon the subject's unique individuality, an impediment to its freedom and enjoyment. As belief in the symbolic order wanes and it becomes increasingly incapable of serving its purpose of providing symbolic efficiency, and as the sovereignty and autonomy of the individual are fetishised, the inevitable result is a widespread regression into the Lacanian Imaginary, with significant consequences for the relativisation concept of social harm.

We see this in the contemporary tendency to give significant primacy to the individual's personal interpretation, feelings, and experience when it comes to issues of harm or identity. Today, we must be increasingly careful not to contradict the individual who feels they have experienced some form of prejudice or harm in an inter-subjective encounter. Instead of consulting shared ethical or moral standards (or trying to construct them), we are often asked instead to try and place ourselves in the shoes of another in a Levinasian fashion, to exchange places with them, to try and feel what they feel as a means of accepting the validity of their experience. As in the Lacanian Imaginary, reality is as you feel it. As Canning and Tombs (2021) have suggested, what the individual experiences as harmful should count as harm in an empirical sense. To do otherwise is to commit the sin of invalidating the individual's personal truth. This is the Imaginary at work, operating in the absence of an efficient Symbolic Order, in which there must be no distinction between personal feeling and reality, and in which the individual's interiority and feelings are recognised and reflected in the external world in a form of perfect unity. We must avoid being too steadfast in our critiques of others for their leisure and consumer habits, fantasies, sexual inclinations, and/or desires – no matter how perverse or destructive – for these are the imaginary essence of identity, the stuff of self-meaning and self-worth, which provide the individual with a sense of being and wholeness, and which we risk stigmatising if we are too stringent in our appraisals. Interestingly, the term often used to describe this crime is that of 'othering'. This hatred of 'othering' is significant here because it marks a clear retreat from the Symbolic Order – which is fundamentally based on 'otherness' – into the Imaginary which endeavours to eradicate otherness in order to attain the impossible return to a primary narcissistic relation. For the subject trapped in the Imaginary, the sense of wholeness and completeness of the self must be protected against any kind of external shared standards, which of course makes it difficult to establish any consistency with regard to establishing what is and is not genuinely harmful, inevitably resulting in interminable emotivist exchanges discussed in previous chapters. This is an argument that we will pick up and elaborate upon in future chapters.

The Pursuit of the Good and the Problem of Enjoyment

Shifting gears, Lacan's thought around the transition from the Imaginary to the Symbolic also has relevance for the third thing we are arguably doing when attempting to identify things that we consider harmful. Namely, imagining some ultimate 'good' to be achieved in the future, and identifying those systemic impediments to its achievement. As I argued in the previous chapter, without some notion of the Good, we are deprived of any evaluative standard or measure against which we determine something to be 'wrong' or harmful. As G.K. Chesterton (1991: 91) once wrote, 'If we have no standard for judging whether anything is right, how on earth can we decide that the world is wrong?' The denial of death discussed above is intimately connected to this imagination of the Good. Any future imagined state of flourishing must first begin with the preservation of life and the sense that our future, the future of our children, our environment, our community, and our country is secure.

But to imagine and strive for some version of the Good is also, fundamentally, to *desire*. It is to imagine the arrival of a utopian condition in which we are individually and collectively enriched, have the opportunity to live full and meaningful lives, and experience a harmonious state of restful contentedness as opposed to a restless anxiety and anger that something profound is absent from our society and our individual lives. In many respects, this reflects a Lacanian psychoanalytic conception of desire that is rooted in *lack*, circling around an idealised but mythical lost object that will fill in the enduring sense of absence at the core of our being. In later chapters, we will deal with the problems and confusion that arise when confronted with individualised and pluralised notions of the good that are, in truth, rooted in *negative liberty*, and the role played by various moral and political philosophical positions, political-economic and cultural machinations in creating this confusion. For now, however, I want to remain focused on how the idea of the Good be inherently susceptible to instability and relativisation by considering its relationship to the *human desire*. To imagine and strive for some version of the good is, fundamentally, to desire; and for many theoretical psychoanalysts, desire is something that can never be satisfied (Freud, 1961; McGowan, 2013).

The insatiable nature of human desire is best explained by returning to the subject's transition from the primary narcissism of the Imaginary and their entry into the Symbolic Order. As we mentioned above, in this period the proto subject comes to the painful recognition that they are not the sole object of the (m)other's desire, and that the attentions and desires of (m)other are often directed elsewhere, towards some other subject or object. For Lacan, the child begins to ask itself, 'what am I in the (m)other's desire? What is it that they want?' It attempts to comprehend the other's desire which, as Žižek (2006: 140–141) emphasises, is an enigmatic, unknowable abyss both to the subject and the Other. Consequently, the infant, Lacan argues, comes to experience itself as *lacking* and as having lost something which can be reclaimed such that they can return to the primary narcissism of the Imaginary in which they exist in a blissful state of unity and wholeness. It is this original sense loss and lack which inaugurates desire. But of course, the child has not lost and is not lacking anything. Its desire is not only inaugurated around something that it does not have, but more importantly, something that *does not and cannot exist* (McGowan, 2013). This is what is described in Lacanian terminology as the *objet petit a*, the 'lost object', or the 'object cause of desire', which is simply the nothingness of lack itself. It is the production of a mythical lost object out of nothingness that generates desire.

The ramifications of this for human desire and enjoyment are tremendous. As a consequence, desire is organised around the perpetual cultivation and experience of dissatisfaction. Plenty of objects stand in for the lost object of our desire. Often, we cannot truly explain why we desire what we desire. Our efforts at explaining why we fall in love with a particular person instead of another or why we desire a particular consumer commodity over other similar commodities are often quite unsatisfactory. We list off a series of qualities, but these are often qualities that other people or other commodities possess, and all we are left with is the feeling that there is something within that person or commodity, some ineffable 'X' or surplus that is more than the mere sum of its qualities that makes the person or thing desirable. This surplus is the *objet petit a*, the mythical lost object that, once captured, will finally address the nagging sense of lack and dissatisfaction. But as McGowan (2016) observes, the moment the object is obtained it ceases to be *the* object, since the lost object does not actually exist. What we enjoy most, therefore, is the *prohibition* of the object of our desire and its pursuit. We enjoy the object most when it is inaccessible to us, because as long as the object remains out of our reach, we do not have to confront the emptiness of our own desire and the fact that it is not *the* lost object of desire. It can remain in its idealised state as *the* lost object, the thing that will fill in the lack at the core of our being. We repeat this process interminably, and this process is what

Freud describes as the death drive. As McGowan (2013: 35) clarifies, '[t]he death drive, despite the implications of the term...is not a drive to die and thereby return to an inorganic state. Rather than the death that occurs at the end of life, the death drive comes out of a death that occurs within life. It is a drive to repeat the experience of the loss of the privileged object that gives birth to the desiring subject'. Without the repetition of this loss, without dissatisfaction, we would cease to be subjects capable of desire.

A scene from the blockbuster movie, *The Blind Side* (2010), displays this process of desire and dissatisfaction perfectly in relation to consumerism. Leigh-Ann Tuohy (Sandra Bullock) is taking her newly adopted son, Michael Oher (Quinton Aaron), shopping for some clothes in preparation for Oher's attendance at a glamorous and elite private school. As they are browsing, Tuohy gives him some advice: 'Well, if there's one thing I know about shopping it's that if you don't love it in the store, you won't wear it. *The store's where you like it the best*'. This line represents the quintessential structure of desire in general, and particularly in relation to consumer capitalism. But it also provides a crucial distinction between *enjoyment* and *pleasure*. Acquisition of the privileged object is the beginning of pleasure, which is a short-lived experience of excitation that occurs at the *end* of our enjoyment and actually marks the *dissolution* of our enjoyment. The apex of our enjoyment is when the commodity is out of our reach, when it still holds 'the promise' of being the lost object of our desire. As soon as we obtain it, its mystical qualities begin to degrade as our pleasure fizzles out until it holds no allure for us and is cast aside. Quite simply, acquiring the object of desire deprives the object of its desirability.

This is precisely why companies like Apple and Samsung can endlessly release new smartphones that are in reality only marginally different from their predecessors and continue to sell them with success. It is equally one of the reasons behind the packaging of the iPhone, which is designed in such a way that the lid to the box cannot be ripped off quickly but must be eased off slowly, only for the phone to be encased within further layers of packaging which must be gradually removed and peeled off with care. This process of unveiling the new commodity and keeping it out of our grasp for as long as possible is so satisfying that, in 2020, Apple saw fit to make an entire television commercial out of it in the advertising campaign for the latest iPhone. When marketing a particular commodity, common sense would suggest that one should *advertise* what the commodity can actually *do*, the new features and capabilities it possesses in order to convince people that its purchase will be worthwhile. However, in the iPhone commercial, none of the features of the phone are displayed or shown off. Indeed, one barely sees the actual phone at all. The entire advert revolves around a man sitting down and removing the phone from the box, rubbing his fingers together, and smacking his lips as he prepares to peel off the plastic screen cover in an almost erotic fashion. What Apple seem to have grasped is that, in reality, what they are selling and what the consumer is buying is not really the phone itself, but rather the spine-tingling experience of anticipatory desire and enjoyment at the very pinnacle of its intensity. The lesson from McGowan (2013) is that capitalist society succeeds through our continuous misrecognition of where our enjoyment truly lies. We continuously misidentify the location of our enjoyment within the object of our desire when, in truth, the location of our enjoyment is in *desire itself* – the pursuit of that which does not exist. If one were to try and design an anti-capitalist advert, it would revolve around what happens moments after the original advert ended and the phone had been unpacked, depicting the profound indifference towards the phone that begins to set in merely minutes, hours, and days after that ecstatic moment of unwrapping.

Away from the realm of consumerism, the 'lost object' perhaps has its most obvious manifestation in political programmes, particularly those organised around nostalgia and the reclaiming of better days gone by. This is particularly pronounced in the politics of the far-right. While commonly depicted as hostile agitators provoking hatred and violence, or as 'white supremacists' espousing an imaginary ethnic superiority, qualitative research of the far-right in the 21st century tells a different story. The contemporary far-right view themselves in a more defensive capacity, existing in a position of cultural and economic *inferiority*, stripped of dignity and security (Winlow et al, 2017). Their view, according to this research, is that there is no place for them in the world of cosmopolitan liberal capitalism. They are not valued or cared about and have been tossed on the scrapheap of history, and therefore view themselves and their politics as a last-ditch vanguard protecting their own communities, jobs, cultural values, and traditions (Telford and Wistow, 2020). In the far-right imagination, at some earlier point in history people and communities like theirs had an unmitigated access to enjoyment that has since been stolen from them, usually by the immigrant other who are now perceived to have direct and unimpeded access to such enjoyment themselves. As Todd McGowan describes, they imagine themselves as having once had 'a direct relation with their privileged object and achieved a perfect satisfaction. We [now] exist in the aftermath of a fall, and from the perspective of the fall, we can see the possibilities for complete satisfaction in the world we have lost' (McGowan, 2013: 42). For the political far-right, if we could only get *back* to that point in time, everything would be alright, and our utopia could be realised. In the USA, this is captured by Donald Trump's slogan 'Make America Great Again', and the 'once was England' trope for groups such as the English Defence League (EDL). Reflecting upon their extensive ethnography among the EDL and other followers of the far-right in post-industrial Britain, Winlow et al (2017) write:

> We sat for hours with EDL supporters discussing these issues. Inevitably, a sense of frustration pervaded our discussions, and we were returned to the same issues again and again. Some of our most cogent respondents talked in considerable detail about neighbourhood decline and the current instability of working-class labour markets. There was often an aching sense of sadness and loss, but these emotions, especially in group discussions, could quickly change into anger and resentment. *Our respondents often struggled to accurately identify what had been lost.* They talked about the loss of community life and stable labour markets, *but they also often seemed to be grasping for something else, something they couldn't quite put their finger on.* Ultimately, it seemed to us, they were saddened by the loss of stability as such. To them everything appeared to be falling apart.
>
> *(Winlow et al, 2017: 106; emphasis added)*

After 40 years of neoliberalism, globalisation, deindustrialisation, and mass unemployment, it is perfectly legitimate for the working class to be nostalgic for a time of greater economic and cultural security, a time of shared ethics, and a time in which they and their communities felt valued for the role they played in a shared political, social, and economic project. We should not make the error common to left-liberal political commentators that nostalgia is entirely regressive (Earle, 2017; El-Enany, 2017; Judah, 2016). As Winlow and Hall (2022) argue, there is great political utility in a politics of nostalgia. Nostalgia can be a key driver for a more progressive, collectivist, and economically fair world. The point is that in the absence of a mainstream leftist-political narrative which locates the decline of post-industrial communities within such political-economic processes, their political *desire* is rooted in the reclaiming of a lost object, a golden era of bountiful prosperity and uninhibited access to enjoyment and satisfaction which, despite never truly existing in the way they imagine, they perceive as having been taken away from them by particular others who now have a privileged access to their lost enjoyment, sometimes resulting in ethno-nationalist politics (Winlow et al, 2017).

It should be noted that this is not the exclusive preserve of the far right. It is arguably just as prevalent in many aspects of contemporary leftist politics, which tend to imagine their utopias as existing in the future in a perpetual state of becoming and realisation; be it Marxist imaginations of a socialist utopia, projects dedicated to ending patriarchal social relations or white hegemony, or the culturally liberal projects of the 20th century dedicated to lifting various forms of social and cultural repression. In terms of their structure, the politics of the far right and the left are almost identical. There is an endless construction of new enemies, new barriers to overcome, and a figure of the 'other' that has unimpeded access to enjoyment and prohibits our enjoyment and realisation of the Good. Once we have gotten rid of immigrants, the '1%', the patriarchy, traditional masculinity, radical Islam, heteronormativity, systemic racism, 'Whiteness', the 'Woke', and so on, the Good can and will emerge. Consistent with the repetitious logic of the death drive, these efforts always seem to undermine themselves, generating and intensifying the very issues they endeavour to combat in a daemonic cycle of repetition (McGowan, 2013; Winlow and Hall, 2013). The attainment of the lost object must forever remain out of reach.

Closer to the focus of this book, the field of corruption and 'anti-corruption' arguably has a similar issue. Sampson (2015) refers to the significant expansion of the term corruption beyond its more traditional rigid sense over the past two decades. The term corruption is no longer limited to the bribery of public officials for a specific purpose. Rather, it has grown to subsume any and all abuse of power under its definitional remit: 'The corruption concept has become inflated, a floating signifier, encapsulating the general decadence of the political regime in which people find themselves' (Sampson, 2015: 439). This is paralleled by the enormous growth of the anti-corruption and compliance industries of regulatory capitalism, constituted by a glut of NGOs, supranational organisations, activists, politicians, academics, audit companies, and compliance departments, all of whom invest an immense amount of libidinal energy in the utopian future of a world unblighted by corruption.

In one respect, this is a mark of progress. Anti-corruption scholars and activists have long criticised the inadequacies of definitions which effectively restrict corruption to the public sector, and more specifically the public sector of nations in the developing world. This ignores the forms of corruption that proliferate in neoliberal Western nations and aids policies which promote increased marketisation and privatisation of public sector domains. Expanding definitions of corruption affords us an opportunity to better understand the reality of this phenomena.

In another sense, however, the flurry of activity against corruption (without much success) indicates the 'lost object' at work. The ideal of a utopian future of a world without corruption can only function as an ideal through its prohibition. The prohibition of the unrealised ideal, the acknowledgment that we are not 'there' yet, constitutes the ideal itself. Therefore, under the guise of tackling corruption, an immense amount of unconscious energy goes into maintaining the ideal as an unrealised one – particularly as anti-corruption shifts from 'movement' to 'industry', as it changes from being a force *in* itself to a force *for* itself (Johnston and Fritzen, 2021). New regulations and procedures for transparency and accountability are implemented with great hope that they will usher in the utopian future imagined. But as soon as they are, the anti-corruption industry approaches the emptiness of the ideal. It fails to deliver on its promise, just as the consumer commodity fails to satisfy the consumer in a lasting way. With hindsight, it is acknowledged that the previous measures in which so much hope was invested were flawed from the outset. Some might even admit that they knew this from the beginning. The conclusion drawn is that more needs to be done; we need to collect more data and implement more regulations and procedures. While generating vast amounts of information, a widening range of literature is acknowledging that such measures have the effect of making things *less* transparent and more opaque as to exactly what is happening with corruption (Hansen and Flyverbom, 2015; Kuldova, 2021; Sampson, 2019; Tsoukas, 1997), thereby leading us *away* from the stated goal, rather than towards its realisation. As Sampson (2015: 44) writes, 'We may not be able to define, nor measure, what it is we are fighting, but there is no doubt that we have to "do something" about "it"'. By continuously expanding the meaning of the term corruption, the anti-corruption industry effectively precludes the possibility of its elimination, thereby facilitating infinite enjoyment of the ideal of an imagined future without corruption by never having to face its emptiness.

The purpose and relevance of these discussions for the object of this book's focus – the concept of social harm – is by now hopefully becoming clearer. If our conception of social harm is at one level rooted in our imagination of some ideal version of the 'good', and if our imagination of the good is tied to the structure of human desire as presented here, then it is clear how vulnerable the concept of social harm is to confusion and relativisation. It is no mere coincidence that, as McMahon (2006) observes, the word Utopia – coined by Thomas More in 1516 – can be translated as 'no place', derived as it is from the ancient Greek *ou* ('no') and *topos* ('place'). We must constantly delay the actual achievement 'the good'. It must not, and indeed *cannot*, ever truly be realised. To do so would be to confront its essential emptiness and to become conscious of the fact that it is not *the* lost object of our desire:

> As we get closer to the ideal of a good society, we simultaneously approach the emptiness concealed within the ideal. The notion of the good does not emerge simply from moral reasoning and speculation about the proper arrangement of society. We develop this notion only through the experience of its prohibition. That is to say, the prohibition of the good doesn't form an obstacle to a pre-existing ideal *but constitutes the ideal as such*.
>
> (McGowan, 2013: 6; emphasis added)

This is the difficulty that faces pseudo-Hegelian political projects or approaches to social harm whose goal is to achieve 'recognition'. As we described above, when the subject enters the symbolic order, the Big Other demands certain things from them, and so long as this demand is satisfied, the Other affords the subject recognition in return. But what theoretical psychoanalysis teaches us is that what the Other explicitly demands is not equivalent to what it *really* wants from the subject. The subject senses that there is something else that the Other *really* wants, a secret desire that is not articulated by the Other's overt commands. The subject becomes a desiring subject by trying to realise this secret, and it is assumed that those who are afforded full recognition have direct access to, and enjoyment of, such a secret. Of course, the truth of the matter is that the desire of the Big Other is in fact an enigmatic abyss. It does not know what it wants. Once full recognition is achieved, it does not bring the satisfaction of 'finally penetrating the secret enclave of the social authority, but instead the disappointment of seeing that this secret does not exist' (McGowan, 2013: 88). Therefore, the pursuit of recognition, McGowan argues, leads only to frustration. Consequently, one must either acknowledge the truth that the secret desire of the Other does not exist, or they must refuse to confront this truth and instead conclude that full recognition is yet to be achieved and more work is to be done.

Subsequently, we can imagine how new barriers – i.e. new 'harms' – to a particular vision of the good or recognition could be created and erected in order to perform this unconscious function of keeping the good or recognition as something yet to be accomplished in the future and in a perpetual state of arrival. Not only would this muddy the waters around what does and does not constitute a legitimate form of social harm, but also many of the prohibitions erected against these new 'harms' to the good could, in themselves, become harmful. Freud grasped this fundamental point in relation to the Soviet Union at a time when the worst of their atrocities had not yet been committed and the West had no meaningful knowledge of those that had already occurred. In *Civilization and Its Discontents,* originally published in 1930, he wrote quite prophetically: 'One only wonders, with concern, what the Soviets will do after they've wiped out their bourgeois' (Freud, 1962: 62).

This is particularly pertinent given that, much like professional politics, social justice, and environmental activism are now big business, described by Costa et al (2021), as 'professional activism'. Entire careers, fame, influence, and fortunes have been made on the back of trying to rectify historic injustices, mitigate various systemic harms, and eradicate them through the realisation of these utopias. Moreover, as Swift (2019) points out in his book on 'leftist hobbyism', leftist politics is also for many a source of personal identity and, in some respects, leisure, rather than an immediate life and death struggle for those involved. Therefore, it is not unreasonable to speculate that as political activism has become increasingly commodified and bound up with personal identity, lifestyle, and leisure, there is plenty of motivation for shifting the goalposts as to whether the 'good' or the recognition being fought for has actually been achieved and whether the harms being fought against have been sufficiently eradicated or negated.

The engaged reader will have recognised an apparent contradiction in my argument so far. In the previous chapter, I argued that we must have a coherent and shared conception of the internal Goods – the *telos* – of human life and various social roles, practices, and institutions, from which we can derive an understanding of harm. I argued that the concept of harm is logically predicated upon some notion of the Good which can provide the evaluative standard against which we measure whether something has been harmed or not. Yet in this chapter, I have appeared to demonstrate that this is in fact an impossibility by using theoretical psychoanalysis to explore the relationship between the teleological ethics of the Good and the nature of human desire. Following the work of various psychoanalytic theorists, I have shown that the Good is symbolised by various 'lost objects', and that our phantasmic enjoyment of the Good is predicated upon its *prohibition* rather than its achievement. In order to find the Good *enjoyable*, it must always remain slightly out of our reach and in a position of becoming and possibility; and this leaves it highly susceptible to relativisation. Consequently, we change our definition of the Good or 'human flourishing' in order to continue our enjoyment and avoid a confrontation with the emptiness of the ideal. We construct new enemies, new barriers, new limits, and new harms that must be overcome in order to achieve the Good and to truly flourish and achieve our *telos*. As McGowan comments in the conclusion to his book, *Enjoying What We Don't Have*, 'There is no path leading from the death drive to utopia. The death drive undermines every attempt to construct a utopia; it is the enemy of the good society' (McGowan, 2013: 283). Therefore, it would seem that as long as we base our conception of harm upon a conception of the Good, we will always be fighting an uphill battle against the relativisation of harm.

How do we resolve this apparent contradiction? First of all, I would argue that the shared notion of the *telos* and the goods *internal* to social practices is somewhat different from the more pluralistic and individualised notions of the good to which our energies are often directed. But we can find a way out of this situation by taking the lessons of McGowan (2013, 2016) and recognising where our enjoyment truly lies. That is, rather than mislocating our enjoyment in the *achievement* of the Good, we fully recognise that our enjoyment (and the wider social good) is derived from their pursuit and incomplete achievement. The act of continuously shifting the goalposts and redefining the 'good' that will satisfy us is both a failure to acknowledge the lack at the core of our being, and a misplaced belief that the lost object can be captured in a way that will provide enduring pleasure, satisfaction, and contentment, finally ridding us of this lack. By fully confronting the truth of the nature of our desire we can avoid this slippage and relativisation because it would fundamentally transform our relationship to our enjoyment of the Good. To borrow from McGowan (2013: 283), 'Rather than being done for the sake of an ultimate enjoyment to be achieved in the future, it [pursuing the Good] would be done for its own sake'.

Taken out of the wider context of McGowan's psychoanalytic political project, this message of doing the good for its own sake is reminiscent of the kind of non-teleological rule-abiding ethics that the likes of MacIntyre (2011) dismisses. As we'll see in more depth in the following chapter, MacIntyre argues that removing the notion of the *telos* separates the relationship between morality and desire and often places them in opposition to one another, consequently depriving the subject of good or motivating reasons for following ethical commands. The answer to the question 'why should I do my duty' becomes the tautologous response, 'because it is your duty'. But this reading of the quote above from McGowan would be flawed. McGowan is not suggesting that we *remove* enjoyment or happiness from the picture as Stoic or Kantian ethics does, but that we identify the true locus of enjoyment, happiness, and human flourishing within its pursuit. By identifying that our enjoyment truly lies in pursuing the *telos* rather than in achieving it we do two important things. Firstly, we retain the *telos* which gives us reasons for following ethical injunctions, thereby keeping the relationship between morality and desire intact. Secondly, we avoid the relativisation of harm that comes from endlessly shifting the goalposts, which itself stems from misidentifying the true locus of our enjoyment in the achievement of the *telos* itself. Consequently, a more accurate rewriting of the quote above would be something along the lines of: 'Rather than being done for the sake of an ultimate enjoyment to be achieved in the future, it [pursuing the Good] would be done for the enjoyment and contentment it currently provides'. But this conundrum is the subject of a later chapter in the book and will be dealt with in more detail in due course.

Homeostasis and the Solicitation of the Trap

As much as human beings attempt to transcend what is and move to what is not, numerous thinkers – such as Spinoza, Freud, Damasio, and Žižek, among others – have observed that we are also often driven by the counterforce of what is sometimes called *conatus*, which can be understood as a condition of homeostasis, security, and calm. This is arguably the fourth thing we are doing when identifying social harms in practice. The late criminologist Jock Young spent a significant portion of his later career discussing ontological (in)security and the unsettling nature of what he described as the 'vertigo of late modernity'. The subject seeks to assuage the traumatic unsymbolisable irruptions and experiences of the Lacanian Real and take up a place within an order of coherent and meaningful symbols through which we can orient ourselves to the world and in which the world around us and our place within it make sense. As Hall (2012b) observes, we actively 'solicit the trap' of the symbolic order rather than being its reluctant subjects. This is ideology, for symbolic orders are always ideological. Ideology or symbolic orders are not, as Marx and Gramsci conceived it, a set of parlour tricks and myths preventing us from seeing things as they really are (see Winlow et al [2021] for a good overview of ideology). Rather, as discussed above, symbolic orders equip us with a more or less internally coherent set of symbols, meanings, and myths that help us experience reality in a coherent way, as opposed to the entirely unsymbolisable, unintelligible and traumatic experiences of the Lacanian Real. We are born into and grow up within these symbolic orders, and the subject, unconsciously terrified of the traumatic return of the Lacanian Real, yearns to stay within the symbolic order in which their lives make sense. Even when the system or symbolic order is actively harmful to the subject or to others, it can be difficult to convince the subject to abandon and transcend that which is familiar and has provided a sense of comfort and protection, or at the very least helped to make their lives and identities intelligible (Hall, 2012b). This is precisely why symbolic orders – which are always ideologically entrenched and make sense within specific historical and social circumstances – continue to persist even when these circumstances undergo profound change, thereby rendering the symbolic order itself redundant and dysfunctional in what Johnston (2008) describes as a condition of *deaptation*. The unconscious drives and anxieties of the subject will often lead them to rationalise, relativise, or disavow the harms generated by the symbolic order.

The present context of what Fisher (2009) describes as *capitalist realism* is perhaps the best example of this. Within capitalist realism, capitalism occupies the horizon of the thinkable. Capitalism is a mature enough political economic system that everyone understands its workings in the most basic way. We understand and have largely come to accept the wage form and that most of us have to toil for a wage while the capitalist takes the surplus profits. As stated previously, we are largely aware of the negative consequences and harms of capitalism: the inequalities it necessarily produces, its environmental destruction, corruption, and commodification of cultural practices and essential public services. None of this is news to us. Bringing this information into the cold light of day and educating the masses of these social arrangements have not jeopardised the continuation of the system as Marxian and Gramscian critiques of ideology anticipated. Žižek's (2000) *reversal of ideology* is arguably a more accurate model of ideology for our times. As discussed in earlier chapters, we are to a greater or lesser extent aware of the harms, but despite this awareness we continue to act in ways that tacitly enable the perpetuation of these harms. We disavow these harms and choose to act as if we do not know, because acting as if we do not know is more comforting than fully confronting the truth of the situation.

The present mode of late capitalism is neither passionately supported by only a small minority, nor does it demand (or even encourage) widespread positive belief and support. Yet it nevertheless plods on through its acceptance as the least worst of all systems (Winlow, 2012). Rather than cultivating a 'politics of fear', it is more accurate to argue that neoliberalism's elites cultivate and maintain an *objectless anxiety*, which Hall (2012b: 367) describes as 'a vague undercurrent of unsymbolised apprehension in which almost any object of fear, internal or external, can be manufactured to suit specific circumstances and political objectives'. A true politics of fear, Hall argues, is too intense, carrying with it the risk that a majority or influential minority might become confident in their identification of the system itself as a legitimate source of objective fear, and go in search of an alternative symbolic order. Rather, through demanding only our acceptance that what we presently have is the least worst of all systems, elites propagate a political *catastrophism* in which all alternatives are dismissed as inevitably leading to totalitarianism, fascism, barbarism, and economic disaster (Winlow et al, 2015). This has been the ideological function of the 'short twentieth century' (Hobsbawm, 1996), characterised by the atrocities of Nazism, Stalinism, Maoism. These were driven by what Badiou (2007) describes as the passion for the Real. As Žižek writes, 'in contrast to the nineteenth century of utopian or "scientific" projects and ideals, plans for the future, the twentieth century aimed at delivering the thing itself – at directly realising the longed-for New Order' (Žižek, 2002: 5). This is why so many politicians of the 'end of history' period presented themselves as non-ideological pragmatists, simultaneously presenting neoliberalism as 'non-ideological' and catastrophising about those who dared to challenge the neoliberal order as dangerous ideologues (Hochuli et al, 2021; Winlow et al, 2015). Such strategies draw on the human yearning for homeostasis to perpetuate harmful systems and circumstances through a logic that amounts to a conservative wisdom of 'better the devil you know'.

However, this is also what makes us adaptable to such a wide variety of systems and symbolic orders. Social constructionist theories have traditionally viewed human biology and neurology as somewhat rigid and unchanging, while social or symbolic orders are infinitely flexible. The philosophy of transcendental materialism, however, argues the opposite (Johnston, 2008). It draws on relatively recent insights from neuroscience that reveal human neurological systems to be characterised by plasticity and malleability, while observing that symbolic order's ideological systems, symbolic customs and codes must actually be quite rigid in order to function efficiently (Johnston and Malabou, 2013). Historically, humanity has shown itself to be extremely adaptable, capable of fitting into radically different social, cultural, theological, and political-economic conditions which have been both harmful and benign in various ways. Drives, desires, and the anxieties at the core of the subject are always in tension with one another, and always accessible to the symbolism of the external world. Certain drives can become prominent while others remain dormant as they are stimulated in different ways by the pre-existing symbolic order. As Hall and Winlow (2015) argue, these symbolic orders can be conservative, hierarchical, and regressive, or they can be reflexive, progressive, and egalitarian if they leave sufficient space in which the subject can freely move. But for the subject driven to avoid a traumatic encounter with the Lacanian Real, any symbolic order is better than no symbolic order at all.

Moving Forward

It is reasonable to argue that throughout history human societies have always relativised, rationalised, or disavowed particular harms. This tendency is consistent across societies with different political economic systems, secular societies, highly religious societies, and in different moral philosophical, ethical, and cultural eras. Nor is this relativisation, rationalisation, and disavowal limited to those who are perpetuating harm. As demonstrated by the brief discussion of the contemporary context of late capitalism towards the end of the chapter, it is something that is often done collectively and even engaged in by the apparent victims of harm themselves; and this chapter has endeavoured to explain why this is the case through the use of various ideas from theoretical psychoanalysis. But what is different about our present moment is twofold. Firstly, as Chapter 1 demonstrated, it is the apparent inability to establish meaningful consensus on what should be legitimately considered harmful at all, let alone how we rank order such harms. Secondly, as Chapter 2 argued, it is that the tools necessary for establishing such a consensus are prohibited to us by liberalism's insistence on the sovereignty of the autonomous individual. As such, we remain trapped in the emotivist deadlocks described in both of the preceding chapters.

The remainder of the book will be dedicated to understanding how we have arrived in this deadlocked position. The previous chapter argued that a more sociological NeoAristotelian notion of the *telos* is integral to the coherence of the concept of social harm, and that the concept of harm is reliant upon some shared coherent notion of the Good. Therefore, it is argued that if we are to understand how the concept of social harm has come to be in this underdeveloped state of disorder, we must understand how the notion of the *telos* came to be moved from the core to the periphery of social, cultural, political, economic, and moral life. The following chapters do so by drawing on some of the psychoanalytic theory discussed so far, and contextually deploying them within developments in religion, cultural, and socio-legal change, politics, economics, and philosophy.

Notes

1 I am aware that Hillyard and Tombs have repeatedly stated that their typology, which was initially set out in *Beyond Criminology*, should not be considered as a meaningful theory or definitional attempt at conceptualising social harm. They emphasise that it is incomplete and lacks a clearly articulated ethical and philosophical basis. Nevertheless, I maintain that their initial typology of social harm and the manner in which they approached it reflects some core truths about the nature of the way in which we conceptualise social harm; something which is perhaps reflected in the way that subsequent typologies seem to consistently circle back to and build upon this original.

2 See the following link for the Trump quote: https://www.theguardian.com/us-news/2016/jan/24/donald-trump-says-he-could-shoot-somebody-and-still-not-lose-voters

3 Reports suggest that as of mid-April 2020, Bezos had increased his net worth by $24bn since the beginning of the pandemic in January 2020.

References

Augustine, S. (1998) *The City of God Against the Pagans*. Cambridge. Cambridge University Press.

Badiou, A. (2001) *Ethics: An Essay on the Understanding of Evil*. London. Verso.

Badiou, A. (2007) *The Century*. Cambridge. Polity.

Becker, E. (1973) *The Denial of Death*. New York. Free Press.

Becker, E. (1975) *Escape from Evil*. New York. Free Press.

Canning, V. and Tombs, S. (2021) *From Social Harm to Zemiology: A Critical Introduction*. Abingdon. Routledge.

Chesterton, G.K. (1991) *The Collected Works of G.K. Chesterton Volume XXXIV: The Illustrated London News 1926-1928*. San Francisco. Ignatius Press.

Copson, L. (2016) 'Realistic Utopianism and Alternatives to Imprisonment: The Ideology of Crime and the Utopia of Harm'. *Justice Power and Resistance*. 1: 73–96.

Costa, A., Vaz, H. and Menezes, I. (2021) 'Exploring the Meanings of Professional Activism'. *Community Development*. 52(2). DOI: 10.1080/15575330.2020.1866049.

Damasio, A. (2000) *The Feeling of What Happens: Body, Emotion, and the Making of Consciousness*. London. Vintage.

Dews, P. (2008) *The Idea of Evil*. Oxford. Wiley.

Dupuy, J.P. (2014) *Economy and the Future: A Crisis of Faith*. East Lansing, MI. Michigan State University Press.

Eagleton, T. (2009) *Trouble with Strangers: A Study of Ethics*. Oxford. Blackwell.

Earle, S. (2017) 'The Toxic Nostalgia of Brexit'. *The Atlantic*. 5th October 2017. Available at: https://www.theatlantic.com/international/archive/2017/10/brexit-britain-may-johnson-eu/542079/.

Ehrenreich, B. (1997) *Blood Rites: The Origins and History of the Passions of War*. London. Granta.

El-Enany, N. (2017) 'Brexit Is Not Only an Expression of Nostalgia for Empire, It Is Also the Fruit of Empire'. Available at: https://blogs.lse.ac.uk/brexit/2017/05/11/brexit-is-not-only-an-expression-of-nostalgia-for-empire-it-is-also-the-fruit-of-empire/.

Ellis, A. (2016) *Men, Masculinities and Violence: An Ethnographic Study*. Abingdon. Routledge.

Embery, P. (2021) *Despised: Why the Modern Left Loathes the Working Class*. Cambridge. Polity.

Fisher, M. (2009) *Capitalist Realism: Is There No Alternative?* Winchester. Zero Books.

Freud, S. (1961) *Beyond the Pleasure Principle*. New York. W.W. Norton & Company.

Freud, S. (1962) *Civilisation and Its Discontents*. New York. W.W. Norton & Company.

Gibney, E. and Wyatt, T. (2020) 'Rebuilding the Harm Principle: Using an Evolutionary Perspective to Provide a New Foundation for Justice'. *International Journal for Crime, Justice, and Social Democracy*. 9(3). DOI: 10.5204/ijcjsd.v9i3.1280.

Hall, S. (2012a) *Theorising Crime and Deviance: A New Perspective*. London. Sage.

Hall, S. (2012b) 'The Solicitation of the Trap: On Transcendence and Transcendental Materialism in Advanced Consumer-Capitalism'. *Human Studies*. 35(3): 365–381.

Hall, S. and Winlow, S. (2015) *Revitalising Criminological Theory: Towards a New Ultra-Realism*. Abingdon. Routledge.

Hall, S., Winlow, S. and Ancrum, C. (2008) *Criminal Identities and Consumer Culture: Crime, Exclusion and the New Culture of Narcissism*. Abingdon. Routledge.

Hansen, H.K. and Flyverbom, M. (2015) 'The Politics of Transparency and the Calibration of Knowledge in the Digital Age'. *Organisation*. 22(6): 872–889.

Harari, Y.N. (2015) *Sapiens: A Brief History of Humankind*. London. Vintage.

Herman, A. (2012) *Freedom's Forge: How American Business Produced Victory in World War II*. New York. Random House.

Hillyard, P. and Tombs, S. (2004) 'Beyond Criminology?' in P. Hillyard, C. Pantazis, S. Tombs and D. Gordon (Eds) *Beyond Criminology: Taking Harm Seriously*. London. Pluto Press: 10–29.

Hobsbawm, E. (1996) *Age of Extremes: The Short Twentieth Century, 1914–1991.* London. Abacus.

Hochuli, A., Hoare, G. and Cunliffe, P. (2021) *The End of the End of History: Politics in the Twenty-First Century.* London. Zero.

Homer, S. (2005) *Jacques Lacan.* Abingdon. Routledge.

Johnston, A. (2008) *Žižek's Ontology: A Transcendental Materialist Theory of Subjectivity.* Chicago. Northwestern University Press.

Johnston, M. and Fritzen, S. (2021) *The Conundrum of Corruption: Reform for Social Justice.* Abingdon. Routledge.

Johnston, A. and Malabou, C. (2013) *Self and Emotional Life: Philosophy, Psychoanalysis, and Neuroscience.* New York. Columbia University Press.

Judah, B. (2016) 'England's Last Gasp of Empire'. *The New York Times.* 12th July 2016. Available at: https://www.nytimes.com/2016/07/13/opinion/englands-last-gasp-of-empire.html.

Kuldova, T. (2021) 'Luxury and Corruption' in P. Donzé, V. Pouillard, and J. Roberts (Eds) *The Oxford Handbook of Luxury Business.* Oxford. Oxford University press.

Lasslett, K. (2010) 'Crime or Social Harm: A Dialectical Perspective'. *Crime, Law and Social Change.* 54: 1–19.

Lee, D. and Nilsson, P. (2020) 'Amazon Auditions to Be 'the New Red Cross' in Covid-19 Crisis'. *Financial Times.* 31st March 2020. Available at: https://www.ft.com/content/220bf850-726c-11ea-ad98-044200cb277f.

Littler, J. (2019) 'Normcore Plutocrats in Gold Elevators: Reading the Trump Tower Photographs'. *Cultural Politics.* 15(1): 15–28.

MacIntyre, A. (2011) *After Virtue.* London. Bloomsbury.

McGowan, T. (2013) *Enjoying What We Don't Have: The Political Project of Psychoanalysis.* Lincoln. University of Nebraska Press.

McGowan, T. (2016) *Capitalism and Desire: The Psychic Costs of Free Markets.* New York. Columbia University Press.

McMahon, D. (2006) *Happiness: A History.* New York. Atlantic Monthly Press.

Milbank, J. and Pabst, A. (2016) *The Politics of Virtue: Post-Liberalism and the Human Future.* London. Rowman & Littlefield.

Nagle, A. (2017) *Kill All Normies: Online Culture Wars from 4Chan and Tumblr to Trump and the Alt-Right.* London. Zero Books.

Pemberton, S. (2015) *Harmful Societies: Understanding Social Harm.* Bristol. Policy Press.

Raymen, T. (2019) 'The Enigma of Social Harm and the Barrier of Liberalism: Why Zemiology Needs a Theory of the Good'. *Justice, Power, and Resistance.* 3(1): 134–163.

Raymen, T. and Kuldova, T. (2021) 'Clarifying Ultra-Realism: A Response to Wood Et. Al'. *Continental Thought & Theory.* 3(2): 242–263.

Raymen, T. and Smith, O. (2021) 'The Post-Covid Future of the Environmental Crisis Industry and Its Implications for Green Criminology and Zemiology'. *Journal of Contemporary Crime, Harm, and Ethics.* 1(1): 63–87.

Sampson, S. (2015) 'The Anti-Corruption Package'. *Ephemera: Theory & Politics in Organisation*. 15(2): 435–443.

Sampson, S. (2019) 'Anti-Corruption: Who Cares?' in S. Arvidsson (Ed) *Challenges in Managing Sustainable Business*. Cham. Palgrave Macmillan: 277–294.

Schwab, K. and Malleret, T. (2020) *Covid-19: The Great Reset*. Geneva. Forum Publishing.

Siedentop, L. (2014) *Inventing the Individual: The Origins of Western Liberalism*. Cambridge. Harvard University Press.

Smith, O. (2019) 'Luxury, Tourism, and Harm: A Deviant Leisure Perspective' in T. Raymen and O. Smith (Eds) *Deviant Leisure: Criminological Perspectives on Leisure and Harm*. Cham. Palgrave: 305–324.

Swift, D. (2019) *A Left for Itself: Left-Wing Hobbyists and Performative Radicalism*. London. Zero.

Telford, L. and Wistow, J. (2020) 'Brexit and the Working Class on Teesside: Moving Beyond Reductionism'. *Capital & Class*. 44(4): 553–572.

The Blind Side (2010) [Film] USA. Warner Bros.

Tsoukas, H. (1997) 'The Tyranny of Light: The Temptations and Paradoxes of the Information Society'. *Futures*. 29(9): 827–843.

Vaishnav, M. (2017) *When Crime Pays: Money and Muscle in Indian Politics*. Yale. Yale University Press.

Wainwright, J. and Mann, G. (2018) *Climate Leviathan: A Political Theory of Our Planetary Future*. London. Verso.

Wakeman, S. (2018). 'The "One Who Knocks" and the "One Who Waits": Gendered Violence in *Breaking Bad*'. *Crime, Media, Culture*. 14(2): 213–228. DOI: 10.1177/1741659016684897.

Winlow, S. (2012) 'Is It OK to Talk about Capitalism Again? Or, Why Criminology Must Take a Leap of Faith' in S. Winlow and R. Atkinson (Eds) *New Directions in Crime and Deviancy*. Abingdon. Routledge: 21–40.

Winlow, S. (2014) 'Trauma, Guilt, and the Unconscious: Some Theoretical Notes on Violent Subjectivity'. *The Sociological Review*. 62(2): 32–49. DOI: 10.1111/1467-954X.12190.

Winlow, S. (2019) 'What Lies Beneath? Some Notes on Ultra-Realism and the Intellectual Foundations of the "Deviant Leisure" Perspective' in T. Raymen and O. Smith (Eds) *Deviant Leisure: Criminological Perspectives on Leisure and Harm*. Cham. Palgrave: 45–66.

Winlow, S. and Hall, S. (2012) 'What Is an "Ethics Committee"? Academic Governance in an Epoch of Belief and Incredulity'. *The British Journal of Criminology*. 52(2): 400–416. https://doi.org/10.1093/bjc/azr082.

Winlow, S. and Hall, S. (2013) *Rethinking Social Exclusion: The End of the Social?* London. Sage.

Winlow, S. and Hall, S. (2018) 'What Price Justice: The Failures of the Left and the Political Economy of the Future'. *Gower Initiative for Modern Money Studies*. Available at: https://gimms.org.uk/2019/01/02/what-price-justice/.

Winlow, S. and Hall, S. (2022) *The Death of the Left*. Bristol. Policy Press.

Winlow, S., Hall, S. and Treadwell, J. (2017) *The Rise of the Right: English Nationalism and the Transformation of Working-Class Politics*. Bristol. Policy Press.

Winlow, S., Hall, S., Treadwell, J. and Briggs, D. (2015) *Riots and Political Protest: Notes from the Post-Political Present*. London. Routledge.

Winlow, S., Kelly, E. and Ayres, T. (2021) 'Ideology and Harm' in P. Davies, P. Leighton and T. Wyatt (Eds) *The Palgrave Handbook of Social Harm*. Cham. Palgrave Macmillan: 37–58.

Yar, M. (2012) 'Critical Criminology, Critical Theory and Social Harm'. In S. Hall and S. Winlow (Eds), *New Directions in Criminological Theory*. Abingdon: Routledge.

Young, J. (2007) *The Vertigo of Late Modernity*. London. Sage.

Žižek, S. (2000) *The Ticklish Subject: The Absent Centre of Political Ontology*. New York. Verso Books.

Žižek, S. (2002) *Welcome to the Desert of the Real*. London. Verso.

Žižek, S. (2006) *How to Read Lacan*. New York. W.W. Norton & Company.

4

THE DECLINE OF THE TELOS

There is a fundamental distinction between Neo-Aristotelian or *eudaimonistic* ethics and what MacIntyre (2002) describes as more 'modern' ethics, which he describes elsewhere as the 'morality of early and late capitalist modernity' or simply as 'Morality' with a capital 'M' (MacIntyre, 2016). This basic distinction can be observed by considering the way in which moral or ethical questions are posed. Neo-Aristotelian[1] or eudaimonistic ethics organised around the idea of the *telos* and human flourishing asks, 'What am I to do if I am to fare well?' More modern ethics, which have rejected the *telos* and have certainly rejected the notion that it should have any role in moral life, asks 'What rules ought I follow if I am to do right?'; and MacIntyre argues that modern ethics 'asks this question in such a way that doing right is made something quite independent of faring well' (MacIntyre, 2002: 81).

To go into a little more detail around this distinction, Neo-Aristotelian ethics sees morality not as a given or as something that can be practised by simply obediently following rules, but as an achievement. Morality and virtue are not distinct from personal happiness, human flourishing, and the achievement of excellence in various social roles and practices but are instead a fundamental and necessary spur to those pursuits (Aristotle, 1976: 66). The ethics of Graeco-Roman antiquity has been broadly described as a

DOI: 10.4324/9781003098546-4

eudaimonistic ethics, in which 'living well' is essential and synonymous with 'happiness'.[2] The individual identifies themselves through their inherited, acquired, and chosen social roles, relationships, and practices. They are mother, son, member of this social community or that community of practice, and they have undertaken a particular vocation or a role within the community. The individual understands themselves and is understood by others according to these inherited, acquired, and chosen social roles, all of which have goods internal to their practice and associated duties and responsibilities. Within a Neo-Aristotelian framework, one cannot truly flourish, excel, and achieve their true Good and *eudaimonia* if they are not practising the virtues required to act in accordance with the goods, responsibilities, and duties of these roles. This is the individual's *telos,* and to fail to pursue and achieve this *telos* is to live a life of frustration and incompleteness in which *eudaimonia* or 'flourishing' is unavailable. Therefore, the notion of the *telos* and *eudaimonia* keeps the relationship between morality, desire, and the Good intact. This moral framework, MacIntyre (2011) argues, was organised around a basic three-part structure. There was, on the one hand, the individual-as-they-happened to-be, and the individual-as-they-could-be-if-they-realised-their-*telos* on the other. Ethics – training in the virtues required to achieve the goods internal to social practices – sit in between these two poles and enables the individual to make the transition from the former to the latter. Unlike more modern ethics, this perspective does not sever the relationship between morality and human flourishing or happiness. For as long as this three-part scheme remains intact, the individual possesses good reasons for choosing to follow the precepts of morality.

By contrast, in its whole-hearted rejection of shared notions of the *telos,* modern ethics or 'Morality' share a number of key characteristics that totally sever the relationship among morality, 'human flourishing', or some grander notion of the Good, thereby reducing morality to obedient rule-following. The first is that our own interests and desires are often seen as an impediment to morality. Oftentimes, we must reject or actively act *against* our interests in order to act in accordance with morality's injunctions. We see this in Kant (1998), who views morality as acting out of a sense of duty to universalisable categorical imperatives, denying ourselves particular desires and interests if for no other reason than to avoid them being inflicted upon ourselves. We see it in Rawls (1971), who can only imagine people acting in an ethical and equitable manner when they are standing behind a 'veil of ignorance'. We see this in the utilitarianism of John Stuart Mill, who wrote that the readiness to serve the happiness of others through the sacrifice of his own happiness or desire is the highest virtue that can be found in humanity. When self-interest and personal desire are in accordance with ethical maxims and rules, it is simply a happy coincidence rather than a necessary interrelation. For deontological positions such as Kant's, however, if we act in accordance with ethical maxims *because* it aligns with our self-interest, we are not acting morally at all.

A good example of this can be found in the early pages of Kant's *Groundwork of the Metaphysics of Morals*. Kant is reflecting on the difficulty posed by those situations in which an action that is performed in conformity with moral duty also happens to be an action that the individual is inclined to perform out of their self-interest. In such a situation, is such action moral? Since Kant argues that an act can only be moral if it is done from duty, rather than self-interest, such situations are troublesome. He uses the example of a shopkeeper:

> For example, it certainly conforms with duty that a shopkeeper not overcharge an inexperienced customer, and where there is a good deal of trade a prudent merchant does not overcharge but keeps a fixed general price for everyone, so that a child can buy from him as well as everyone else. People are thus served *honestly;* but this is not nearly enough for us to believe that the merchant acted in this way from duty and basic principles of honesty; his advantage required it; it cannot be assumed here that he had, besides, an immediate inclination toward his customers, so as from love, as it were, to give no one preference over another in the matter of price. Thus the action was done neither from duty nor from immediate inclination but merely for purposes of self-interest.
>
> *Kant, 1998: 11*

There are two interrelated things we should take note of from the above which are of interest in understanding the distinction between modern and Neo-Aristotelian ethics. The first is the use of inclinations and interests, which are spoken of in rather one-dimensional and economic terms. The second is Kant's deep pessimism about the human subject. While Kant was certainly optimistic about the capacity for human reason, his anthropological assumptions conceive of human beings as fundamentally egoistic and self-interested (Milbank and Pabst, 2016). For Kant, it is the shopkeeper's duty to not overcharge their customers. But we cannot believe that the shopkeeper did so out of duty and basic principles of honesty. The shopkeeper did so because it was in their economic self-interest to do so. If the inexperienced customer discovered that they had been overcharged, they would know the shopkeeper is a dishonest con artist and would take their business elsewhere and encourage others to do the same. It would seem, therefore, that the only way in which we could know of the shopkeeper's true motivations was if they had no other competitors in business and *still* declined to overcharge an inexperienced customer. Then, Kant would argue, it could be conceived as a moral act done out of duty.

But notice that in this situation, there are still only two options. There is only the shopkeeper's duty on one side and their self-interest on the other.[3] This is no doubt a product of Kant's Lutheran upbringing, and we will expand on the role of religion in shaping moral philosophy in more detail later. Kant's moral philosophy rejects God as a legitimate moral authority because for Kant, it is the individual, through the ability to reason according to the categorical imperative, that is morally sovereign. The individual only ought to do what God commands if it is right. But if the individual can determine whether what God commands is right, then they have no need for God's divine instructions on what they ought to do, and they are in fact following their own reason rather than God's command. Hence why, for Kant, the rational moral being obeys nobody but themselves. To obey any external authority is to be guilty of heteronomy, which is why the *telos* of eudaimonia is considered as equally useless for the moral agent as divine command (MacIntyre, 2002). But while Kant rejects God as a legitimate moral authority, the *content* of Kant's notion of morality is nevertheless inherited from and reflective of his Christian background, and he clearly inherits Lutheran anthropological assumptions about the essentially sinful, egoistic, and fallen nature of humanity, which he recasts in secularised terms (MacIntyre, 2011; Vanden Auweele, 2013). For humanity after the Fall, morality is an epic internal struggle between one's duty and desire. Since humanity is sinful, its desires are corrupt. Therefore the individual's desires and moral duty can never truly align.

The difference with Neo-Aristotelianism or a *eudaimonistic* ethics could not be starker. As we alluded to in earlier chapters, a Neo-Aristotelian point of view looks at the shopkeeper as a functional social role in a community, with goods internal to itself that serve the social community of which it is a part, in precisely the same way that there are goods internal to being a doctor, a politician, or a publican. A good shopkeeper therefore prioritises these goods internal to the role of shopkeeper, such that declining to overcharge an inexperienced customer is not done out of some future calculation of economic self-interest *or* an abstract sense of 'duty' that is entirely disconnected from their various social roles, but simply because overcharging a customer is not what a good shopkeeper would do and would hamper the shopkeeper's ability to flourish as both a shopkeeper, a member of the community, and as a human being more generally. This is why a Neo-Aristotelian perspective can escape the tautologous nature of Kantian ethics or the crude cost-benefit analysis of utilitarianism. If the shopkeeper were to ask a Kantian why they should do their duty and not overcharge a customer, the Kantian would simply reply, 'because it is your duty according to the categorical imperative'. If the shopkeeper were to ask a utilitarian, the utilitarian would respond, 'because a loss of reputation might affect your business in the future', leading the shopkeeper to weigh up the likelihood of detection and its negative ramifications against the benefits of overcharging the customer. The Neo-Aristotelian perspective, however, can always provide the shopkeeper with good reasons by suggesting that failing to do as a good shopkeeper would do would lead to a life of emptiness, frustration, dishonesty, and suspicion in which true friendship (in the traditional sense of the term) is absent and it is difficult to achieve human flourishing. 'Interest' and happiness here are conceived in much broader terms than simply economic well-being or egoistic pleasure or desire. Indeed, it is no accident that the term 'interest' came to acquire an almost exclusively economic and egoistic meaning in the 17th and 18th centuries (Hirschman, 1977), at precisely the same period in which this more obedient, rule-following conception of morality ascended to a dominant position (MacIntyre, 2016).

This leads us onto another characteristic of modern ethics or 'Morality'. Its maxims are highly abstract and individualistic in the sense that they are universally binding on all individuals *as individuals* rather than in terms of their social roles, functions, or relationships. This is a product of a wider process occurring throughout Christendom that we will explore in more depth later, which abstracted the individual from the various social roles, communities, and relationships which had historically constituted the entirety of identity, and instead promoted the individual in relation to God as a separate social role that took primacy over all others. While these other social roles did not vanish or cease to be important, they were nevertheless to remain secondary (Siedentop, 2014). As such, the notion of moral 'duty' came to take on a radically different character (Anscombe, 1958). The duty of adhering to the maxims of this modern ethics is no longer a matter of performing one's duty as a parent, political leader, or member of a community of practice. Instead, moral duty is conceived in more abstract terms, and as ethical maxims were secularised and no longer conceived as divine commandments, they lost any external authority, such that the performance of duty is done for its own sake and its performance is its own reward. 'In a sublime tautology', Eagleton (2009: 113) writes, 'we should be moral simply because it is moral to be so'.

This self-referential and tautologous nature is a further shared characteristic of the rules of 'Morality' and is related to their presentation as abstract, universal, and exceptionless. Modern ethics' shared rejection of both the *telos* and divine authority means that they cannot be reduced to any fundamental principle or purpose. We cannot do anything but will them. To try and justify the rules of morality in terms of some greater shared end that they serve suggests that there could come a time or situation in which it was more beneficial *not* to follow the rules of morality. Given that the rules of morality are presented as universally binding on all individuals and are without exception, attempting to justify such rules would negate their universal and exceptionless nature. Therefore, by divorcing Morality from social roles, functions, and relationships, and the consequent lack of connection with shared aims or purposes, the individual is largely deprived of any reasons for following them because the divorce throws MacIntyre's three-part ethical framework, described above, out of balance. In the absence of the *telos,* we are simply left with human persons and their desires as they happen to be in their untutored state on the one hand, and the ethical precepts and maxims of morality on the other. Without the third component of the individual-as-they-could-be-if-they-realised-their-telos, the two parts of this moral scheme are in complete opposition to each other. Consequently, 'the injunctions of morality, thus understood, are likely to be ones that human nature, thus understood, has strong tendencies to disobey' (MacIntyre, 2011: 55).

This relates back to arguments made in earlier chapters around the superego and the guilt function. Recall that the superego functions effectively by promising that adherence to the commands of the superego will bring enjoyment in the future, and inflicting guilt upon the subject for failure to adhere to these injunctions. Obey the word of God and paradise will be yours in the afterlife. Work hard at school, defer immediate gratification, and when you grow up you will have a good job and a prosperous and enjoyable life. These are the commands of the traditional superego. But by separating both the individual and the notion of duty from their social roles and by separating ethics from *eudaimonia*, the superego struggles to carry out its functions under a deontological ethics. A deontological ethics certainly cannot promise enjoyment or *eudaimonia* since duty should be undertaken for its own sake, and in an increasingly liberal-individualistic society in which the legitimacy and authority of morality are called into question, it will equally struggle to inflict guilt given that its ethics are disconnected and abstracted from any social roles. To quote MacIntyre (2002: 90), '[i]t is when we detach a man from his social roles, but still leave him with the concept of "duty", that the concept is necessarily transformed', such that is it not uncommon in everyday moral discourse for a response to the question 'Why ought I do that?' to simply be 'Because you ought', with no further reason forthcoming (*ibid.* 83–84). A Neo-Aristotelian ethics, on the other hand, enables the superego to fulfil its functions far more effectively. The Neo-Aristotelian superego can not only promise enjoyment through the notion that adherence to its ethics will lead to *eudaimonia*; but it can also more effectively carry out the guilt function as its ethics are connected to one's concrete social roles, practices, and responsibilities. Transgression of its ethics means that one has failed as a parent, a professional, a friend, and so on. Together, this makes the Neo-Aristotelian superego far more robust and effective.

Another shared feature of Morality is that its rules or maxims are never as exceptionless and unconditional as they are presented to be. As numerous moral philosophers have pointed out with their infamous 'trolley problem', in reality, we are often confronted with situations which challenge the exceptionless nature of these moral rules and which those moral frameworks are largely incapable of resolving. Such that allegedly exceptionless moral injunctions such as 'do not kill', 'do not commit acts of torture', or 'never violate the individual's right to free speech' come to acquire a long list of contextual and situation-specific allowances which undermine their allegedly exceptionless nature (Dews, 2008). Similarly, utilitarian maxims of Bentham and Mill, which suggest that we pursue whatever will bring the greatest happiness or pleasure to the greatest number, fall flat because of the heterogeneous nature of 'happiness' or 'pleasure' (Anscombe, 1958). As MacIntyre asks of utilitarianism, 'But which pleasure, which happiness ought to guide me?' (MacIntyre, 2011: 77). On these questions, utilitarianism has no answers. It attempts to devise a new teleology for moral choices without a coherent notion of human flourishing running through it, replacing the telos of human flourishing with a completely heterogeneous telos of 'happiness' or 'pleasure' such that there can be no justifiable decisions for or against our choices.

This ties into an additional problem, alluded to in previous chapters, that the maxims of modern ethics are fundamentally negative. They tell us what *not* to do and provide an *a priori* list of behaviours to avoid but remain entirely silent in terms of what we should do and how we should go about our lives (Eagleton, 2009: 115). This is what makes Morality entirely compatible with liberal individualism and at home within liberal modernity. As our own moral authorities, we are sanctioned to live in any way we please, so long as it is compatible with the various rules of morality. But as we have seen, we can always formulate the categorical imperative or the harm principle in such a way that exceptions can be found to apparently exceptionless and unconditional rules in ways that do not break the internal coherence or structure of the categorical imperative. 'It follows that in practice', MacIntyre (2002: 191) argues, 'the test of the categorical imperative imposes restrictions only on those insufficiently equipped with ingenuity'. Anscombe (1958) similarly highlights the absurdity of 'legislating for oneself', in which every reflective decision reaches a majority vote of 1-0. There are, of course, huge variations within 'modern' ethics in terms of the content of its ethical maxims, and we will return to the finer details of various ethical positions in more depth later. But 'modern' ethics nevertheless shares these basic characteristics, among some others (for more, see MacIntyre, 2016: 114–120). Together, the combination of the inability to give reasons for following particular moral injunctions, the ability to create a series of caveats to supposedly exceptionless rules, and the outright prohibition on the establishment of a shared notion of the Good drives and perpetuates the manipulative and emotivist nature of moral and zemiological debate in contemporary society.

I am concerned with this distinction between Neo-Aristotelianism and 'modern ethics' because in previous chapters I have attempted to demonstrate that the concept of social harm, if it is to have any coherence and be fully functional, is inextricably entangled with a more Neo-Aristotelian or *eudaimonist* perspective. As an evaluative concept, social harm must have a more positive ethics – a coherent notion of the Good from which an understanding of harm is derived. Nor can the concept of social harm be built on abstract ethical principles. Rather, it demands an understanding of the *telos* of institutions and ecosystems and the goods internal to social roles, social practices, and their functions in order to ascertain whether they are flourishing or not. The chief problem is that the systematic study of social harm has emerged in a social context in which the dominant conception of ethics is that of the more modern variety described above which, working in concert with liberalism's autonomous individualism, prohibits such considerations.

This is an underlying tension that is arguably reflected in the most prominent conceptualisations of social harm to date. A significant number of these conceptualisations refer to and make use of the *language* of human flourishing or some notion of the Good. But in terms of the actual content of their conceptualisations, they also revert to an approach that is reminiscent of some variant of 'Morality'. Pemberton's (2015) approach speaks about social harm as the compromising of human flourishing but builds his conceptualisation of human flourishing on a human needs model that is underpinned by Rawlsian principles of justice, which is itself a form of deontological liberalism (Sandel, 1982). Yar's (2012) approach, rooted in a Hegelian theory of recognition, talks about basic prerequisites for human flourishing and even makes mention of Aristotelianism. However, with reference to Sayer's (2003) 'qualified ethical naturalism', which suggests that certain basic needs and vulnerabilities '*necessarily grounds moral imperatives* and social demands' (Yar, 2012: 61), Yar falls back on an almost Kantian ethics which treats recognition through respect for human rights, love, and self-esteem as borderline categorical imperatives, the transgression of which should be considered as an instance social harm. But as we have seen in discussing Kant above, these moral imperatives for recognition that form the basis of Yar's conceptualisation of social harm can quite easily turn into hypothetical imperatives of 'always give recognition to the Other except when…', thereby relativising the concept of social harm. Gibney and Wyatt (2020) talk of the *summum bonum* – the 'highest good' – but then retreat to a more utilitarian terrain by attempting to fix John Stuart Mill's utilitarian 'harm principle' by suggesting that the *summum bonum* is merely the 'survival of life' and that harm should be reconceived as anything that makes life more fragile.

The only exceptions to this are Lasslett's (2010) approach which explicitly (and erroneously) rejects ethics as having any place in the conceptualisation of social harm, and Garside (2013) who attempts to flesh out and build upon Lasslett's (2010) approach. Although, as Pemberton (2015) rightly observes, Garside's introduction of Meszaros draws on ideas of essential human needs and notions of human fulfilment, leaving Garside closer to Pemberton's approach than the author perhaps intended or realised. As demonstrated at the outset of chapter two, even the question posed by zemiologists when conceptualising social harm is reflective of this more modern ethics. It asks 'what *is* social harm' in an abstract way, seemingly in hope of devising some universal law-like zemiological principle that would be akin to moral philosophy's categorical imperative.

This means that all of these conceptualisations of social harm quickly run into problems they cannot resolve, some of which we have already identified in both this chapter and previous chapters. Therefore, we need to understand how the traditional notion of *eudaimonia* or human flourishing – the happiness of virtue (McMahon, 2006) – came to be ousted from the core of social, cultural, and moral life and moved to its periphery. How did morality and 'happiness' or eudaimonia come to be divorced from one another to the extent that not only is our present conception of 'happiness' so different from Aristotle's *eudaimonia* that it scarcely translates, but that to live morally or to do the moral thing is, as with Kant, to act against our desires and what will make us happy? We need to understand how the subject came to be severed from their natural relationships and social roles, and how these roles became subordinated to the primary social role of the autonomous individual to such a degree that ethical maxims were largely abstracted from the social and cultural order, practices, and communities to which they were (and are) being applied. How did such social roles and their associated ethical duties and responsibilities come to be seen as burdensome weights upon our individuality and happiness, rather than being seen, as they were in antiquity, as key to the *telos* of human flourishing? We need to understand how it became almost compulsory to talk in the language of individualised negative liberty and increasingly difficult and unfamiliar to speak in more teleological and eudaimonistic terms. For the Stoics, achieving *eudaimonia*, 'living well', and 'flourishing' were considered synonymous with 'living in accordance with nature', by which they meant living in accordance with one's inherited, acquired, and chosen social roles. The likes of Cicero and Epictetus developed complex, flexible, and personalised means of determining what one should do in order to 'live well' and achieve one's *telos* of *eudaimonia* along these lines (De Lacy, 1977; Visnjic, 2021). But today, when zemiologists refer to 'human flourishing' – the compromising of which is considered to constitute social harm – it is not referred to in terms of individuals seeking *eudaimonia* or 'flourishing' according to their inherited, acquired, and chosen social roles. Rather, it refers to the individual in a more abstract sense, separate from all social ties, with the capacity to pursue their privately defined notion of human flourishing. As such, 'human flourishing' becomes hollowed out into a rather meagre term that is largely devoid of content and reduced to a checklist of general human needs.

Where to Start?

If our task is to understand how the *telos* moved from the core to the periphery of social and moral life, then at what point in history should we begin in documenting this transition? It is unclear as to at what precise point in history it became difficult, even alien, to speak in truly teleological or *eudaimonistic* terms. One reason for this lack of clarity, put forward by MacIntyre, is that within a culture long dominated by philosophical liberalism and ethically influenced by the moral philosophy of the Enlightenment, the decline of the *telos* is:

> celebrated historically for the most part not as loss, but as self-congratulatory gain, as the emergence of the individual freed on the one hand from the social bonds of those

constraining hierarchies which the modern world rejected
at its birth and on the other hand from what modernity has
taken to be the superstititions of teleology.

MacIntyre, 2011: 39

Another reason for this lack of clarity is that, as with most significant transformations, it did not happen abruptly as the result of one
particular event, but extremely gradually, circuitously, and non-
linearly over the course of around 1800 years (MacIntyre, 2011). This
makes picking a historical starting point for such an analysis incredibly difficult, given that there are so many junctures in history which
could be – and have been – considered as suitable starting points.
Nevertheless, there are a couple that are worthy of particular mention.

We could, for instance, go back as far as the 4th century BCE for
an appropriate starting point. The ethical systems of Aristotle and
Plato were very much rooted, and made sense within, the context of
the autonomous and 'democratic' Greek *polis* or city-state. But at
this time, the local autonomy of the civic life of the *polis* was being
undermined by the emergence of distant imperial powers, first of
Macedonia and later Rome, effectively reducing these city-states
into a series of colonies (Siedentop, 2014). Their independence was
reduced to administration and organising taxes rather than deciding
on policies through rational public debate; and while there were still
public assemblies, they were largely without substance (MacCulloch,
2010). The circumstances within which notions of the *telos* and the
primacy of reason were functional were therefore undergoing profound change, to the extent that the new scale of social organisation
and the shift from local city-states to large military empires was
plunging the symbolic order of the *polis* into a dysfunctional condition of what Johnston (2008) describes as *deaptation* (Visnjic, 2021).
As Siedentop (2014: 52) writes, 'Rome was like a giant theatre or
stage, with the citizens of subjugated and dependent cities reduced
to mere spectators sitting on its benches. They were ceasing to be
actors on their own stages. Their inherited roles were jeopardized'.

This had a substantial influence on philosophical, ethical, and
religious thought. The power of these external empires not only
undermined the assumed natural superiority of the *polis'* citizen
class, but challenged the privileged status of reason, *logos,* and teleological thinking as the key to understanding nature and social
reality. Greater emphasis was placed upon power and the force of

the *will*, which was being experienced as triumphing over reason. Platonic philosophy began to consider questions around the source of all being – the Absolute – a first cause, the power of which was beyond comprehension. The decline of local autonomy to decide on shared goods and ends and the nature of the Good life meant that philosophers turned their ethical thinking inwards as well, placing greater influence upon the will and the interiorisation of moral life. This is said to be reflected in Stoicism, which MacIntyre (2002, 2011) argues trended away from the notion that doing what was right should lead one towards their *telos* of *eudaimonia*. Instead, he argues, Stoicism advocated a strict obedience to moral law in which the passions are entirely subjugated to a right and upstanding will that is in conformity with virtue. Doing what is right should be done for its own sake irrespective of whether it leads to happiness or good health, and Christianity and more modern rule-based moralities such as that of Kant can detect some of their ancestries in Stoicism (MacIntyre, 2002, 2011). Indeed, Visnjic (2021) argues that it was the Stoics who invented the notion of duty, which they called *Kathêkon,* providing the ancient antecedent for Kant's notion of moral duty.

However, Visnjic (2021) is quick to assert that Kantian duty and Stoic duty should not be simply conflated. There are significant differences in the Stoic and Kantian ethical systems, and MacIntyre is arguably wrong in his contention that the Stoics abandoned the *telos* and that they should not be considered a *eudaimonistic* form of ethics. As the likes of De Lacy (1977) and Visnjic (2021) have identified, the Stoic notion of duty remained intimately bound up with a consideration of social roles, which have a prominent role to play in Stoic ethics in terms of how one discovers their *Kathêkon* or 'duty'. Cicero in *De Officiis* outlined four *'personae'* that every human being is alleged to have and should consider when discovering their *Kathêkon*. All human beings have the first *personae* in common – that of being a rational and social animal. The second *personae* refer to each individual's nature, both physical and temperamental. The third *personae* are those things we have inherited; natural social relationships and roles, membership of a particular community, wealth and positions of privilege which carry with them associated ethics and responsibilities. The fourth *personae* consist of those social roles we have chosen for ourselves in life, for instance our vocation. We should, so the likes of Cicero and Epictetus argue, endeavour to make our actions conformable with each of these four *personae* in our lives. These should guide us in practical moral deliberation, and living virtuously in accordance with our inherited, acquired, and chosen social roles will lead us to our *telos* or final end of *eudaimonia*. This Stoic method of discovering one's duty is highly particular, flexible, and practical and in this regard is distinct from a Kantian conception of duty which makes no appeal to particular social roles and divorces duty from human desires or well-being entirely (De Lacy, 1977; Visnjic, 2021). Therefore, this Stoic method of discovering one's duty is arguably far closer to MacIntyre's (2011) own Neo-Aristotelian approach to virtue than has been recognised. Moreover, it remains a *eudaimonistic* ethics in other important respects. Happiness and 'living well' or in accordance with virtue are considered synonymous; such happiness is, as with Aristotle, distinct from mere pleasure, enjoyment, and wealth; and *eudaimonia* is considered to be the final end and *telos* of life.

This is not to say that the teleological ethos of Aristotle was not losing its appeal or in any kind of jeopardy in this new context of distant imperial rule. It was, and this much has been well documented. In the realms of religion, Judaism was rapidly rising in popularity as a growing Jewish diaspora brought Judaism into close contact with Hellenistic culture. Within Judaism, the law is simply Yahweh's will. 'I will be who I will be!', as God said to Moses. God's power is incontestable and unfathomable, and this image of an inaccessible and inscrutable God dictating the moral law corresponded with the experience of being ruled by a distant and irresistible imperial power. 'It was as if the trials of dealing with Roman power were being projected onto a universal screen' (Siedentop, 2014: 53). But despite the collapse of the *polis* within which Aristotelian ethics were rooted, a modified teleological and *eudaimonistic* ethics nevertheless persisted through the Stoics and survived for several centuries.

Another potential starting point for the decline of the *telos* is the birth of Christianity. This is because Christianity's most fundamental innovation – the moral equality of all souls before God – initiated a religious, moral, and socio-cultural revolution (MacCulloch, 2010). Siedentop (2014) argues that from our present context it is easy to underestimate just how radical a move this was, for it challenged the entire social order of antiquity. Today, we more or less think of 'society' as an association of individuals. We have the power to vote, with each vote held to count just as much as any other vote in principle if not always in practice. We possess an individual will.

Inherited and acquired social roles – such as parent, child, sibling, or member of some political community or community of practice – can be 'put on' and 'taken off' as we choose, and we remain intelligible as an individual separate from these natural relationships and acquired roles. We are typically conceived of as individual human beings first, over and above our various social roles, to the extent that in the contemporary context certain inherited aspects of our identity are seen by some as oppressive weights upon our individuality that are to be shirked and resisted (see Winlow and Hall, 2012, 2013). While there are inherited socio-structural privileges which give certain groups advantageous access to positions of leadership or prestige, we intuitively reject the idea that certain people are, by their very 'nature' and status, inherently superior to others for the performance of this or that role. Certain politicians might continue to hold such elitist views privately, but to publicly extol the belief that certain demographics are naturally superior or inferior to others would be to commit electoral suicide. This is precisely why there is such anger and fury when systemic privileges place people who appear entirely incompetent into positions of prominence. Today, even the British monarchy is largely symbolic rather than reflecting any widespread belief that members of the royal family are, by their nature, inherently superior to the 'commoner'. All of this, as we will see, is arguably a legacy of Christianity's emphasis on the moral equality of souls.

This basic intuition of moral equality was thoroughly alien to the world of antiquity. As is well established, the teleological ethics of Aristotle and the entire social order of the *polis* were built on an assumption of natural inequality (De Ste Croix, 1981).[4] The very notion of an 'individual' distinct from their inherited social roles and identities would have been largely unintelligible (Siedentop, 2014). Hobbes' idea of the 'mushroom person' – the isolated individual in the state of nature who has no natural relationships and must figure out how to live with others – would have been extremely difficult to comprehend. It was a world whose institutions, inhabitants, and their understanding of themselves, others, and the cosmos more generally was entirely structured by their natural relationships, roles, and inherited statuses which carried with them an assumption of natural inequality. Everything had a *telos* – an end, purpose, or final cause that was bestowed by nature and towards which it should naturally strive.

Reason was believed to be capable of identifying the *telos* of each thing, that end or purpose towards which it naturally tends, and great emphasis was placed upon the power of reason and oratorical argument (*logos*) to decide on policy in the public assemblies of the 'democratic' *polis* (city-state). Given that reason provided the key to understanding the social and natural order more generally, it was considered among the highest faculties in the world of antiquity, if not *the* highest. It could command reality. But reason was only attainable by a select few – the philosophers and citizens of the polis – who by their nature possessed these superior attributes which made knowledge and capacity to be governed by reason possible. This, not uncoincidentally, placed them in positions of power. For Plato, only a select few could have knowledge of the Ideal Forms, the truer and higher versions of reality, through an excellence of the soul. For Aristotle, only the citizens of the *polis* could have knowledge and command of the virtues to achieve *euadaimonia* or 'human flourishing' and believed that slaves were, by nature, 'living tools'.

The conceptions of freedom with which we are familiar mirror Berlin's (2002) two concepts of liberty, in which we have the negative freedom from authorities or sovereign powers to do more or less as we please, and the positive freedom to choose who governs us and how much they govern. In contemporary society, we think of the hedonistic consumer as free, in the sense that they have the autonomy to choose as they wish free from taboos or judgement – hence the contemporary obsession with 'stigma' and 'destigmatisation'. But in antiquity, the hedonistic consumer would not have been considered free, but enslaved to their passions. Freedom in this period, as we have touched upon, was bound up with notions of virtue and moral excellence, and one was 'free' if they had the capacity to choose wisely and in accordance with their *telos* and true good. The dominant imagery was that of ascendency and the dominant ethic that of perfectionism, as the citizens of the *polis* sought to ascend to a purer level of thought and being. Everything had its 'proper place' in this natural order of things (MacIntyre, 2002).

Jesus' teachings, on the other hand, were explicitly anti-elitist and in stark contrast to both ancient Hellenistic ethics and the Sadducees and the Pharisees – two of the most prominent Jewish factions in Palestine at the time. The Sadducees were a wealthy Jewish aristocracy who found a distinct advantage to Roman rule, operating the temple with Roman support and drawing temple priests from a small group of wealthy privileged families. While opposed to the Sadducees, the Pharisees – whose name meant 'separated ones' – were elitist in their own way. They despised their Roman rulers and took a somewhat self-righteous pride in the strict observance of Jewish law, displaying naked contempt for those they deemed to be 'ritually unclean' (Shelley, 2013). Jesus, by contrast, espoused a message of forgiveness, love, repentance, humility, and a trust in the mercy of God; often preaching to the poor and using parables which often spoke to the reality of poverty experienced by his listeners. Jesus also preached about the impending end of the world and the coming kingdom of God. The kingdom of God of which Jesus spoke was not necessarily a local or geographical realm, but rather a spiritual realm that represented God's sovereign will acting through the individual by way of divine grace. This is a more personal and individualistic relationship with God, in which the individual's status as a child in God's kingdom is set above and apart from their inherited roles and relationships to family, community, and polity. In the Gospel of Matthew (10:35–39), Jesus says to his apostles:

> For I am come to set a man at variance against his father, and the daughter against her mother, and the daughter in law against her mother-in-law. And a man's foes shall be they of his own household. He that loveth father or mother more than me is not worthy of me: and he that loveth son or daughter more than me is not worthy of me. And he that taketh not his cross, and followeth after me, is not worthy of me. He that findeth his life shall lose it: and he that loseth his life for my sake shall find it.

Jesus is not suggesting that individuals not love their family, but simply that their devotion should first and foremost be to God. The individual should abandon and reject their family if it is what the service of God requires. This is a significant departure from the world of antiquity, in which the individual could scarcely be intelligible when separated from their natural relationships and inherited social roles and status within the wider social and political community. Instead, Christianity is in many respects inventing a new primary social role – the individual – emphasising 'individual agency over corporate agency, conscience over inherited social roles' (Siedentop, 2014: 76). Personal allegiance to God is to take precedence. In this, the role-based notion of the *telos* and *eudaimonia* took another blow, and Jesus' message further separated the individual from the inherited social roles and community within which the idea of the *telos* made sense. Furthermore, the notion that reason is capable of determining the *telos* of human life and the perfectionist ethos to a teleological morality was seen as a self-righteous human arrogance that was in contrast to the humility and faith in the divine wisdom of God championed by Jesus and his followers. Reason could help with the discovery of truth, but it could not establish truth in and of itself.

St Paul took this idea of a more personal relationship and commitment to God a step further in his notion of 'the Christ'. Rather than being merely a saviour or liberator of the Jews, Paul gave the term a new meaning which positioned the Christ as a saviour of all humanity (MacCulloch, 2010). In Jesus, Paul saw God acting through human agency, developing the idea of a God that is potentially present within every believer – 'The Kingdom of God is within you' as Jesus said to the Pharisees (Luke 17: 21). In contrast to God as an external coercive force, this was an inner and mystical union of divine will and human agency through which we can all become 'one in Christ'. Paul draws on the image of God as the Father to infer the brotherhood of all humanity (Siedentop, 2014). As Paul wrote in his letter to the Galatians, 'For ye are all the children of God by faith in Christ Jesus. For as many of you as have been baptized into Christ have put on Christ. *There is neither Jew nor Greek, there is neither slave nor free, there is neither male nor female; for you are all one in Christ Jesus*' (Galatians 3: 26–28; emphasis added).

Here, Paul is announcing an entirely new universal ethic – *the moral equality of all souls* – in diametric opposition to the original teleological assumption of natural inequality. Being 'one in Christ' liberates the individual from their inherited social roles and through faith elevates the individual over and above them. But it is important to note that this individualism is not the atomising individualism of liberalism, which dissolves social bonds and natural relationships, often viewing them (including and perhaps especially religion) as archaic and arbitrary constraints upon individuality, or views forms of human association merely as self-interested protection against the violent anarchy of individual wills (Deneen, 2018; Milbank and Pabst, 2016). Rather, it is a new conception of social association, one organised around loving individual wills who are collectively guided in shared faith and belief in God, as opposed to a social order determined by one's birth or 'nature' or inherited status.

Nevertheless, liberalism's individualism would not have been possible or even conceivable without Paul's earlier innovations.

The perfectionist ethic of the *telos,* with its image of ascending to a higher form of moral virtue and truth through the power of reason, simply did not chime with Christianity's ethos of humility, the moral equality of souls, and the belief that ultimate truth lay with God alone and was beyond human comprehension. Overturning the assumption of natural inequality and that everything had its place according to its nature or telos opened up space for reflection on human nature in early Christian thought. Most specifically, reflections on the power (or lack thereof) of human reason and the will. It was Augustine of Hippo, later to become Saint Augustine, who was most prominent in these reflections in the late 4th and early 5th century CE. Augustine's ideas around human nature, reason, and the will were acutely shaped by his own biography and experiences, and we get the clearest sense of Augustine's ideas in this area through his classic text, *Confessions,* which can only be described as a spiritual autobiography that outlines his life and journey to becoming a devout Christian believer.

Despite being raised a Christian by his mother, Augustine was not initially moved by religion. He was initially drawn to Manichean beliefs while studying in Carthage and subsequently being employed at a university in Milan as a teacher and rhetorician. During his time in Milan, Augustine was not averse to the perfectionist notion of the *telos* and the imagery of human flourishing and ascendency towards a 'higher' nature. He spent time in civilised and intellectual circles and was impressed by what intellectually cultivated minds could achieve, finding the idea of moving towards 'perfection' through the power of the intellect highly seductive (Shelley, 2013; Siedentop, 2014). Indeed, it is acknowledged within the academic literature that the *eudaimonistic* ethics of the Stoics had a significant influence on Augustine, early Christian thought, and ethics in the early middle ages more generally; but as we will see, such *eudaimonistic* ethics were subject to modifications which significantly transformed their character and distanced them from their antecedents in Graeco-Roman ethics and philosophy (Rasimus et al, 2010; Visnjic, 2021). This was a product of Augustine being a man of extreme passions, who felt there was an internal war of higher and lower natures taking place within his soul – which perhaps explains the appeal of Manicheanism's binary thought. While a learned man committed to the pursuit of truth, he nevertheless found himself immersed in a range of what he describes as 'worldly activities'. He vigorously pursued high status and wealth, succumbed to gluttony, and found sexual temptations and lustful desires particularly difficult to resist as he described himself as 'firmly held in the thralldom of women' (Augustine, 1966: 197). Sex in particular, Shelley (2013) describes, was Augustine's 'defiling passion' from which he felt rescued by God's divine will. Therefore, while Augustine was influenced by the eudaimonists and agreed with their contention that virtue was essential to 'living well', he transformed the entire structure of eudaimonistic ethics in so many respects that one cannot describe him as a *eudaimonist* in any meaningful way. For starters, the notion that *eudaimonia* could be achieved through human reason and without the intervention of divine grace to buttress the frail human will was unacceptable to Augustine and thoroughly discordant with his personal experience. This informed his redefinition of virtue as 'right reason' and living in accordance with one's nature and social roles, to virtue as the love of God and faithfully obeying the word of God. Finally, consistent with the logic of Christianity more broadly, he rejected the notion that eudaimonia could be achieved in this life on earth. For Augustine, 'earthly life was a pilgrimage toward our true heavenly home' (Davis, 1992: 45–46). This heavenly home was the true human *telos*. The fallen nature of humanity, inexorably caught up with defiling passions and sin among even the most virtuous, meant that the state of *eudaimonia* could only be experienced in the afterlife.

In *Confessions*, Augustine documents the events leading up to his overpowering conversion experience in which, upon reading a passage by St Paul that spoke to him, 'all the darkness of doubt dispersed as if by a light of peace flooding into my heart' (Augustine, 1966: 225). In telling his account, we find a template for Augustine's understanding of the essential depravity and weakness of the human will, the insufficiency of reason, and the necessity for divine grace to support and prop up the human will. What is most important to identify in Augustine's conversion experience is that prior to his conversion Augustine admits of becoming convinced, at a rational and intellectual level, of God's truth:

> I no longer had the excuse which permitted me to think that the reason why I had not yet given up the world to serve Thee was that my perception of truth was uncertain; for, now, it

also was certain. But, still earthbound, I refused to fight under Thy command, and I feared as much to be freed of all my burdens, as one should fear to be hindered by them.

Augustine, 1966: 207

Despite this, Augustine could not bring himself to leave behind his sinful passions and devote himself to God. His will was not strong enough, '[t]hus my two voluntary inclinations, one old and the other new, one carnal and the other spiritual, were engaged in mutual combat and were tearing my soul apart in the conflict' (Augustine, 1966: 207). He allegorically described it as akin to someone trying to awaken themselves but continually succumbing to the ease and comfort of sleep. At a rational and intellectual level, Augustine confessed that he knew of God's truth and that the right path was the way of God. He similarly expressed a desire and willingness to turn his life over to the service of God. But despite these commands of the will towards the mind, his mind would not carry out his will:

> The mind commands the body and is immediately obeyed; the mind commands itself and is resisted. The mind commands the hand to be moved and its readiness is so great that command can hardly be distinguished from enslavement. Yet, the mind is the mind, while the hand is the body. The mind commands the mind to will; it is not something else, yet it does not do it. What is the source of this monstrosity? What purpose does it serve? It commands, I say, that the will-act be performed, and it would not issue the command unless it willed it, yet its command is not carried out. But, it does not will it completely, and so it does not command it completely. [...] So, it does not command with its whole being; therefore, its command is not fulfilled. For, if it were whole, it would not command that it be done; it would already be done. Hence, it is not a monstrosity to will something in part and to oppose it in part; it is rather an illness of the mind, which, though lifted up by truth, is also weighed down heavily by habit; so it does not rise up unimpaired.
>
> *Augustine, 1966: 217–218*

And of course, it was sexual temptations that plagued Augustine most strongly, despite the fact that earlier in the text he conceded that such indulgences – or 'burdens' as he describes them – were no longer bringing him any satisfaction or pleasure:

> What held me were the trifles of trifles and vanities of vanities, my former mistresses, plucking softly at the garment of my flesh and whispering: 'Do you send us away?' and: 'From this moment unto eternity, we shall not be with you, and: 'From this moment unto eternity, this and that will not be permitted you.' What suggestiveness was there in that phrase, 'this and that' – O my God, what suggestiveness! May Thy mercy avert its gaze from the soul of Thy servant! What sordid things, what indecencies, did those words suggest!
>
> *Augustine, 1966: 222*

From the standpoint of theoretical psychoanalysis, Augustine is exhibiting classic signs of what Lacan would describe as *jouissance* or what Freud termed the death drive (Freud, 1961). He is trapped within what Freud describes as 'daemonic cycles of repetition' that fail to satisfy him and are leading him off-course in the absence of a central master narrative to his life; and Augustine resists the termination and resolution of these cycles of repetition in the same way that Freud observed his patients resisting psychoanalytic treatment. Other theorists who have employed the death drive in relation to destructive and self-harmful behaviours have suggested that the death drive is actually drawing the subject unconsciously towards the achievement of a *symbolic death,* in which one's present symbolic life and identity is destroyed and something different can emerge and be built in its place (McGowan, 2013; Winlow, 2014). We can certainly see that in Augustine's autobiographical journey in *Confessions.*

However, in the absence of a clear conception of the unconscious and its drives, Augustine arrives at different conclusions. The intellect and the will alone are insufficient to lead one towards a true and ethical life. The fallen nature of humanity – Augustine describes humanity and himself as 'sons of Adam' – means that we are simply too depraved, too sinful, and our wills too weak to be able to rely on the intellect, reason, and human will alone. For Augustine, the gift of divine grace is necessary to prop up the flawed human will; and if the human will is depraved then the intellect cannot be trusted either: 'My mind, questioning itself upon its own powers, feels that it cannot rightly trust its own report' (Augustine, 1966: 306). The idea of ascendency towards perfection or the *telos* through reason and the intellect was becoming increasingly absurd to Augustine.

Even more absurd to Augustine was the notion that such *perfection* was available only to a select few by their nature. Immediately prior to his own conversion experience, Augustine recalls he and his friend being told of the conversion experience of two public servants at the imperial court who, upon reading *Life of Anthony* and learning of the Egyptian monks who resisted the temptations of the world, decided to abandon their secular ambitions and dedicate their lives to the service of God instead. Upon hearing this, Augustine felt a burning sense of shame, turning to his friend, and exclaiming:

> What is wrong with us? What does this mean, this story you heard? *Unlearned men* are rising up and storming heaven, while we with our teachings which have no heart in them, here we are tumbling about in flesh and blood! Is it because they have led the way that we are ashamed to follow, yet are not ashamed of the fact that we are not following?
>
> *Augustine, 1966: 215; emphasis added*

Here we see the assumptions of natural inequality and the *telos* further inverted. 'Unlearned men' were courageous and humble enough to 'storm heaven', while Augustine and his friends with all their intellectual powers and education were still 'tumbling about in flesh and blood', 'in thralldom' to their most base desires. Walking through his gardens later, Augustine heard the voice of a child singing 'take it and read it' over and over. Finding this peculiar, Augustine took it to be a divine commandment from God telling him to open a book and read the first passage he found, culminating in his conversion experience:

> And so I went hurriedly back to the place where Alypius was sitting. I had placed there the copy of the Apostle [Paul] when I had got up from the place. Snatching it up, I opened it and read in silence the first passage on which my eyes fell: 'Not in revelry and drunkenness, not in debauchery and wantonness, not in strife and jealousy; but put on the Lord Jesus Christ, and as for the flesh, take no thought for its lusts.' No further did I desire to read, nor was there need. Indeed, immediately with

the termination of this sentence, all the darknesses of doubt dispersed, as if by a light of peace flooding into my heart.

Augustine, 1966: 225

It was as if this passage from Paul was written especially for Augustine. As Siedentop (2014: 101) writes, '[t]he fall of man is not a second-hand story for him. Augustine sees himself in the human species and the human species within himself. The equality of our plight underpins everything he wrote as a Christian' (Siedentop, 2014: 101).

Therefore, it would seem that the birth of Christianity and early Christian philosophy could be a perfectly adequate starting point for our analysis of the decline of the *telos*. We can certainly see the distance travelled from the teleological ethics of the *polis* prior to these developments. There, reason was given ultimate privilege with its capacity to determine goods, ends, and the *telos* of all things through discourse and debate within the qualified democracy of the Greek *polis*. Every individual had a *telos* according to their inherited status and social roles, and it was inconceivable that the individual could achieve eudaimonia, 'flourishing', or 'living well' apart from these social roles. Living virtuously in accordance with one's roles and achieving eudaimonia were inextricably synonymous with one another. With the emergence of Christianity, we move to a message that completely opposes the perfectionist ethos of teleological ethics and antiquity's assumptions of natural inequality. Jesus espoused humility and trust in a merciful divine power and obedience to his commands. St Paul develops a more distinct conception of the individual separate from their inherited roles and social relationships, and his notion of being 'one in Christ' emphasised the moral equality of souls in contrast to the assumption of natural inequality. While Paul's individualism is not the atomised individualism of liberalism which presents so many contemporary challenges, liberalism's individualism would not be possible without Paul's earlier interventions and innovations. Finally, Augustine's reflections on the weakness and depravity of the human will downplays the power of reason, the intellect, and the human will to live in accordance with virtue without the intervention of divine grace. He rejects the imagery of 'ascendency', human flourishing, and 'excellence' that are so key to Aristotelian ethics, viewing these as a self-righteous arrogance discordant with Jesus' emphasis upon humility and faith in a merciful God.

Perhaps most importantly, for humanity after the Fall, eudaimonia cannot be achieved in this life, and the *telos* of humanity is relocated to the afterlife and is to be found only in death. The significance of this cannot be understated. Moving *eudaimonia* and the *telos* to the afterlife did not sever the relationship between morality and desire. After all, the individual still lives virtuously and according to the dictates of God in order to achieve *eudaimonia* in heaven. But it does transform the *experience* of the relationship between morality and desire in this earthly life in a way that moves closer to and is arguably the antecedent of 'modern ethics', in that acting virtuously is seen as acting *against* our earthly passions and desires which we can only hope to educate and control with the intervention of divine grace. As numerous scholars of religion have pointed out, Augustine is one of the most influential writers of the Christian tradition, and his theological system has had a lasting influence on Christianity and, by extension, Western civilisation more generally. His understanding of human nature, particularly his ideas around sin and grace, would have a profound impact upon religious and philosophical thought. Most directly in terms of Lutheranism, Calvinism, and the Reformation, but also more indirectly on later political and moral philosophy as well, as we will come to see later (Milbank and Pabst, 2016; Shelley, 2013).

Nevertheless, this starting point is an imperfect and imprecise one for a number of reasons. For starters, the primacy of inherited social roles and relationships, the notion of the *telos,* and assumptions of natural inequality did not simply disappear overnight, and the political, economic, socio-cultural, and legal structure of society meant that these ideas co-existed somewhat uncomfortably alongside Christianity and its moral intuitions (Siedentop, 2014). Furthermore, Aristotelianism underwent a revival in the 12th and 13th centuries, as Aristotle's works were rediscovered and translated, culminating most famously in Thomas Aquinas' *Summa Theologica*, which attempted to synthesise Aristotle's work with Christianity (MacCulloch, 2010). Aquinas insisted that good reason never leads the individual away from God's truth. By watering down Augustinian ideas around the totalising depravity and weakness of the human will and re-emphasising virtue as the Christian *telos,* Aquinas' work carved out greater space for the cultivation and improvement of earthly life. The perfect happiness of eudaimonia could still only be found in the afterlife. But in the meantime,

Aquinas argued, it remained possible to prepare for this through the cultivation of an *imperfect* eudaimonia in this life, climbing a ladder towards heavenly eudaimonia and restoring images of ascendency and a pseudo-perfectionist ethos of teleology (McMahon, 2006). So it was not a case of a linear disappearance of such ideas.

Aristotelianism was finally renounced once and for all through the Reformation, and when Martin Luther renounced the Catholic Church and its sale of indulgences he renounced it for its Aristotelianism, describing Aristotle as a 'buffoon who misled the Church' and favouring Augustinian ideas of sin and grace. Similarly, Thomas Hobbes in *Leviathan* explains the Reformation as stemming partly from bringing philosophy and the 'doctrine of Aristotle' into religion. Furthermore, as others have argued, while many important Enlightenment philosophers rejected or kept their religious upbringings at arms length, when it comes to the *content* of their moral philosophy their ideas often reflected the religious beliefs in which they were raised (MacIntyre, 2011; Vanden Auweele, 2013). Kant and Kierkegaard were raised as Lutherans; Diderot was a Jansenist; and Hume and Adam Smith were Presbyterians (an offshoot of Calvinism). These are precisely the denominations which dismissed human virtue entirely, conceiving of an originally sinful, egotistic, selfish human nature along Augustinian lines that was thoroughly incompatible with a teleological ethics, acting as a precursor to liberalism.

Not that we should mourn the decline of the teleological ethics of the ancient *polis*. It was after all a highly elitist and wholly repugnant ethics that endorsed slavery, the oppression of women, tacitly accepted all manner of other practices and beliefs which, by today's standards, we would rightly reject. This older teleological thinking and its metaphysical assumptions stands in stark contrast to the more sociological Neo-Aristotelianism advocated by MacIntyre (2011) that has been suggested in previous chapters to be of central importance in establishing some coherence around the concept of social harm. The point is that the events described in this chapter set in motion processes which would gradually prohibit *any* notion of the *telos* from playing a role in our collective ethical, political, economic, and socio-cultural life, with its absence ultimately impoverishing the concept of social harm to the point of incoherence. These processes were given added impetus by cultural-legal processes and economic changes which we will explore in the chapters that follow. While Christianity emphasised the primacy of the individual in relation to God over and above their inherited, acquired, and chosen social roles, these changes increasingly severed individuals from their roles in practice, introducing an anxiety in the subject which was conducive to economic, profit-oriented, and competitive-individualistic subjectivities which are anathema to any kind of Neo-Aristotelianism.

Notes

1 It is necessary at this point to mention Aristotle's abhorrent metaphysical views around human subjects and inequalities. Aristotle believed in the idea of natural inequality and aristocracy and therefore had no qualms with issues of slavery among other things. For Aristotle, slaves were incapable of practical reasoning and the attainment of *eudaimonia* or 'flourishing' by virtue of their 'nature'. It can be taken as a given that these aspects of Aristotle's thought should be (and are) wholeheartedly rejected. However, as MacIntyre (2011) observes, Neo-Aristotelianism draws heavily upon Aristotle's philosophy of ethics without being wedded to these metaphysical commitments, and we can discard these commitments without it necessarily effecting the validity or utility of Aristotelianism, so long as we provide a new ontological foundation for the *telos*.

2 It is customary to acknowledge that while *eudaimonia* has often been translated to 'happiness', the contemporary meaning ascribed to the term 'happiness' fails to truly capture the meaning of eudaimonia. For Aristotle, happiness is not merely enjoyment, pleasure, wealth, or other such experiences. Rather, it is a condition of doing and living well, in accordance with reason and virtue. It is a state higher than mere pleasure, enjoyment, prestige, or success. Hence, why it is often described as 'human flourishing' and is therefore significant for the concept of social harm given that numerous authors have used the term 'human flourishing' (see Pemberton, 2015; Yar, 2012), albeit in a way that is quite distant from the original moral philosophical meaning of the term.

3 It should be noted that Kant concedes that it would be insufferable for duty not to eventually end in happiness. MacIntyre (2002: 189) argues that this amounts to 'a tacit admission that without some such notion [of happiness or the Good], not morality itself, but the Kantian interpretation of it scarcely makes sense'.

4 While this book has advocated the importance of some kind of teleology to the concept of social harm, it is necessary to say that it is certainly not this particularly repugnant teleology of antiquity. As MacIntyre (2011) emphasises, it is possible to develop a more sociological teleology, which looks at the ends and purposes of social roles, practices, and institutions without inheriting assumptions of natural moral inequality. The purpose of this discussion is to explore how the notion of the *telos* came to be purged from social, cultural, and moral life over time, setting in motion events that have prevented its re-entry and have contributed to the relativisation and obfuscation of the concept of social harm.

References

Anscombe, G.E.M. (1958) 'Modern Moral Philosophy'. *Philosophy*. 33(124): 1–19.

Aristotle (1976) *Ethics*. London. Penguin.

Augustine, St. (1966) *Confessions*. Washington, DC. The Catholic University of America Press.

Berlin, I. (2002) *Liberty*. Oxford. Oxford University Press.

Davis, S. (1992) 'Early medieval ethics' in L. Becker and C. Becker (Eds) *A History of Western Ethics*. London. Psychology Press.

De Lacy, P.H. (1977) 'The Four Stoic Personae'. *Illinois Classical Studies*. 2: 163–172.

De Ste Croix, G.E.M. (1981) *The Class Struggle in the Ancient Greek World*. Ithaca, NY. Cornell University Press.

Deneen, P. (2018) *Why Liberalism Failed*. New Haven, CT. Yale University Press.

Dews, P. (2008) *The Idea of Evil*. Oxford. Wiley.

Eagleton, T. (2009) *Trouble with Strangers: A Study of Ethics*. Oxford. Blackwell.

Freud, S. (1961) *Beyond the Pleasure Principle*. New York, NY. W.W. Norton & Company.

Garside, R. (2013) 'Addressing Social Harm: Better Regulation versus Social Transformation'. *Revista Crítica Penal y Poder*. 5: 247–265. Special Issue: Redefining the Criminal Matter.

Gibney, E. and Wyatt, T. (2020) 'Rebuilding the Harm Principle: Using an Evolutionary Perspective to Provide a New Foundation for Justice'. *International Journal for Crime, Justice, and Social Democracy*. 9(3). doi: 10.5204/ijcjsd.v9i3.1280.

Hirschman, A. (1977) *The Passions and the Interests: Political Arguments for Capitalism before Its Tritumph*. Princeton, NJ. Princeton University Press.

Johnston, A. (2008) *Žižek's Ontology: A Transcendental Materialist Theory of Subjectivity*. Chicago, IL. Northwestern University Press.

Kant, I. (1998) *Groundwork of the Metaphysics of Morals*. Cambridge. Cambridge University Press.

Lasslett, K. (2010) 'Crime or Social Harm: A Dialectical Perspective'. *Crime, Law and Social Change*. 54: 1–19.

MacCulloch, D. (2010) *A History of Christianity*. London. Penguin.

MacIntyre, A. (2002) *A Short History of Ethics*. Abingdon. Routledge.

MacIntyre, A. (2011) *After Virtue*. London. Bloomsbury.

MacIntyre, A. (2016) *Ethics in the Conflicts of Modernity*. Cambridge. Cambridge University Press.

McGowan, T. (2013) *Enjoying What We Don't Have: The Political Project of Psychoanalysis*. Lincoln, NE. University of Nebraska Press.

McMahon, D. (2006) *Happiness: A History*. New York, NY. Atlantic Monthly Press.

Milbank, J. and Pabst, A. (2016) *The Politics of Virtue: Post-Liberalism and the Human Future*. London. Rowman and Littlefield.

Pemberton, S. (2015) *Harmful Societies: Understanding Social Harm.* Bristol. Policy Press.

Rasimus, T., Engberg-Pedersen, T. and Dunderberg, I. (Eds) (2010) *Stoicism in Early Christianity.* Grand Rapids. Baker Academic.

Rawls, J. (1971) *A Theory of Justice.* Cambridge, MA. Harvard University Press.

Sandel, M. (1982) *Liberalism and the Limits of Justice.* Cambridge. Cambridge University Press.

Sayer, A. (2003) '*Restoring the Moral Dimension in Social Scientific Accounts: A Qualified Ethical Naturalist Approach*', paper presented at the International Association for Critical Realism Annual Conference, Amsterdam, online at: www.lancs.ac.uk/fass/sociology/papers/sayer-restoring-the-moral-dimension.pdf.

Shelley, B. (2013) *Church History in Plain Language.* Nashville, TN. Thomas Nelson.

Siedentop, L. (2014) *Inventing the Individual: The Origins of Western Liberalism.* Cambridge, MA. Harvard University Press.

The Holy Bible, Galatians 3: 26–28. King James Version (2020). Abbotsford, WI. Zeiset.

The Holy Bible, Luke 17: 21. King James Version (2020). Abbotsford, WI. Zeiset.

The Holy Bible, Matthew 10: 35-39. King James Version (2020). Abbotsford, WI. Zeiset.

Vanden Auweele, D. (2013) 'The Lutheran Influence on Kant's Depraved Will'. *International Journal of Philosophy & Religion.* 73: 117–134.

Visnjic, J. (2021) *The Invention of Duty: Stoicism as Deontology.* Boston, MA. Brill.

Winlow, S. (2014) 'Trauma, Guilt, and the Unconscious: Some Theoretical Notes on Violent Subjectivity'. *The Sociological Review* 62(2): 32–49. doi: 10.1111/1467-954X.12190.

Winlow, S. and Hall, S. (2012) 'What Is an 'Ethics Committee'? Academic Governance in an Epoch of Belief and Incredulity'. *The British Journal of Criminology.* 52(2): 400–416. https://doi.org/10.1093/bjc/azr082.

Winlow, S. and Hall, S. (2013) *Rethinking Social Exclusion: The End of the Social?* London. Sage.

Yar, M. (2012) 'Critical criminology, critical theory and social harm'. In S. Hall and S. Winlow (Eds), *New Directions in Criminological Theory.* Abingdon: Routledge.

5

MORALITY AND DESIRE

Let us begin this chapter by recapping the journey we have made
so far. In Chapter 1, we explored how the concept of social harm,
operating as it currently does within a wider culture of emotivism,
is in a severely underdeveloped condition which prevents our ability
to anchor the meaning of the concept in a way that provides it with
coherence and consistency. In Chapter 2, we examined the nature
of the concept of social harm more closely, and it was argued that
in order to say with confidence and good reason that something
or someone has been harmed we must have some comprehension
of the nature or *telos* of that thing. The conclusion drawn was that
a Neo-Aristotelian way of thinking about human life, social roles,
and social practices is essential to social harm's conceptual coherence
and the avoidance of the interminable emotivist battles discussed in
Chapter 1. But it was acknowledged that within a culture broadly
influenced by liberal philosophy, we are unaccustomed to such
thinking and arguably prohibited from thinking in such ways due
to liberalism's reticence towards a discussion of shared goods and
ends. Within a liberal culture, there can be little agreement on what
the Good might be, or to what ends we should be directing our
energy. Such matters lie within the private realm of the sovereign
individual. All we can hope to agree on are the *rules* which govern
the manner in which we pursue our privately defined notions of the
Good.

DOI: 10.4324/9781003098546-5

We can see the unsatisfactory nature of such a rule-oriented culture when the conduct of a corporation, institution, or prominent individual is under some kind of legal or moral scrutiny. The usual defence offered up is that the conduct under scrutiny did not breach any laws; that their behaviour 'technically' complied with and fell within the boundaries of various rules and regulations governing conduct in that field or industry, and that they have diligently followed procedure and therefore cannot be fairly accused of any wrongdoing. But this explanation that all the rules have technically been followed is never experienced as convincing. Such explanations do not assuage the sense that some harm or wrongdoing has occurred. Nevertheless, it is a defence that cannot seem to be defeated, often engendering a feeling of impotence with the only recourse being endless reviews and revisions of the rules, procedures, and regulations that are currently in place. Hence the tendency over the past couple of decades to call for ever greater commitment to principles of 'transparency' and 'accountability' to restore public confidence in the wake of the latest government, corporate, or financial scandal; a call which, as researchers have observed, seems to breed rather than diminish suspicion and cynical distrust (Hansen and Flyverbom, 2015; Tsoukas, 1997).

Situations such as these, which are a commonplace feature of contemporary politics, economy, and 'good governance', are an example of the distinction made at the outset of the previous chapter between Neo-Aristotelian morality and more modern rule-oriented 'Morality' and legal culture. This is a culture in which morality and law are conceived as two distinct and separate realms, and the rules governing the conduct of a particular social role or institution are increasingly divorced from the *telos* of that particular social role or institution. At times, we continue to think in Neo-Aristotelian terms, evaluating the conduct of a particular figure or institution according to the *telos* of that institution or the individual's social role. But we occupy a culture that is so habituated to conceiving of morality as obedient rule-following and viewing law, morality, and desire as separate and distinct realms that this more teleological thinking lacks any meaningful arena in which it can be formally expressed, taken seriously, and acted upon.

This is perhaps most clearly manifested in the arena of corruption and politics. Corruption, as defined by Nye (1967: 966) is 'behaviour which deviates from the formal duties of a public role because of private-regarding (personal, close family, private clique) pecuniary or status gains; or violates rules against the exercise of certain types of private regarding influence'. Therefore, corruption rests on a clear distinction between private interest and public good. But as Bukovansky (2006) argues, given that the notion of the 'public good' has little normative purchase in contemporary society and is largely a rhetorical device that is relatively bereft of meaningful content, and given that political actors are conceived of as 'economically rational' and self-interested actors such that there is relatively little expectation that they will act in accordance with the *telos* of their public roles, 'how we determine whether or not a selfish act was corrupt depends ultimately on whether it broke a law. A corporate campaign contribution can be distinguished from a bribe only by reference to a law' (Bukovansky, 2006: 197). Therefore, even in the arena of politics in which the ideal of the *telos* of a politician retains some purchase in the public consciousness, we can do nothing other than impotently refer to 'rules', 'procedures', and governmental committees – a series of bureaucratic 'little others' that are to guide the postmodern subject (see Winlow and Hall, 2012).

It is worth mentioning that the moral philosophy of Graeco-Roman antiquity is notable for its relative *lack* of discussion of routinised and universally applicable 'rules'. There is little mention of them in Aristotle's *Ethics*, and in the Athenian *polis,* law and morality are not considered separate realms as they are in modernity (MacIntyre, 2011). Adam Smith actually criticised the Stoics for their failure to 'lay down many precise rules that are to hold good unexceptionally in all particular cases' (Smith, 2002: 387). But rules to coerce a particular type of conduct were largely superfluous and alien to a moral system in which *eudaimonia* and living virtuously were inextricably linked, and in which one discovered what one should do by reflecting on one's social roles on a situation-by-situation basis rather than appealing to abstract universal laws. As Visnjic (2021) points out, the lack of discussion of rules within these moral systems was not an oversight or a failure, but rather a *rejection* of the idea of rules as being a good guide for conduct. Smith's criticism of the Stoics is representative of the fact that he occupied a moral culture that already separated morality and desire, viewing morality as a set of rules that are to be obediently followed in opposition to one's desires.

Consequently, it was determined in the previous chapter that our task was to understand how the notion of the *telos* came to be moved from the core to the periphery of social, political, economic, and moral life, such that the separation of morality and desire could be possible. There is a clear parallel here with Hall's (2012a) theory of the *pseudo-pacification process*, which explores how *agape* – an unconditional love, solidarity, and communal altruism – was similarly moved from being a core value to a peripheral 'insulating sleeve'; thereby creating the ideal cultural-ethical conditions in which a nascent market economy could flourish, one which required what Hall describes as pseudo-pacified subjectivities geared towards non-violent but ruthlessly aggressive competitive individualism in economic and consumer markets. Therefore, while we began exploring the marginalisation of the *telos* in the previous chapter by looking at the emergence of Christianity and its basic moral intuitions and assumptions about human nature, Hall's pseudo-pacification process – which starts in the period around the late Middle Ages and early modernity – is of arguably even greater significance for understanding the decline of the *telos* and the separation of morality and desire.

The Pseudo-Pacification Process

In order to make sense of Hall's pseudo-pacification process, it is necessary to briefly acknowledge the socio-economic context that was its predecessor. In medieval England up until the Black Death the separation of economy from the household or family unit, which Weber (2002) held to be a pre-requisite for the emergence of capitalism, had not yet taken place. In this period, land was the principal object of economic value and desire, while family and community – and their protection through communal altruism, solidarity, and, if necessary, violence – were the principal sites of identification, security, honour, and social reputation (Hall, 2020). Crucially, property was collectively 'owned' by the entire family unit and inheritance was shared rather than being owned by and bequeathed to individuals, meaning that there was no ability to disinherit families and children (MacFarlane, 1978). Production was largely for the purpose of family consumption rather than trade or profit. Farm labour was family labour, and economic activities were geared not towards wealth creation but to merely satisfying the natural wants and needs of the family (Polanyi, 2001; Sombart, 1915). Economic activity was clearly connected to the *telos* of one's natural relationships and acquired social roles, with their being strong emphasis from the Church on Aquinas' notion of a 'sufficient livelihood' according to one's station in life, something that was thoroughly normalised and accepted through custom. To seek more than this was not enterprise, but the deadly sin of avarice, and acquisitive economic motives were treated with significant suspicion by the Church. Labour was considered necessary and honourable, and the craftsman made and sold according to the maintenance of a sufficient livelihood. The activities of the merchant trader, on the other hand, aimed not merely at livelihood but profit (Tawney, 1948). The medieval merchant trader, much like today's commodity traders who barter the world's resources on a far grander scale (Farchy and Blas, 2021), bought in order to sell dearer without making any change or improvement to the commodity. Their interest was purely acquisitive and individualistic, divorced from any wider public spirit or charity and therefore viewed as a parasitic means of livelihood (Hirschman, 1977). Expedient access to certain goods via traders meant that they were tolerated, but with a begrudging wariness, and they were submitted to limits and restrictions at every turn, with warnings against the perils of such economic activities.

Communities worked in concert with Church authorities on establishing a just and fixed price for goods to prevent both overcharging, price undercutting, and hoarding to raise prices (Hall, 2020). Bookkeeping was careless, and exact measurements and precise calculations were not a feature of economic activities in this time period. Greater emphasis was placed upon quality – the goods internal to these 'economic' activities – rather than precisely calculating costs, labour time, and expenses:

> As for work itself, for the peasant and the craftsman alike it was lonely, patient effort. Man lost himself in his work. He lived in it, as the artist does; he loved it so, that he would much rather not have parted with his handiwork…the potter strove hard not to be tempted by the trader's offers for his pipe. But if it had to be sold, then the commodity was to be worthy of its makers. The peasant, like the craftsman, had put something of himself into his product; and in its making the rules of art were obeyed'.
>
> *(Sombart, 1915: 18–19)*

Usury, while more commonplace and tacitly accepted among the elite, was prohibited among the peasant and the craftsman to prevent their easy exploitation (Tawney, 1948). As Hudson's (2018) history of debt has shown, throughout history usury has been the primary means through which wealthy moneylenders have dispossessed the masses of their property and reduced them to permanently indebted labourers. In this context, there are powerful emotional ties with one's home and geographical area, with people linked by strong ties of community and kinship. Hall (2020: 22) remarks that 'we can discern the beginnings of a manifested *agape*, the attempt to diffuse the social ideal of care in the family and community outwards into the broader economy, to operate in the interests of social justice and civility'. We must, of course, resist an over-romanticism here and acknowledge that this was also a period marked by naked and shameless feudal expropriation and additional *corvée* duties, and this system arguably helped preserve the maintenance of seemingly natural inequalities in which society was conceived as a grand social organism, with each playing their naturally allotted part (Tawney, 1948). But for our purposes, the point remains that this was a period in which morality and (economic) desire were in conformity with, rather than opposed to, one another, operating under broadly Thomistic lines.

An orthodox view of medieval history and the rise of capitalism is that such arrangements began to give way in dramatic fashion in the 16th and 17th centuries, as England moved from a peasant to a market capitalist society. But more recent historical research which underpins Hall's theory of the pseudo-pacification process suggests that such arrangements were undergoing change far earlier. Dyer (2000) observes that the nobility, both lay and clerical, were more concerned with war, prayer, hunting, and courtly entertainment than they were with managing the estate, which was seen as a tedious chore that was to be delegated to their inferiors. The preferred method was to lease out manors for fixed rents, generating most of their income from these rates and the sale or exchange of surplus demesne produce (Brenner, 2003). This created a space for the emergence of more entrepreneurial peasants, artisans, and craftsmen. As Dyer (2000) argues, contrary to popular historical narratives which are little more than romanticised myth, it is not necessarily true that the peasantry uniformly resisted the drift towards more marketised economic relations. Rather, numerous medieval historians and documents indicate an ascending and aspirational tendency in late medieval England. As far back as the 13th century, around 20% of people lived in urban or small towns which were centres for trade, and peasants required profits from crafts and trade in order to pay rents to the aristocracy (Siedentop, 2014), while Dyer (2000) estimates that around a third of the population living in town and country earned wages that were often paid in cash. Between 1275 and 1500, England's internal trade was responsible for around one quarter of gross national product (GNP). As Tawney writes:

> It was not the lords of great estates, but eager and prosperous peasants, who in England first nibbled at commons and undermined the manorial custom [...] It was not great capitalists, but enterprising gildsmen, who began to make the control of the fraternity the basis of a system of plutocratic exploitation, or who fled, precocious individualists, from the fellowship of borough and craft, that they might grow to what stature they pleased in rural isolation.
>
> *(Tawney, 1948: 78–79)*

Turning our attention to land and property, the introduction of laws of primogeniture and the sweeping enclosure movement shifted the unit of ownership from the collective family to individuals, with documentary evidence indicating that by at least the 14th century, the individual was the most common unit of ownership. Property was frequently sold outside the family for economic gain during the lifetime of the owner, thereby disinheriting children, and there was a highly active market in land (MacFarlane, 1979). When property was bequeathed within the family it was bequeathed to specific individuals. This legally and culturally driven dissolution of the family, inherently sexist as it favoured sons, created a more insecure and uncertain existence for children. Those last in line or out of favour with their parents could be cast out of the geographically bound productive-defensive unit of family, land, and community and into the competitive marketplace (Hall, 2012a, 2014, 2020). As Dyer (2000) observes, it would be wrong to project the image of a relatively rigid and immobile society too late into the medieval period. After the plague in the middle of the 14th century, serfs moved about a great deal, and the suburbs that developed on the edge of town originated from 'the flow of relatively poor immigrants anxious to gain an income from the employment and commercial opportunities provided by the town' (ibid., 2000: xiv). The use of landless wage labourers was commonplace by at least the 14th century, with some historians suggesting that this was widespread practice even earlier (Brenner, 2003; MacFarlane, 1979). As Hall (2020: 24) writes, 'the relations of sociability, security, and love conditional only on the defence of the family's honour and land were tainted by what could be described as a norm of institutionalised betrayal'.

At this point in Hall's analysis, the role of psychoanalytic theory coalesces with the historical narrative. As we explored in Chapter 3, ultra-realists such as Hall draw on Lacanian psychoanalytic theory to argue that at the core of subjectivity lies nothing other than a powerful, structuring absence that inspires deep anxiety, one which is assuaged by the active solicitation of a coherent symbolic order through which meaning can be established and the individual can understand and orient themselves to the external world (Hall, 2012b). However, the symbolic order of customs, codes, religious, and neighbourly ethics that had previously governed economic activities and tried to spread the social idea of *agape* into the economy more widely was becoming *deaptative* as the legal, economic, and socio-cultural circumstances in which this symbolic order made sense was vanishing. Therefore, the legally and culturally driven dissolution of the family/community unit meant that it ceased to be the basis of identity, subjectivity, honour, and existential security. This abiding sense of loss became the *objet petit a*, the unnameable lost object of desire which propelled the subject to look outwards towards the nascent economic markets for a replacement:

> The legally driven splitting of the family, and with it the geo-graphically bound ethnic community, corresponds with the splitting of the individual ego and the redirection of its identification processes, from the family and community outward to the world of the commercial market in which offspring were forced to engage in pacified economic competition against each other as their traditional mode of security and status was disrupted.
>
> *(Hall, 2014: 17–18)*

The individual was physically and economically dislocated from the productive-communal unit of the family. Household and community were separated from economic matters (Polanyi, 2001), and for socially disembedded and economically insecure individuals who had been cast out into a marketplace that demanded increasingly competitive-individualistic subjectivities, there could be no comfortable relationship between morality and their economic desires. Their economic activities were no longer connected to the *telos* of their social roles and natural relationships, and in this new cultural and economic context, the Aristotelian and Stoic notion of the happiness of virtue – that morality and living virtuously are an indispensable precondition of *eudaimonia* – was an increasingly deaptative idea that was frankly dangerous to one's economic security and earthly happiness. Economic desire, morality, and happiness were no longer being thought of as complimentary parts of a single scheme, but increasingly as separate individual provinces which were often in conflict with one another (Tawney, 1948). In order to avoid a traumatic re-encounter with the Lacanian Real, not to mention material impoverishment, the subject had to flexibly adapt to these new circumstances and identify with the emerging principles and requirements of the new order by pursuing material wealth and socio-symbolic status as a precarious, insecure, and, most importantly, *individualised* source of security. Hall (2020) argues that this process is akin to cell division, a socioeconomic tumour that spread throughout the social body as we witness the primary object of economic desire shifting from land to money, and the source of social status and distinction shifting from the defence and service of land and community to individual performance within the nascent competitive market economy. This was intensified by the emergence and symbolic significance of an increasingly complex consumer culture (Sassatelli, 2007), evidential in the diaries and documents of not just the elite, but the lower orders as well (Thomas, 2009).

Hall's interest, of course, is in explaining the decline of physical violence and homicide and the concomitant rise in other forms of acquisitive and entrepreneurial criminality from the Middle Ages through to late modernity. But the relevance of his argument for our purposes here is self-evident. He provides a corrective to Elias' (1994) argument that this is part of an overall 'civilising process', to argue instead that this was part of a broader *pseudo-pacification process*. Hall (2012a) suggests that the violent subjectivities of pre-capitalist societies were not fully pacified and grown out of, but instead were preserved, pseudo-pacified and put to work by the nascent market economies as the underlying energy upon which a capitalist society would be built. Indeed, historical research by Ward-Perkins (2005), Maddern (1992), and Dyer (2000) provides plenty of empirical evidence to suggest that after the fall of the Roman Empire, England became a decentralised and largely ungoverned paraspace replete with violence, hence the emphasis on close and affective communal ties and the violent defence of land and community. The violent and thymotic energies that disrupted trade routes and private property rights were *pseudo-pacified* into aggressive and intensely competitive but non-violent activities and forms of socio-symbolic activity in the modes of work and consumption. As Hall observes, capitalist societies cannot properly function in either extreme of indiscriminate violence or strong ethical pacification, but rather rely upon the perpetual cultivation of a dynamic tension between the poles of pacification and stimulation which would provide the ideal pseudo-pacified subjectivities for a market society to flourish:

> The historical evidence does not point to a general 'civilizing process' … but a complex psychosocial process in which direct and unashamed violence and intimidation were gradually sublimated into a multitude of criminalized and legalized forms of exploitation, deception, and appropriation, which ran alongside and in tension with what can only be described as a sort of insulating sleeve of ethico-legal restraints, like the thick but flexible insulation around an electrical wire carrying a powerful current.
>
> *(Hall, 2012a: 32)*

Therefore, Hall argues, Calvinist Protestantism may have institutionalised this competitive individualism, but it was not its 'spirit' or core driver as Weber (2002) had argued. Rather, Protestant ethics were a footbrake to try and keep under control powerful drives of lack within anxious, economically insecure, and socially disembedded individuals that were already being harnessed and stimulated by economic, legal, and socio-cultural changes (Sombart, 1915). This is arguably why Calvinism, and not the Lutheranism from which it sprang, became the dominant form of Protestantism following the Reformation. Luther despised economic individualism and covetousness in all of its guises. He disdained economic individualism as enthusiastically as he despised the commercialisation of religion through the Catholic Church's sale of indulgences, which could absolve the individual of past sins and reduce the time spent in purgatory after death (MacCulloch, 2010). In these respects, Luther was a socio-economic conservative, a man who looked backwards to a more 'distributivist' and medieval economic order (Chesterton, 2009), and whose conception of an ideal society was more medieval than that of most thinkers of the Middle Ages, due to his dismissiveness towards the economic and commercial developments of the previous two centuries as a relapse into paganism (Tawney, 1948). The socio-cultural and political background that coloured Luther's thought was that of the peasant village and small market town described earlier, in which economic activities were carried on for household subsistence rather than individualistic enterprise, and in which commerce and finance were peripheral matters rather than central to the entire economic system.

Calvinism, by contrast, took for granted the existence of a relatively advanced and individualist mode of economic organisation. It was a largely urban movement that was carried from nation to nation by merchant traders and workmen for whom the more traditional scheme of social and economic ethics had long ceased to have much relevance to the practicalities of their social lives and economic activities (Walzer, 1965). Founded in Geneva, Calvinism spread and gained its most loyal adherents in large business centres of the day, such as Antwerp, Amsterdam, and London among others. It was not the case that Calvinism conceded the economic realm as free from the moralising influence of religion. Calvinism had its own rigorous rules around how economic affairs should be conducted. But it did not automatically view commercial enterprise with hostility and suspicion and accepted large-scale commerce, credit, and financial institutions as an expedient and unavoidable feature of the economic realm they were seeking to moralise and temper, thereby developing its social ethics to operate within, rather than oppose, these realities (Tawney, 1948; Walzer, 1965). The older form of Christian ethics was effectively *deaptative* (Johnston, 2008), applicable to a world that no longer existed. As Calvin wrote to a correspondent, 'What reason is there, why the income from business should not be larger than that from landowning? Whence do the merchant's profits come, except from his own diligence and industry?' (cited in Tawney, 1948: 113).

Virtue Dismissed

Despite their many respective divergences, what the theological out-looks of Lutheranism and Calvinism shared was a deeply pessimistic and Augustinian understanding of human nature. Original sin was so extreme and corrupting that it was impossible for humanity to reason its way towards a virtuous life and society, thereby dismissing outright any notion of the *telos* or a connection between morality and desire (Milbank and Pabst, 2016). As we saw at the end of the previous chapter, Aristotle was described by Luther as a 'buffoon who misled the church'. Unlike Aquinas, Luther and Calvin could see no reconciliation between Aristotelianism and Christianity. Since humanity was irretrievably corrupted after the Fall, so was their reason. Neither of these things, therefore, could be trusted to provide the individual with any comprehension of their true end. About the ends of life, human reason must be silent and defer solely to faith and the impenetrable and unfathomable will of God. In his commentary *On Galatians*, Luther writes:

> We comfort the afflicted sinner in this manner: Brother, you can never be perfect in this life, but you can be holy. He will say: 'How can I be holy when I feel my sins?' I answer: You feel sin? That is a good sign. To realize that one is ill is a step, and a very necessary step, toward recovery. 'But how will I get rid of my sin?' he will ask. I answer: See the heavenly Physician, Christ, who heals the broken-hearted. *Do not consult that Quackdoctor, Reason. Believe in Christ and your sins will be pardoned.*
>
> *(Luther, 2012 [1535])*

Recall MacIntyre's (2011) three-part moral scheme, outlined near the outset of the previous chapter, which gives the subject good reasons for following the injunction of morality. It was made up of the individual-as-they-happened-to-be on the one hand and the individual-as-they-could-be-if-they-realised-their-*telos* on the other. Ethics played the intermediary role of guiding the individual from the former to the latter, the achievement of which would lead the individual to *eudaimonia* or 'human flourishing' – the happiness of virtue. While Augustine's ideas of sin and grace weakened this relationship by relocating *eudaimonia* to the afterlife, the scheme was not entirely severed. Firstly, Catholicism retained the idea that through faith in God and through good works, one could earn their place in heaven – or at least minimise the time spent in purgatory (MacCulloch, 2010). Secondly, while it was accepted that humanity could not achieve heavenly eudaimonia in this life, the Fall of Adam was not so totally corrupting that humanity could not work towards an *imperfect* eudaimonia on Earth (McMahon, 2006). The Reformers, outraged over the sale of indulgences and generally disdainful of the role played by ecclesiastical authorities as an intermediary between Christians and God, rejected these ideas wholeheartedly. Good works had no role to play. For Luther, the individual was 'justified by faith alone' rather than by their actions. It is possible for Good works to be done without good faith and for all manner of motives (Shelley, 2013), and here we see an obvious prelude to Kant's deontological ethics in which an act is only moral if it is done from a sense of moral duty.

Calvinism's doctrine of predestination was even more severe. God had already decided who was among the elect and who was condemned to damnation. Therefore, Calvinism was a theology concerned less with personal salvation and the reconciliation of the individual with God, and more with fostering religious obedience. As Walzer (1965) observes, it was a social and moral doctrine concerned with worldly affairs, rather than a personal and transcendent one concerned with the saving of souls. Humanity after the Fall had not only become estranged from God but also estranged from society. The individual was an asocial, egoistic, greedy, and domineering animal rather than a naturally political or social one. As Calvin (cited in Walzer, 1965: 31) commented: 'I say that the nature of man is such that every man would be lord and master over his neighbours and no man by his good will would be a subject'. He wrote that 'we know that men are of so perverse and crooked a nature, that everyone would scratch out his neighbour's eyes if there were no bridle to hold them in' (Calvin cited in Walzer, 1965: 33). Calvinism, therefore, was in many respects a concretely practical and political theology concerned with coping with the aftereffects of the Fall of Adam. It instilled a certain pragmatism that, as we will see, comes to exert a powerful influence on later political and moral thought.

The socio-economic changes discussed earlier in this chapter created an economic context which was increasingly less compatible with MacIntyre's three-part moral scheme. As economic and cultural activities became more individualistic in nature and were separated from the household and the *telos* of one's social roles within the family and community, the link between morality and desire was weakened. Through the Reformation, we see the (re) introduction and intensification of a conception of human nature which makes MacIntyre's three-part moral scheme seem not just impossible, but hopelessly naïve and dangerous. The Reformers dismiss the notion of the *telos*, and that following one's *telos* will lead to eudaimonia. Humanity is a wretched animal, one that is fundamentally asocial, selfish, greedy, and subject to its most base passions. Human beings base nature and corrupted reason means that it is incapable of discerning and acting towards the collective Good, independent of God. Therefore, as we observed in the last chapter, the rejection of the *telos* reduces MacIntyre's three-part scheme to a two-part scheme. We have humanity as it happens to be on the one hand and the injunctions of morality on the other, with the relationship between these two parts being quite unclear. The commands of morality are ones that human nature, as it is understood from a Lutheran and Calvinist view and operating within an increasingly competitive-individualist economic and commercial context, will be most inclined to disobey and circumvent. Morality, consequently, completes its transformation from being that which will lead to one's happiness and without which one cannot truly flourish, to a form of obedient rule-following abstracted from one's social roles and practices. This is what transforms the notion of moral duty into a tautology, in which the reason provided for why we should do our duty is simply that it is our duty.

In the absence of the *telos*, which could give the individual good reasons for following the injunctions of morality, the question then became how to foster moral compliance such that there is at least a simulacrum of political and economic harmony. As Hirschman's seminal text demonstrates, through the latter stages of the Renaissance and the Enlightenment, various answers were given to this question, all of which revolved around the repression, manipulation, or *harnessing* of humanity's depraved passions. Calvin's response, the likes of Hirschman (1977) and Walzer (1965) argue, was of the repressive and coercive variety, in which the state – an agency of God's sovereign will – would be tasked with restraining the most dangerous passions. But even in Calvin's own thought, we can see precursors to the idea of 'harnessing', rather than merely restraining the passions, and using one vice to check another to bring about a greater good and harmony, an idea that would be developed and expanded upon by key thinkers and would become key to the moral legitimisation of capitalism (Dupuy, 2014; Hirschman, 1977). As Tawney argues, Calvin wondered:

> Was it not possible that, purified and disciplined, the very qualities which economic success demanded—thrift, diligence, sobriety, frugality—were themselves, after all, the foundation, at least, of the Christian virtues? Was it not conceivable that the gulf which yawned between a luxurious world and the life of the spirit could be bridged, not by eschewing material interests as the kingdom of darkness, but by dedicating them to the service of God?
>
> *(Tawney, 1948: 119)*

Overall, the naturalisation of a pessimistic view of human nature resulted in a pragmatism that gripped moral and political thought through the 17th century and the Enlightenment, particularly as faith began to wane in the ability of traditional moral philosophy or religion to restrain the destructive human passions. Indeed, while much has been attributed to Calvinism's frugal asceticism as a key religious and cultural driver of capitalism's growth, the atmosphere of this time was not necessarily as austere and non-materialistic as it is sometimes depicted, and it is unrealistic to suggest a sharp divide between a rigorously Puritan era which gave impetus to capital accumulation through industriousness and thrift, and a more hedonistic, materialistic, and Godless era that was to follow (Sassatelli, 2007). On the contrary, the expansion and growth of markets and accumulation required a more general diffusion of consumer desire throughout the social body in order to create demand; and there is ample historical evidence to suggest that there was a significant degree of hedonistic materialistic and an actively competitive and comparative consumer culture in this period at the precise moment in which Protestant asceticism was supposed to be constraining it (Sombart, 1915; Thomas, 2009).

Harnessing the Passions

Therefore, as the 16th, 17th, and 18th centuries progressed, it seemed increasingly fanciful that the asocial and avaricious competitive individualist would curtail their actions due to the appeals of moralising philosophers or at the urgings of the Church (Hirschman, 1977). Consequently, there was a recurrent call in this period to treat 'man as he really is', with the overwhelming feeling that by talking about how humanity *could* be or *ought* to be, moral philosophers had wished away the reality of humanity as subject to base passions and selfish individualism rather than confronting these alleged realities head-on. Machiavelli's *The Prince* was an early notable expression of this pragmatic realism, in which the 'effectual truth of the matter' which the prince has to deal with is far more important than the 'imagined republics and principalities that have never been seen nor known to exist in reality' (Machiavelli, 2005: 53):

> For there is such a distance between how one lives and how one ought to live, that *anyone who abandons what is done for what ought to be done achieves his downfall rather than his preservation.* A man who wishes to profess goodness at all times will come to ruin among so many who are not good. Therefore, it is necessary for a prince who wishes to maintain himself to learn how not to be good, and to use this knowledge or not to use it according to necessity.
>
> *(ibid.: 53; emphasis added)*

A century later, at the outset of his *Political Treatise*, Spinoza is even more fervent and sharp-tongued in his criticism of philosophers and their utopian imaginations of society and humanity:

> Philosophers conceive of the passions which harass us as vices into which men fall by their own fault, and, therefore, generally deride, bewail, or blame them…And so they think they are doing something wonderful, and reaching the pinnacle of learning, when they are clever enough to bestow manifold praise on such human nature, as is nowhere to be found, and to make verbal attacks on that which, in fact exists. *For they conceive of men, not as they are, but as they themselves would like them to be* […] it has come to pass that, instead of ethics, they

have generally written satire, and that they have never conceived a theory of politics which could be turned to use.

(Spinoza, 2016 [1677]: 11; emphasis added)

Vico, writing 50 years later, quotes Spinoza almost verbatim. But
he goes further, to suggest – as we will explore in greater depth
momentarily – that through harnessing the passions through legislation, rather than merely prohibiting them, indulgence of the passions and self-interest can bring about the common Good:

> Philosophy considers people as they ought to be and hence is
> useful only to the very few who want to live in the Republic of
> Plato, rather than sink into the dregs of Romulus. Legislation
> considers people as they really are, in order to direct them to
> good purposes in society. Out of ferocity, avarice, and ambi-
> tion, the three vices which plague the entire human race, it
> creates armies, trade, and courts, which form the might, afflu-
> ence, and wisdom of commonwealths. Thus, from three great
> vices, which otherwise would certainly destroy all the people
> on the earth, legislation creates civil happiness. This axiom
> proves that divine providence exists and that it acts as a divine
> legislative mind. For out of the passions of people intent on
> their personal advantage, which might cause them to live as
> wild and solitary beasts, it makes civil institutions which keep
> them within human society.

(Vico, 1999 [1725]: 78)

There are a number of key points worth taking from the above
quotes. First is the pessimism masquerading as pragmatism in regard
to the human subject, which Milbank and Pabst (2016) argue to be
the now-secularised theological assumption underpinning contemporary liberal individualism. At the risk of belabouring the point,
by this stage of early modernity, the idea of the human *telos* and the
notion that morality and virtue are integral to the achievement of
happiness or eudaimonia has been wholeheartedly rejected. It is a
period populated by thinkers who understand human beings not
in terms of their natural relationships, social backgrounds, communities, and commitments, but as individuals in isolation from
all of these things, whose private desires and interests are distinct
from – and largely in opposition to – the interests of collective

public life. In the middle of the 17th century, Hobbes' (2017 [1642]) discussion of the state of nature in *De Cive* describes individuals as mushrooms who spring out of the earth entirely independently without any engagement with one another. These mushroom people are not citizens of a community or members of a family. They are pure individuals without any natural relationships. Their first and foremost problem is to ensure their own existence and survival (Lutz, 2012), and it is conceded that human beings are egoistic, self-interested, individualistic creatures who are largely governed and overwhelmed by 'the passions' of avarice, glory, praise, gluttony, and ambition among other things.

Secondly, we see in all three accounts the separation of politics from morality. Politics, as a Neo-Aristotelian conceives it, is a fundamentally moral activity, a social practice with a *telos* and goods internal to itself in which 'excellence' or 'flourishing' is only achievable when the politician adheres to those internal goods and the virtues necessary to attain them. For the thinkers discussed above, it is not. For Machiavelli, the politician must be prepared to abandon ethics in order to effectively carry out political functions. Ethics is a hindrance rather than a necessary spur to these activities; while Spinoza in the latter part of the excerpt quoted above seems to consider ethics to be something entirely distinct from – even in opposition to – a 'useful' theory of politics. Politics, therefore, is reconceived not as a moral activity but a technical one, concerned with careful management and administration, judged according to the achievement of particular outcomes.

This brings us onto the third point, alluded to above, that is specific to the final excerpt. Here, Vico builds on the likes of Spinoza and Machiavelli to put forth the idea of *harnessing* the passions. It had become accepted that humans were largely at mercy to their base 'passions'. Faith had been lost in the ability of religion or the state to repress and prohibit them, or the ability of morality to cultivate virtue. Therefore, for Vico, trying to cultivate virtue or repress the passions was an exercise in futility. Better that the wild passions be *harnessed* through legislation and careful management such that they bring about the 'overall good' for society. This was to become a dominant idea of the age, one that would become integral to capitalism's legitimisation and the shaping of liberal economic thought (Dupuy, 2014; Hirschman, 1977). Bernard Mandeville, whose poem *The Fable of the Bees* and the subsequent essay is considered by many to be the precursor to laissez-faire, provides a more extensive elaboration. He begins his essay, which is in essence a defence of his famous poem, in a similar vein to Vico, critiquing those who preoccupy themselves with humanity as it should be, and asserting his belief that human beings are creatures entirely subject to their passions:

> One of the greatest reasons why so few people understand themselves, is, that most writers are always teaching men what they should be, and hardly ever trouble their heads with telling them what they really are. As for my part... I believe man (besides skin, flesh, bones that are obvious to the eye) to be a compound of various passions, that all of them, as they are provoked and come uppermost, govern him by turns, whether he will or no. To show that these qualifications, which we all pretend to be asham'd of, are the great support of a flourishing Society, has been the subject of the foregoing Poem.
>
> *(Mandeville, 1988 [1732]: 76)*

The chief task for the moralists, clergy, and law makers, Mandeville argues, has always been to convince people to conquer rather than indulge their appetites and to prioritise the public good over their private interests or desires. The very fact that these two spheres can be separated shows how far we have strayed from the teleological ethics of the Stoics or Aristotle, for such an argument is only possible when self-interest is conceived in individualistic terms as separate from one's social roles and *telos,* and in which morality is conceived of 'doing right' rather than 'faring well'. Regardless, since Mandeville thought it was entirely illogical to assume that any individual would voluntarily act against their own inclinations or place the good of the collective over their own, the moralists, clergy, and law makers adopted a cunning tactic to encourage compliance. Namely, they have recognised the sinful pride and vanity of human beings, 'and observing that none were either so savage as not to be charm'd with praise, or so despicable as patiently to bear contempt, justly concluded that flattery must be the most powerful argument that could be used to human creatures' (Mandeville, 1988 [1732]: 77). This is the rationale behind those who extol the virtues and excellence of human nature, who speak of what people are capable of when they control their passions, and that this capacity to do so is what makes humanity a 'higher' and superior creature, distinct from mere animals and 'beasts'. One particular passage is worth quoting at length:

> Having by this artful way of flattery insinuated themselves into the hearts of men, they began to instruct them in the notions of honour and shame; representing the one as the worst of all evils, and the other as the highest Good to which mortals could aspire. Which being done, they laid before them how unbecoming it was the dignity of such sublime creatures to be solicitous about gratifying those higher qualities that gave them the pre-eminence over all visible Beings. They indeed confess'd, that those impulses of nature were very pressing; that it was troublesome to resist, and very difficult wholly to subdue them. But this they only used as an argument to demonstrate how glorious the conquest of them was on the one hand, and how scandalous on the other not to attempt it.
>
> To introduce, moreover, an emulation amongst Men, they divided the whole species into two classes, vastly differing from one another: The one consisted of abject, low-minded people, that always hunting after immediate enjoyment, were wholly incapable of self-denial, and without regard to the good of others, had no higher aim than their private advantage; such as being enslaved by voluptuousness, yielded without resistance to every gross desire, and made no use of their rational faculties but to heighten their sensual pleasure. These vile grov'ling wretches, they said, were the dross of their kind, and having only the shape of men, differ'd from brutes in nothing but their outward figure. But the other Class was made up of lofty high-spirited creatures that, free from sordid selfishness, esteem'd the improvements of the mind to be their fairest possessions; and setting a true value upon themselves, took no delight but in embellishing that part in which their excellency consisted; such as despising whatever they had in common with irrational creatures... and making a continual war with themselves to promote the peace of others, aim'd at no less than the publick welfare and the conquest of their own passion.
>
> *(Mandeville, 1988 [1732]: 77–78)*

For Mandeville, traditional morality and theology are one giant confidence trick. It is a manipulation that exploits human vanity and weakness for fawning praise by telling them that they possess a higher nature that it would be wasteful not to pursue. It simultaneously shames the individual into compliance, and then places individuals in comparison and competition with one another by dividing 'the whole species into two classes', one to be despised for its low-minded hedonism and the other to be praised for its unselfish virtuousness. Mandeville's view of society is undeniably a cynical one, an aggregation of vain and self-interested individuals tied together not by their natural relationships, love, or commitment to their social roles and community, but by envy, competitive comparison, and guilt. He presents the moralists, clergy, and lawgivers almost as misanthropes who despise humanity and therefore conspire to simultaneously flatter, shame, and inflict guilt on people for their desires. Mandeville, on the other hand, presents himself as accepting of people as they really are, warts and all. There is a parallel to be drawn with contemporary discussions around stigmatisation. Today, when one critiques the harms of rising levels of obesity, gambling addiction, binge drinking culture, or paedophilia (or to use today's sanitised parlance, 'minor-attracted persons'), there is a tendency for the critique itself to be condemned as harmful for it risks 'stigmatising' these groups and their sense of self-worth.

Mandeville believes we should all drop the pretence. Especially given that, for him, the traditional contention that indulging our passions and self-interest has no benefit to society is plainly false. On the contrary, the central lesson of the *Fable* is that 'private vices, by the dextrous management of a skilful politician, may be turned into publick benefits' (ibid.: 231). Even the very worst in society, by pursuing their private self-interest, indulging their passions and even engaging in outright criminality, serve the public good. As Hirschman (1977) points out, Mandeville scarcely goes into detail about the process by which private vices are transformed into public benefit. Consequently, in its raw form, the 'harnessing' solution is 'marred by an element of alchemical transformation rather out of tune with the scientific enthusiasm of the age' (ibid.: 20). Only with regard to one particular 'vice' did Mandeville offer much detailed elaboration: the general desire for and consumption of material goods, wealth, and luxury. He lists off a string of examples around how even the 'worst' of society do something for the public benefit.

Thieves and robbers, for example, provide trade for blacksmiths and locksmiths who make weapons, locks, and gates to guard against intruders. Without these criminals, 'half the Smiths of the nation would want employment; and abundance of workmanship (which now serves for ornament as well as defence) is to be seen everywhere both in town and country, that would never have been thought of, but to secure us against the attempts of pilferers and robbers' (Mandeville, 1988 [1732]: 98). He urges the reader 'to look upon the Consumption of things, and he'll find that the laziest and most unactive, the profligate and most mischievous are all forc'd to do something for the common good'. While they are gluttonous and wasteful, endlessly consuming and destroying material goods, this habit provides a great deal of employment and trade: 'The Labour of Millions would soon be at an End, if there were not other millions, as I say, in the *Fable*, "Employ'd, To see their Handy-works destroy'd"' (ibid.: 98). The same argument is applied to the highwayman who solicits the 'common harlot', who in turn purchases stockings, dresses, gloves, and shoes, providing work for the textiles dealer, tailor, and merchants. Prostitution, Mandeville argues, even guards against rape and sexual harassment!

> The passions of some people are too violent to be curb'd by any law or precept; and it is wisdom in all governments to bear with lesser inconveniences to prevent greater. If courtezans and strumpets were to be prosecuted with as much rigour as some silly people would have it, what locks or bars would be sufficient to preserve the honour of our wives and daughters? [...] Some Men would grow outrageous, and ravishing would become a common crime. Where six or seven thousand sailors arrive at once, as it often happens at Amsterdam, that have seen none but their own sex for many months together, how is it to be suppos'd that honest women should walk the streets unmolested, if there were no Harlots to be had at reasonable prices?
>
> *(Mandeville, 1988 [1732]: 102–103)*

It is worth noting that with the exception of this final farfetched example, the 'public benefits' that are to be derived from indulging and harnessing these private vices are conceived of in exclusively economic terms. It is here that we begin to see a narrowing of the aims around the collective Good down to economic and material well-being; for the abandonment of the *telos* and the acceptance of people as naturally egoistic and self-interested with such diversely incompatible desires means there cannot be an overall Good to which we collectively strive. Even where the good is not spoken of in economic terms, it is discussed as the mere absence of *a priori* evils (i.e. rape or war) rather than the *presence* of anything, which would become a feature of liberalism's negative politics (Badiou, 2001; Deneen, 2018).

Nevertheless, at the time, Mandeville's brazenly open declaration that 'private vices have public benefits' was still considered too scandalous to be palatable. It seemed to be suggesting that vices such as greed, gluttony, lust, and so on were somehow good in and of themselves, which, needless to say, was a significant departure from basic ethical intuitions that were deeply rooted in centuries of philosophical and theological thought and tradition. Furthermore, the question remained as to by what process the otherwise irrepressible passions were to be harnessed and controlled.

The answer to both of these issues was to be found in the idea of the countervailing passion (Hirschman, 1977). While the passions had traditionally been uniformly denounced and placed in opposition to the virtues or reason, in the 17th and 18th centuries, the passions were to undergo a partial rehabilitation. It was surmised that passions could only be defeated or tamed through other passions. Therefore, rather than denouncing all of the passions uniformly, they were divided up, with more 'innocuous' passions placed in opposition to those that were thought to be more dangerous and corrosive, with the former capable of keeping the latter in check. For example, in Hume's essay *Of Refinement in the Arts*, he acknowledges that luxury and the desire for material goods have its dangers. But it also provides a check and balance against the evil of 'sloth', which for Hume is far more pernicious:

> By banishing vicious luxury, without curing sloth and an indifference to others, you only diminish industry in the state, and add nothing to men's charity or their generosity. Let us, therefore, rest contented with asserting that two opposite vices in a state may be more advantageous than either of them alone; but let us never pronounce vice in itself advantageous.
>
> *(Hume, 1994 [1752]: 114)*

Hirschman lists off a whole host of minor and major thinkers in the 18th century for whom 'the idea of engineering social progress by cleverly setting up one passion to fight another became a fairly common intellectual pasttime' (Hirschman, 1977: 26). With regard to economic matters, this idea of the countervailing passion became even more palatable when the passion of avarice ceased to be understood as a passion at all and was instead described under the blander term of 'interest'. This was an accomplishment of Adam Smith, and not merely an insignificant case of semantics. Accepting that people were subject to their passions was to also accept that they were, to a significant degree, volatile and unpredictable. While the idea of the countervailing passion was nevertheless appealing as a means of trying to harness and manage the passions, there was still the sense that one was attempting to govern forces that were not entirely under control. Smith's semantic accomplishment, Hirschman argues, was to transform the passion of avarice into something different entirely by endeavouring to show that when individuals follow their interests – now conceived in purely economic terms – they become cold, calculating, and, most importantly, predictable:

> The insatiability of *auri sacra fames* [hunger for gold] had often been considered the most dangerous and reprehensible aspect of that passion. By a strange twist, because of the preoccupation of post-Hobbesian thinking with man's inconstancy, this very insatiability now became a virtue because it implied constancy. Nevertheless, for this radical change in valuation to carry conviction, and to effectuate a temporary suspension of deeply rooted patterns of thought and judgment, it was necessary to endow the "obstinate" desire for gain with an additional quality: harmlessness.
>
> *(Hirschman, 1977: 56)*

Collectively, these ideas around the countervailing passion, harnessing the passions, and the transition of economic self-interest from being a 'passion' to merely predictable 'interest' that could serve the public good, enabled classical liberalism to accelerate the process of deconstructing the traditional Symbolic Order and its various prohibitions and impediments upon individual economic and consumer desires. Of course, as the final line of Hirschman's quote above indicates, economic self-interest nevertheless had to be viewed as innocuous and imbued with a relative harmlessness in order to be firmly accepted as an outright positive virtue rather than reluctantly tolerated as expedient and unavoidable. Despite all the talk of economic individualism's constancy and predictability, this was still a system being driven forward by intense interpersonal competition, anxiety, and insecurity.

A counterforce was needed and was to be found in the sentimentalist moral philosophers. As numerous scholars have observed, this was a period in philosophy that placed a marked emphasis on sentiment and feeling as much as reason (Eagleton, 2009; Hall, 2012a; MacIntyre, 2002). Commerce and money-making was declared as *doux* – roughly translated as soft and gentle – and as something which polishes and civilises the manners. Samuel Johnston famously wrote 'There are few ways in which a man can be more innocently employed than in getting money' and Francis Hutcheson advocated the 'calm desire for wealth' (Hirschman, 1977). Whereas previously, money-making was considered synonymous with the wild and destructive passion of avarice, here 'the interests' were conceived as having an ideal combination of being a passion that was both strong but also calm and gentle. Hume emphasised that we must 'distinguish betwixt a calm and a weak passion; betwixt a violent and a strong one' (Hume, 2007: 269), and money-making for Hume was a perfect example of how a calm *and* strong passion such as commerce and economic self-interest could allegedly overpower violent passions of hedonism and pleasure (Hume, 2020 [1752]). Individuals must ruthlessly compete and pursue their self-interest in the economic realm, but these activities are to be conducted with a surface veneer of civility. Even Montesquieu, who could not in any other way be compared with the sentimentalist philosophers, and whose thought was in many respects out of keeping with his time, nevertheless placed a great deal of emphasis on 'gentleness' more generally, discussing it in relation to a wide range of topics. In relation to economic activities, he wrote: 'Commerce cures destructive prejudices, and it is an almost general rule that everywhere there are gentle mores, there is commerce and that everywhere there is commerce, there are gentle mores' (Montesquieu, 1989 [1748]: 338). Commerce was seen as bringing cultures together and civilising rude and barbarous customs, and the influence of this idea persists today in the view of economic unions such as the EU fostering cosmopolitan tolerance, or of economically advanced neoliberal countries as progressive and morally advanced in comparison to the backwards and corrupt nations of the developing world. This is the aforementioned pseudo-pacification process working, and an early example of commercial humanism. Capitalism with a warm human face.

Interpersonal relations and social activities were permeated with elaborate displays of politeness, warm feeling, and intimacy, such that how one entered a room and greeted others was of utmost importance and could inspire total admiration or disdain. It was a period of highly tuned sensibility, deep feeling, and sympathy with others. As both Eagleton (2009) and Hall (2012a) acknowledge, it was a moral culture of the Lacanian Imaginary. Such benevolence and fellow feeling was not to be extended to the realms of the Symbolic Order, of laws or policies, or social roles that could regulate or prohibit certain types of individual economic conduct. What we are, who we are, our social roles and natural relationships that are rooted in the Symbolic Order should not govern us. This outright rejection of the *telos* was the basic conclusion of Hume's famous is-ought problem, which claimed that we can never derive what we *ought* to do or what we *ought* to avoid from factual statements about what and who we *are*. In Hume's view, reason, our natural relationships, our social and symbolic roles cannot provide us with any direction as to what we should want. Reason simply guides us as to the best possible means of attaining whatever we happen to desire, which is the meaning behind Hume's belief that reason is a 'slave of the passions'. The (im)morality of something is not to be ascertained by reason but is to be measured by the feelings it stirred in the breast (Hume, 1983 [1751]). There was to be no distinction between 'seems to me' and 'is in fact', a personalised relativism that conveniently emerged in a period of rapid economic growth which wished to establish new markets and expand existing ones without the stultifying prohibitions of the Symbolic Order:

> Throughout their works, eighteenth century benevolentist and sentimentalist philosophers […] seemed to be busy in an attempt to construct an intermediary realm, a middle deck that housed a social club where a fragile artificial bonhomie could be orchestrated between the boiler-room of reptilian economic predation and the bridge of dutiful obedience to restrictive norms and laws cobbled together from the detritus of deracinated and relocated values. We should feel for each

other, extend sympathy, listen to each other's problems and share each other's dreams, have fun and romance, but only in the clubhouse dedicated to such contrived sentimental activities; to extend our fellow-feeling elsewhere – especially in economic transactions – was personally naïve and socio-economically destructive.

(Hall, 2012a: 236–237)

Human desire – previously sidelined as a totally corrupting influence – has now come back to the fore. Through a circuitous route, the passions have been rehabilitated, and the individual's feelings and natural inclinations are once again seen in a positive light. But where, in an Aristotelian scheme, human desire's role in morality was previously connected to the *telos* of the individual's social roles, practices, and relationships – and therefore the stabilising influence of the Symbolic Order – this time, they return to morality in a way that is completely divorced from these stabilising influences. Rather, they retreat from the Symbolic Order into the Imaginary, in which all that morality consists of is spontaneous feeling and sentiment of individuals detached from their social roles and relationships, making consistency impossible and relativism endemic in a way that pre-empts the contemporary culture of emotivism.

This brings us back to the moral philosophy of Immanuel Kant, which we touched upon in the previous chapter and is essentially a riposte to the sentimentalists in general and David Hume in particular. Kant famously credits Hume with rescuing him from his 'dogmatic slumber' (Kant, 2004: 10). As we have seen, for the sentimentalists, we are slave to our passions. The passions, rather than reason, are what motivate us to action and inaction. Morality is rooted in the feelings it spontaneously generates in ourselves and others and consequently this subjectivises and relativises morality to the extent that there are no moral facts, only moral opinions. For a man as heavily influenced by religion as Kant, this was unpardonable for a couple of reasons. For starters, Kant believed that human beings are free and rational agents, capable of autonomous reason, and that freedom is essential to morality. If there is no freedom to morally reason, if we are merely slave to our passions and sentiments, then there can be no moral responsibility or real blameworthiness of our actions. Secondly, Kant firmly believed that there were in fact universal moral facts and truths that could be derived

through logic, and in his formulation of the categorical imperative, he endeavours to give human beings the means to exercise this
rationality in a consistent way. A test for establishing obligations that
all rational agents have simply by virtue of being rational agents; a
law that they must follow. In Lacanian terms, Kant's philosophy was
effectively an effort to wrestle morality out of the Imaginary and back
into the Symbolic Order of universal laws (Eagleton, 2009). But it was
a Symbolic Order that was to be firmly organised around the rational
individual as sovereign and as the source of moral authority. To obey
any external authority, to be guided by anything outside of our free
and rational logic – be that our passions, divine command, or any
particular shared conception of the good, ends, or purposes – is to be
guilty of a wrong-headed heteronomy. The telos has been successfully
evacuated from moral life and the individual is now centre stage.

We have already discussed Kant's deontological moral philosophy
in the previous chapter and its shortcomings: its tautologous nature,
its inability to provide the individual with good reasons for obeying
the categorical imperative, the relative emptiness of the test, and its
comparison with a Neo-Aristotelian ethics which has been argued
to be a superior and necessary basis for the concept of social harm.
Therefore, I will refrain from repeating that discussion again here
(see MacIntyre, 2002, 2011 for more extensive discussions). But it
was worth briefly mentioning Kantian moral philosophy in contrast
to Hume and the sentimentalists at this point because it is arguable
that our contemporary culture – particularly with regard to social
harm – is simultaneously sentimentalist *and* deontological. It is sentimentalist in its emphasis on feelings, individual desires, personal
experience, and interpretation. It is sentimentalist in its *emotivist* character and its tendency to be a manipulative culture in this respect as
discussed in Chapter 1. But it is also deontological in its emphasis
on obedient rule-following, human rights, law, and the attempts of
scholars to establish timeless and universal *a priori* principles for the
concept of social harm much in the same way as Kant did for morality. Moreover, in both sentimentalist and deontological schemes, the
individual is morally sovereign (albeit in very different ways), and the
idea of a shared notion of the Good is eschewed as a basis for morality.

Consequently, we can arguably diagnose our zemiological culture as having one foot in the Lacanian Imaginary and another in
the Symbolic. Recall that the Imaginary is the realm of manipulation, the attempt to exert control over the mirror image, and

achieve perfect unity and wholeness between the self and the external world. In precisely the same way, the culture of emotivism is a manipulative culture which tugs at sentiment, feeling, and deploys powerful emphasis upon personal experience and identity to coerce the opinion of those in the external world to conform with their own. By contrast, as mentioned above, Kant's moral philosophy based on universal law, duty, and obligation is firmly of the register of the symbolic order, but in a relatively inefficient way that cannot provide the subject with good reasons for following these injunctions. This is what makes it susceptible to the Imaginary's gymnastics and flexibility. This can be witnessed by the fact that our culture increasingly attempts to *merge* sentimentalist emotivism with universal law. It endeavours to make law – a tool of the Symbolic – serve the feelings, interpretations, perceptions, and mis-identifications of the narcissistic Imaginary. To provide just a couple of examples, the police and the Crown Prosecution Service (CPS) define hate crime as: 'Any criminal offence *which is perceived by the victim or any other person*, to be motivated by hostility or prejudice, based on a person's disability or perceived disability; race or perceived race; or religion or perceived religion; or sexual orientation or perceived sexual orientation or transgender identity or perceived transgender identity' (CPS, 2017, emphasis added). Similarly, law, policy, and practice to tackle corruption is frequently based on the Corruption *Perception* Index (CPI), as produced by Transparency International, which is nothing more than an aggregation of impressions and perceptions as to the extent to which a particular nation is corrupt.

How has our zemiological culture come to acquire this paradoxical deontological-sentimentalist character, which endeavours to make the institutions of the Symbolic Order the servant of the Imaginary? The answer, it will be argued, is through liberalism, the economic and cultural variants of which have come to collectively dominate contemporary political, economic cultural, moral, and intellectual life.

References

Badiou, A. (2001) *Ethics: An Essay on the Understanding of Evil*. London. Verso.

Brenner, R. (2003) *Merchants and Revolution: Commercial Change, Political Conflict, and London's Overseas Traders 1550-1653*. London. Verso.

Bukovansky, M. (2006) 'The Hollowness of Anti-Corruption Discourse'. *Review of International Political Economy*. 13(2): 181–209. DOI: 10.1080/09692290600625413.

Chesterton, G.K. (2009) *Three Works on Distributism*. Scotts Valley. Createspace Independent Publishing Platform.

CPS (2017) 'Hate Crime'. Available at: https://www.cps.gov.uk/crime-info/hate-crime.

Deneen, P. (2018) *Why Liberalism Failed*. New Haven. Yale University Press.

Dupuy, J.P. (2014) *Economy and the Future: A Crisis of Faith*. East Lansing. MI. Michigan State University Press.

Dyer, C. (2000) *Everyday Life in Mediaeval England*. London. Hambledon and London.

Eagleton, T. (2009) *Trouble with Strangers: A Study of Ethics*. Oxford. Blackwell.

Elias, N. (1994) *The Civilising Process*. Oxford. Blackwell.

Farchy, J. and Blas, J. (2021) *The World for Sale: Money, Power and the Traders Who Barter the Earth's Resources*. London. Random House.

Hall, S. (2012a) *Theorising Crime and Deviance: A New Perspective*. London. Sage.

Hall, S. (2012b) 'The Solicitation of the Trap: On Transcendence and Transcendental Materialism in Advanced Consumer-Capitalism'. *Human Studies*. 35(3): 365–381.

Hall, S. (2014) 'The Socioeconomic Function of Evil'. *The Sociological Review*. 62(2): 13–31.

Hall, S. (2020) 'Consumer Culture and English History's Lost Object' in S. Hall, T. Kuldova and M. Horsley (Eds) *Crime, Harm and Consumerism*. Abingdon. Routledge: 21–38.

Hansen, H.K. and Flyverbom, M. (2015) 'The Politics of Transparency and the Calibration of Knowledge in the Digital Age'. *Organisation*. 22(6): 872–889.

Hirschman, A. (1977) *The Passions and the Interests: Political Arguments for Capitalism before Its Triumph*. Princeton. Princeton University Press.

Hobbes, T. (2017 [1642]) 'De Cive' in D. Baumgold (Ed) *Three Text Edition of Thomas Hobbes' Political Theory: The Elements of Law, De Cive, and Leviathan*. Cambridge. Cambridge University Press.

Hudson, M. (2018) *And Forgive Them Their Debts: Lending, Foreclosure and Redemption from Bronze Age Finance to the Jubilee Year*. Dresden. Islet.

Hume, D. (1983 [1751]) *An Enquiry Concerning the Principles of Morals*. Indianapolis. Hackett.

Hume, D. (1994 [1752]) 'Of Refinement in the Arts' in K. Haakonssen (Ed) *David Hume: Political Essays*. Cambridge. Cambridge University Press: 105–114.

Hume, D. (2007) *A Treatise of Human Nature: Volume 1*. Oxford. Oxford University Press.

Hume, D. (2020 [1752]) 'Of Interest' in E. Fuller (Ed) *A Source Book on Early Monetary Thought: Writings on Money Before Adam Smith*. Cheltenham. Edward Elgar Publishing.

Johnston, A. (2008) *Žižek's Ontology: A Transcendental Materialist Theory of Subjectivity*. Chicago. Northwestern University Press.

Kant, I. (2004) *Prolegomena to Any Future Metaphysics: With Selections from the Critique of Pure Reason*. Cambridge. Cambridge University Press.

Luther, M. (2012 [1535]) *Commentary on the Epistle to the Galatians*. Milton Keynes. Authentic Publishers.

Lutz, C.S. (2012) *Reading Alasdair MacIntyre's After Virtue*. London. Continuum Publishing Group.

MacCulloch, D. (2010) *A History of Christianity*. London. Penguin.

MacFarlane, A. (1978) 'The Origins of English Individualism: Some Surprises'. *Theory and Society*. 6(2): 255–277.

MacFarlane, A. (1979) *The Origins of English Individualism: The Family, Property, and Social Transition*. New York. Cambridge University Press.

Machiavelli, N. (2005 [1532]) *The Prince*. Oxford. Oxford University Press.

MacIntyre, A. (2002) *A Short History of Ethics*. Abingdon. Routledge.

MacIntyre, A. (2011) *After Virtue*. London. Bloomsbury.

Maddern, P. (1992) *Violence and Social Order: East Anglia 1422–1442*. Oxford. Oxford University Press.

Mandeville, B. (1988 [1732]) *The Fable of the Bees or Private Vices, Publick Benefits*. Indianapolis. The Online Library of Liberty.

McMahon, D. (2006) *Happiness: A History*. New York. Atlantic Monthly Press.

Milbank, J. and Pabst, A. (2016) *The Politics of Virtue: Post-Liberalism and the Human Future*. London. Rowman & Littlefield.

Montesquieu (1989 [1748]) *The Spirit of Laws*. Cambridge. Cambridge University Press.

Nye, J.S. (1967) 'Corruption and Political Development: A Cost-Benefit Analysis'. *American Political Science Review*. 61(2): 417–427.

Polanyi, K. (2001) *The Great Transformation: The Political and Economic Origins of Our Time*. Boston. Beacon Press.

Sassatelli, R. (2007) *Consumer Culture: History, Theory, Politics*. London. Sage.

Shelley, B. (2013) *Church History in Plain Language*. Nashville. Thomas Nelson.

Siedentop, L. (2014) *Inventing the Individual: The Origins of Western Liberalism*. Cambridge. Harvard University Press.

Smith, A. (2002 [1759]) *The Theory of Moral Sentiments*. Cambridge. Cambridge University Press.

Sombart, W. (1915) *The Quintessence of Capitalism*. New York. E.P. Dutton & Company.

Spinoza, (2016 [1677]) *A Political Treatise*. Exercere Cerebrum Publications.

Tawney, R.H. (1948) *Religion and the Rise of Capitalism*. Middlesex. Pelican Books.

Thomas, K. (2009) *The Ends of Life: Roads to Fulfilment in Early Modern England*. Oxford. Oxford University Press.

Tsoukas, H. (1997) 'The Tyranny of Light: The Temptations and Paradoxes of the Information Society'. *Futures*. 29(9): 827–843.

Vico, G. (1999 [1725]) *The New Science*. London. Penguin Classics.

Visnjic, J. (2021) *The Invention of Duty: Stoicism as Deontology*. Boston. Brill.

Walzer, M. (1965) *The Revolution of the Saints: A Study in the Origins of Radical Politics*. Cambridge. Harvard University Press.

Ward-Perkins, B. (2005) *The Fall of Rome and the End of Civilization*. Oxford. Oxford University Press.

Weber, M. (2002) *The Protestant Ethic and the Spirit of Capitalism*. Oxford. Blackwell.

Winlow, S. and Hall, S. (2012) 'What Is an "Ethics Committee"? Academic Governance in an Epoch of Belief and Incredulity'. *The British Journal of Criminology*. 52(2): 400–416. https://doi.org/10.1093/bjc/azr082.

6

DISAVOWED LIBERALISM

We have taken a long and circuitous journey over the last two chapters, and if we are to avoid losing our bearings it is worth reminding ourselves of their relevance to the core purpose of this book. Chapter 2, if you recall, argued that the starting point for any zemiological enquiry should be an epistemological question. Namely, how can we know with confidence and good reason that something or someone is being harmed, or that some structure, individual, institution, or process is perpetrating social harm? In order to know this, it was argued that we must have some under-standing of the nature of these things, of how they are supposed to work, develop, and function so that we can know when they are flourishing and when they are not. Essentially, we must have an understanding of their *telos*, and it was argued that a shared notion of the Good rooted in the *telos* of human beings, social roles, prac-tices, and institutions was essential if the concept of social harm is to be functional. *A priori* principles of harm that are independent of any particular conception of the Good will not do. However, the problem is that this notion of the *telos* and a shared and robust notion of the Good, while not entirely lost, has certainly been marginalised and is now prohibited from exerting a meaningful influence over the most important aspects of political, economic, and cultural life. We now occupy a society thoroughly committed

DOI: 10.4324/9781003098546-6

to an abstract individualism, pluralism, and a postmodern cynicism towards all collective identities and norms. We lack a shared notion of the Good, while social mores, customs, or any form of normativity is increasingly described as a kind of socio-cultural despotism over the individual. Trying to establish a universally agreed upon understanding of what is and is not socially harmful within this liberal-pluralist context is like trying to climb a mountain that has no summit.

The previous two chapters, therefore, have been dedicated to tracing the events and developments that have contributed to this gradual marginalisation of the *telos* from economic, social, and cultural life; surveying religion, philosophy, and legal, economic, and cultural changes. Collectively, these developments not only pushed the notion of the *telos* to the margins but also created a fundamentally different world. A more individualistic world, one in which the legitimacy of all political and religious authorities were being called into question. Quite simply, they created the economic, cultural, and moral context in which liberalism's domain assumptions and key characteristics could be formed.

While I have already discussed the barrier of liberalism to zemiological coherence in Chapter 2 and elsewhere (see Raymen, 2019), this chapter takes a closer look at liberalism and what it means for the concept of social harm. First, it outlines how liberalism's domain assumptions completely shut the door on the notion of the *telos* and a Neo-Aristotelian ethics, thereby continuing and completing the journey we have taken over the past several chapters. Secondly, it explores how these domain assumptions are present in specific strands of more recent political and academic thought. These strands have shaped our wider zemiological and moral culture, contributing to its simultaneously deontological and sentimentalist character that was alluded to in the previous chapter. But it will also be argued that they have contributed significantly to contemporary thinking around the concept of social harm and social harm research in critical criminology and zemiology more generally. As the title of this chapter suggests, underpinning a lot of research that invokes the language of harm is a disavowed and possibly unconscious attachment to certain key domain assumptions of philosophical liberalism.

Liberalism's Domain Assumptions

Liberalism has acquired a reputation for being notoriously hard to pin down (Losurdo, 2011; Zevin, 2021). It is true that what liberals have said and believed in different times and places has diverged and different variants of liberalism have emerged along particular political, economic, and cultural lines in response to specific and historically contextual issues, such that some might claim it is folly to refer to liberalism as a unified doctrine. There are many culturally liberal leftists who, at least rhetorically, claim to despise the political-economic commitments of neoliberalism – although the widespread support from the political left to remain in the quintessentially neoliberal European Union should call the strength of this opposition into question (Winlow et al, 2017). There are equally many committed neoliberals who have also espoused culturally conservative values, despite those values being directly undermined by their economic commitments. To confuse matters further, in the US the term 'Liberal' often refers to those who advocate greater economic intervention by the state, while 'Conservatives' are those who advocate a greater economic libertarianism which Europeans more accurately describe as liberal. At their core, both the Conservative Party in the UK and the Republican Party in the US have been economically liberal for quite some time, with genuine philosophical conservatives operating on the margins. It is equally unhelpful that many liberals have avoided the term altogether, often describing themselves as something other than 'liberal'; an observation made by the openly liberal writer for *The Economist,* Edmund Fawcett (2014), and one that arguably applies to a significant portion of the academic social sciences.

'Liberal', therefore, has been employed – not inaccurately – to describe corporate capitalist goliaths and hippy counterculture activists alike. Of course, as numerous intellectuals and commentators now acknowledge, the surface-level opposition between economic liberals of the right and the cultural liberals of the left masks a deeper synergy that has allowed liberalism to dominate politics, economics, the arts, culture, and large swathes of the social sciences for the past 50 years (Deneen, 2018; Milbank and Pabst, 2016; Pabst, 2019; Winlow and Hall, 2013; Zamora and Behrent, 2015). In fact, once some key domain assumptions have been established, liberalism as an over-arching term becomes relatively straightforward to understand, and it becomes clear that the political, economic, and cultural 'divergences' that have made liberalism seem like a smorgasbord of otherwise incompatible figures are not nearly as great as they appear.

Perhaps the most significant of these domain assumptions is liberalism's anthropological assumptions, which are largely inherited from proto-liberal thinkers. Quite simply, liberalism views human beings at their essence as fundamentally isolated, autonomous, rational, and self-determining creatures. It thinks of the individual as separate from their natural relationships and social roles. At their essence, human beings are not sons, daughters, siblings, or members of a community, but first and foremost self-interested individuals radically independent from all of these things. For liberalism and its ethics, there must be a self that is prior to and more than a mere collection of their social roles and characteristics that are shaped by their present position in the world.

We can see these assumptions in the thought experiments of liberal and proto-liberal thinkers, who tend to strip the individual of all other extraneous 'social' details when confronting an issue such as politics, ethics, or justice. This is true of Rawls' 'original position', in which the subject stands behind a 'veil of ignorance' unaware of any of their social characteristics or position in society, and in this abstracted state must rationally decide on the fairest principles of justice that would best help individuals achieve their various conflicting ends. This is equally true of the subject in Kant's deontological ethics which informs Rawls' liberal egalitarianism. Kant's endeavour to develop *a priori* ethical principles independent of any particular ends, purpose, or conception of the good necessitates the imagination of a rational subject with an autonomous will that exists prior to and independent of all experience. We see the same tendency in Hobbes' state of nature and his notion of 'natural man'. In the state of nature, there is no society, culture, ethics, family, government, or law. The individual is equated to a mushroom that springs out of the ground, coming to full maturity without any engagement with others (Hobbes, 2017). The 'natural individual' is fundamentally rational and self-interested, motivated by the fear of death and the desire to dominate others, and on these grounds agrees to the social contract out of self-interest. Of course, Hobbes' imagination of the state of nature has never existed in actuality, and the idea of the original social contract itself is littered with self-contradictions. The social contract is supposed to be the story of how human beings come to share social norms and standards. It is the original foundation of the social, the genesis of all shared rules and standards of conduct. But the idea of the contract presupposes an existing convention or understanding of a set of words and rules as binding upon individuals, an understanding which, according to Hobbes' fictitious state of nature, could not exist because the original contract founded such shared rules and standards (MacIntyre, 2002: 132). It is a functional origin myth. Just as Adam and Eve's banishment from the Garden of Eden facilitates Christianity's assumption of humanity as 'fallen', Hobbes' state of nature is a functional origin myth that enables liberalism to imagine human beings as autonomous and rational creatures abstracted from their natural relationships.

This idea of the individual as isolated, rational, and non-relational is important for and closely related to liberalism's transformation of the concept of freedom. As we mentioned in earlier chapters, the meaning of 'freedom' in antiquity was much different to our basically liberal understanding of freedom today. The ancient conception of liberty was not just the freedom to choose, but an ability to choose wisely in accordance with one's *telos* by controlling and disciplining one's passions, and possessing this freedom aided the individual in the more demanding pursuit of human flourishing (Visnjic, 2021). It was a *substantive* conception of freedom with content and direction, rather than a merely *formal* conception of freedom in which the individual possesses the right to do and choose however they please within the limits of law (Milbank and Pabst, 2016). The individual who indulged their base whims and fancies was not considered 'free', but in thrall to their basic desires and therefore barred from the attainment of human flourishing. Freedom, therefore, was fundamentally about the education of one's desires and the freedom to identify one's true end and Good, which was inextricably bound up with their membership of a particular community and their inherited and acquired social roles and practices (Deneen, 2018; MacIntyre, 2011). It was the presence of virtuous wisdom rather than the mere absence of constraint, and as such was understood as something that was *achieved* rather than something that was 'possessed' as a formal right. The idea of freedom as 'self-mastery' evokes this sense of achievement and accomplishment. When one 'masters' a particular skill, it indicates the attainment of a certain level of excellence through practice and education and also indicates a certain shared standard or criteria by which we can judge whether someone has 'mastered' that particular skill. This is what is traditionally meant by 'positive liberty'. Although as we will see, even this is distorted by liberal thinkers such as Constant, Mill, and Berlin in ways that are inherited by contemporary zemiologists.

Liberalism's conception of freedom, on the other hand, is much different in a number of interrelated ways. As we have seen, on the teleological view, freedom is viewed as a means to the achievement of a greater end or good. On the liberal view, by contrast, freedom is thought of as a good and an end in itself. This is because the liberal idea of freedom is also rooted in an autonomous voluntarism. This is where liberalism's aforementioned anthropological assumptions are important. For liberalism, what is most important is not the ends we choose but our capacity to freely choose them rather than them being given to us; and this capacity is found in a self – the isolated mushroom individual – that exists separate from and prior to all of our inherited and acquired relationships and conditions (Sandel, 1982). Political authority, social roles, law, institutions, traditions, customs, and even morality do not have any natural claims upon the individual's actions or desires. The legitimacy of all of these things is dependent upon whether or not they have been freely chosen and consented to by the individual, free from all external influence or consideration. This is an important point regarding liberalism's alleged neutrality. While liberalism often claims to be neutral on *what* we should choose, it is far from neutral when it comes to *how* we should choose (Deneen, 2018). The basis upon which we evaluate institutions, community membership, social norms, our personal desires, or even personal and familial relationships should be, first and foremost, that of individual choice and self-interest.

Consequently, liberalism tends to encourage tentative commitments and loose bonds which are always subject to revision according to the individual's desires and self-interest. As Deneen (2018: 48) so pithily summarises, in the liberal imagination we are wholes apart, rather than parts of wholes. For early liberal thinkers like Constant (2011 [1816]) the 'freedom of the ancients' – in which all citizens of the *polis* had a direct and influential say in matters of government and public policy in comparison to modern societies – is not only impractical in large complex modern nation states, but it also comes at too high a price. While the people of antiquity had great political sovereignty, Constant argues, they were also completely subjected to the 'authority of the community'. Their actions were determined by their social roles and the mores, customs, ethics, and traditions of the ancient *polis*, which regulated and issued guidance in almost all areas of life. 'All private actions were submitted to a severe surveillance', and among the ancients, 'the individual, almost always sovereign in public affairs, was a slave in all his private relations' (ibid.: 6). We should not, Constant warns, sacrifice individual liberty for political liberty. For Constant, individual liberty is the truest form of freedom, and this is guaranteed by an element of political liberty, albeit reduced. Asking people to 'sacrifice, like those of the past, the whole of their individual liberty to political liberty, is the surest means of detaching them from the former and, once this result has been achieved, it would be only too easy to deprive them of the latter' (ibid.: 15). Furthermore, Constant assumes that the political sovereignty of the ancients would be experienced as a burdensome inconvenience to modern individuals, pulling them away from more prized private endeavours of commerce, speculation, and pursuit of pleasures from which the modern individual 'does not wish to be distracted ... other than momentarily, and as little as possible' (Constant, 2011 [1816]: 9). What modern people wanted most was freedom and agency to carry out their lives as they saw fit. As a political philosophy, liberalism was conceived as a rebellion against traditional political and religious authority, tradition, and cultural custom.

While Constant's essay is supposed to be a comparison of the 'freedom of the ancients' and the 'freedom of the moderns', this is a somewhat disingenuous description. What Constant actually does is project a modern liberal understanding of freedom into the past by failing to acknowledge that freedom in antiquity was about more than exercising greater political sovereignty. It was, as we have already mentioned and seen from the discussion of Aristotelian and Stoic ethics, about the ability to choose how to live well, how to choose wisely, and achieve human flourishing, all of which necessitated wider social considerations. By projecting his formal notion of freedom as a natural right that one possesses onto ancient societies which conceived of freedom as something that is *achieved*, Constant sees in the 'authority of the social body' (ibid.: 6) only unwanted and unwarranted impositions stifling and oppressing the subject, rather than as a source of guidance in how to achieve one's *telos*.

It is worth noting, however, that Constant is guilty of a contradiction in his own writing. While he defends steadfastly a formal, negative conception of liberty, he does concede that there is a danger. The danger is that 'absorbed in the enjoyment of our private independence, and in the pursuit of our particular interests, we should surrender our right to share in political power too easily' (Constant, 2011 [1816]: 17). The individual would not care for such important matters and would be concerned only with their private pleasures and trivialities. But we should not fear, because human beings are (and should be) naturally geared towards higher pursuits that bring us happiness. As he writes:

> Is it so evident that happiness, of whatever kind, is the only aim of mankind? *If it were so, our course would be narrow indeed, and our destination far from elevated.* There is not one single one of us who, if he wished to abase himself, restrain his moral faculties, lower his desires, abjure activity, glory, deep and generous emotions, could not demean himself and be happy. No, Sirs, I bear witness to *the better part of our nature,* that noble disquiet which pursues and torments us, that desire to broaden our knowledge and develop our faculties. *It is not to happiness alone, it is to self-development that our destiny calls us*; and political liberty is the most powerful, the most effective means of self-development that heaven has given us.
>
> *(Constant, 2011 [1816]: 17)*

While faithfully defending the right of the individual to choose as they please, Constant cannot countenance the idea that the individual might freely elect to withdraw from important matters of politics. Therefore, confronted with problems that he cannot resolve, Constant feels compelled to selectively return to the language of ascendency, excellence, and self-improvement, towards a conception of the true good and end of human lives. Effectively, Constant is trying to produce a hybrid by blending a formal, negative liberty with substantive freedom. Of course, this is a fundamental contradiction, and as post-liberal scholars have observed, 'it is impossible for a theory grounded on a formal definition to defend any exception to the formal extension of liberty, or any special pleading on behalf of customary mores as opposed to the indifferent operation of law. For this can always be deplored by the consistent liberal as improper delimitation of choice' (Milbank and Pabst, 2016: 34).

This fear and wariness around the improper delimitation of choice is palpable throughout liberal thought and leads us onto a further domain assumption of the liberal imagination: that power and authority can never be trusted to behave well, whether that power be in the form of governments, organised religion, social custom, or even the political will of the masses. Despite often being erroneously equated with democracy, liberalism's relationship with the popular will has always been a deeply conflicted and ambivalent one (Zevin, 2021). What John Stuart Mill called the 'tyranny of the majority' was described as being 'among the evils against which society requires to be on its guard' (Mill, 2003: 76). This continues to be seen today as numerous democratic elections, referendums, and popular opinion on major political and social issues have conflicted with the preferences of the liberal intelligentsia. When this has occurred, the tendency has been to depict the *demos* – particularly the working class – as lacking intelligence, easily duped and manipulated, or inherently bigoted, with the overall attitude being reminiscent of Bertolt Brecht's satirical poem in which the preference would be to dissolve the people and elect another (Embery, 2021; Winlow and Hall, 2022). Therefore, while there is a tendency for the term 'liberal' to evoke an image of an optimistic person with great faith in human reason, individuality, and progress, in actuality liberalism is philosophically underpinned by a dual pessimism, one that takes a rather gloomy view of either the individual, power and authority, or both (Milbank and Pabst, 2016).

For what we might today broadly describe as the liberals of the right, the individual is viewed as fundamentally egoistic, greedy, and self-interested – an inheritance of liberalism's disavowed roots in Christianity (Siedentop, 2014). As we saw in the last chapter, these more glum characteristics are considered to be so powerful and inevitable that it is assumed they cannot be educated or transcended in favour of more collectivist and altruistic dispositions. Consequently, they must be harnessed such that they can be geared towards positive outcomes of creativity, invention, and progress. Right-wing liberalism, as Milbank and Pabst (2016: 27) observe, is so distrustful of the motivations of the self-interested individual that it seeks social order primarily through the public instrument of the legally enforceable contract, while humanity's naturally egoistic and domineering character is also precisely what makes political and religious authority so dangerous.

The liberal left, on the other hand, typically takes a more romantic and Rousseauian view of the individual. In an almost complete inversion of Hobbes and Locke, the individual in their natural state – isolated from all social relations – is inherently good. Things such as bigotry, greed, and selfish competitiveness are not natural qualities but rather inevitable by-products of association with others and the entry of the individual into a social context. Social relations, traditions, and community encourage comparison and division which corrupt the otherwise good and natural individual. Therefore, the liberal left, particularly since the 1960s, has continuously sought to emancipate the individual from the yoke of social norms, institutions, traditional communities, and their shared standards and values, which are often depicted as useless artifices that are regressive and oppressive, corrupting the otherwise naturally good individual and their freedoms (Wolin, 2010). This is the dual pessimism of liberalism. While the liberals of the right tend to take a pessimistic view of the individual, the liberal left take a similarly pessimistic view of the social and deep social commitments. When it comes to the state, the best it can be is a protector of rights, a guarantor of freedoms, and an architect for market competition – the economic manifestation of such freedoms. At the outset of his book *Liberalism: The Life of an Idea*, Fawcett outlines the liberal utopia:

> The liberal dream was a myth of order in a masterless world: a peaceful, prosperous place without father figures or brotherhood, chieftains or comrades, final authorities or natural born friends. It was an appealing myth, shaped by distrust of powers, monopolies, and authorities, by faith that the human ills of warfare, poverty, and ignorance were corrigible in this world, and by unbreachable respect for the enterprises, interests, and opinions of people, whoever they were.
>
> *(Fawcett, 2014: 4–5)*

Therefore, in many respects liberalism is quite a cold and aloof doctrine. Its vision of an ideal world is characterised by the absence of love or intimacy. It is, as above, a world without father figures, brotherhood, comrades, or natural-born friends, and characterised only by the presence of an atomised and isolating cynical mistrust of the other. In general, the tendency is to view all forms of social authority as a potential form of despotism, and consistent with its anthropological assumptions, liberalism frequently pits the individual as separate from and in opposition to 'society'. In fact, as Mill argued, 'society' can be an even more dangerous tyrant than authoritarian and oppressive governments:

> But reflecting persons perceived that when society is itself the tyrant—society collectively, over the separate individuals who compose it—its means of tyrannizing are not restricted to the acts which it may do by the hands of its political functionaries. Society can and does execute its own mandates: and if it issues wrong mandates instead of right, or any mandates at all in things with which it ought not to meddle, it practises a social tyranny more formidable than many kinds of political oppression, since, though not usually upheld by such extreme penalties, it leaves fewer means of escape, penetrating much more deeply into the details of life, and enslaving the soul itself. Protection, therefore, against the tyranny of the magistrate is not enough: there needs protection also against the tyranny of prevailing opinion and feeling; against the tendency of society to impose, by other means than civil penalties, its own ideas and practices as rules of conduct on those who dissent from them; to fetter the development, and, if possible, prevent the formation, of any individuality not in harmony with its ways, and compel all characters to fashion themselves upon the model of its own. There is a limit to the legitimate interference of collective opinion with individual independence: and to find that limit, and maintain it against encroachment, is as indispensable to a good condition of human affairs, as protection against political despotism.
>
> *(Mill, 2003: 76)*

Unsurprisingly, both Mill and liberal thought more generally reject the notion of the *telos*, or the idea that there is some shared Good or standard of excellence and flourishing to which human beings should aspire. Mill is deeply critical of the 'ancient commonwealths' and 'ancient philosophers' and their 'vested interests in each other's moral, intellectual, and physical perfection' (ibid.: 152). This amounts to paternalism, which is an unconscionable despotism, and the 'despotism of custom is everywhere the standing hindrance to human advancement' (ibid.: 134). 'So monstrous a principle' Mill writes, 'is far more dangerous than any single interference with liberty' (ibid.: 152), and 'emancipation from that yoke [of custom] ... constitutes the chief interest of the history of mankind' (ibid.: 134–135). The individual should be absolutely sovereign in matters that concern themselves and requires rights against society from interfering or having a say over their actions, pursuits, and desires.

But what standard is to be employed for justifying interference? It is here that Mill outlines his famous 'harm principle':

> That principle is, that the sole end for which mankind are warranted, individually or collectively, in interfering with the liberty of action of any of their number, is self-protection. That the only purpose for which power can be rightfully exercised over any member of a civilized community, against his will, is to prevent harm to others. His own good, either physical or moral, is not a sufficient warrant. He cannot rightfully be compelled to do or forbear because it will be better for him to do so, because it will make him happier, because, in the opinions of others, to do so would be wise, or even right.
>
> *(Mill, 2003: 80)*

What is most notable about the above quote is how the second half of the excerpt deprives the harm principle of any substance. We can intervene against the actions of another if it is to prevent harm to other people. But then the question remains: how are we to discern whether or not an individual is going to be harmed? Mill explicitly rejects any shared notion of the Good for human beings, any standard of human flourishing or excellence, as a monstrous form of paternalistic despotism. In Mill's own words above, the individual's 'own good, either physical or moral, is not a sufficient warrant'. We cannot intervene because it would be better for the individual, because it would make them happier, or because it would be wise. To do so would be a violation of human dignity, and there is to be no collective deliberation on such matters because these are the preserve of the sovereign individual. Therefore, in setting out these limitations, Mill deprives the harm principle of any criteria for intervention. The above passage is entirely self-negating, and the harm principle becomes empty of meaning.

Interestingly, in the latter part of *On Liberty*, Mill recognises this shortcoming and, like Constant, almost reverts to a Neo-Aristotelian position which considers the *telos* of social roles and practices in order to resolve it (a *telos* that he has already rejected). In those situations in which a person, 'through intemperance or extravagance', becomes unable to pay their debts or provide for their families, then they are worthy of moral opprobrium. A person whose addictions cause pain or misery to the lives of their loved ones or renders them incapable of carrying out their domestic roles or public duties is equally worthy of condemnation. In such situations, 'the case is taken out of the province of liberty and placed in that of morality or law' (Mill, 2003: 145). Notable here is that the 'province of liberty' is considered as something distinct from that of morality, consistent with the tendency of liberal modern ethics to separate morality from desire. But of greater interest is the blatant contradiction in Mill's thought. Is this not society imposing itself upon the individual? Does this not espouse a normative understanding of what is required of social roles; a vision of social and moral excellence which determines what ends an individual should pursue and what desires they should avoid? These understandings of the duties and responsibilities of certain social roles and practices are informed by ethical custom, the sway of which was described earlier as a monstrous despotism and a profound danger to all human liberty. Here, Mill is at odds with his own principles, and while he equivocates and accepts traditional understandings of social roles and practices and their legitimate moral claims upon individual liberty, a little more than a century later the more libertine elements of the postwar left would not.

Irrespective of their equivocations and contradictions, both Mill and Constant unwaveringly maintain that the individual should be absolutely free in those matters which concern *only themselves*. Again, this is reflective of liberalism's anthropological assumptions of the individual abstracted from all social relationships; for are there truly any such practices that concern only oneself? Even if the individual is completely isolated and without friends or family, their demand for a particular service or product creates an industry that will affect others. How, then, are we to classify the conduct of bookmakers, drug dealers, or the producers and purveyors of alcohol whose business certainly has an impact on others? Mill actually confronts this issue when discussing the prohibition of alcohol in the US, conceding that 'trading is a social act'. But, Mill argues, the infringement he is complaining of is not upon the liberty of the trader but the liberty of the consumer, for to prohibit the trading of alcohol is to infringe on the liberty of the individual to consume it. Incapable of resolving this issue within the principles Mill himself has set out, he arbitrarily rules that the negative liberty of the individual must triumph. Of course, as Mill well knew, this suited capitalism perfectly and has been the basic logic underpinning the assumption of harmlessness and the relativisation of the harms emerging from various industries.

This profound distrust of the notion of the *telos*, of ascendency, of achieving a condition of excellence and human flourishing, has persisted and arguably intensified throughout liberal thought. Mid-20th century liberals, such as Isaiah Berlin, cynically viewed it as nothing more than a dangerous front for potential despots who wished to manipulate individuals towards their own ends and interests, degrading individuals and human dignity in the process. In his essay *Two Concepts of Liberty*, he addresses the dangers of the traditional idea of positive liberty. He talks about how a 'dominant self' is identified with 'reason, with my "higher nature" [...] with my "real" or "ideal", or "autonomous" self, or with myself "at its best"'. This is to be contrasted with one's 'lower' nature, which is 'swept by every gust of desire and passion, needing to be rigidly disciplined if it is ever to rise to the full height of its "real" nature' (Berlin, 2002: 179). Berlin's heavy use of scare quotes around these terms is indicative of this cynicism. This 'true self' associated with one's 'higher nature', Berlin argues, provides manipulative and despotic individuals with justification for oppressive control over the individual. It 'renders it easy for me to conceive of myself as coercing others for their own sake, in their, not my, interest. What [...] this entails is that they would not resist me if they were rational and wise as I and understood their interests as I do' (ibid.: 179–180).[1] Once we take this view, Berlin argues, such individuals are 'in a position to ignore the actual wishes of men or societies, to bully, oppress, torture them in the name, and on behalf, of their "real" selves' (ibid.: 180). They can do so 'in the secure knowledge that whatever is the true goal of man (happiness, performance of duty, wisdom, a just society, self-fulfilment) must be identical with his freedom – the free choice of his 'true', albeit often submerged and inarticulate self' (Berlin, 2002: 180). For Berlin, this is true of all social 'wholes' of which the individual is considered a part, and he lists off tribes, races, Churches, States, and communities as guilty parties. They are not sources of enrichment, belonging, identity, or support, but fundamentally manipulative institutions whose claims upon the individual should be curtailed and ought not be too closely embraced but kept at arm's length. This has roots in early liberalism's contestation of absolutist political rule and religious authority, but it has since been extended to a wide range of traditions, customs, and institutions which exert any normative influence or demand upon the individual. For Berlin, the individual is 'the author of values ... the ultimate authority of which consists precisely in the fact that they are willed freely' (Berlin, 2002: 183). As we will see shortly, in the contemporary social sciences and left-liberal politics, 'normativity' itself has become a dirty word; something to be eradicated for its capacity to label, stigmatise, and be exclusionary.

We might applaud this rejection of the overweening paternalism of the *telos* and a shared idea of human flourishing as preserving human dignity and autonomy. But as Milbank and Pabst (2016: 17) argue, this is a delusion. For the alternative to treating individuals as souls to be nurtured and cultivated is actually a far more patronising mode of paternalism, one which reduces individuals to bodies to be externally managed and manipulated through various impersonal bureaucratic processes, incentives, targets, and wars over which the 'autonomous' individual has little say in informing, all the while claiming – disingenuously – to respect their autonomy and freedom of choice (Graeber, 2015). This is certainly true of neoliberal governments who, being certain that the free market is the only guarantor of true human freedom, have consistently waged wars in the name of human rights, human dignity, and human freedom in exactly this vein. For prominent neoliberal thinker Ludwig von Mises, the nation state 'employs its power to beat people into submission solely for the prevention of actions destructive to the preservation and the smooth operation of the market economy' (Von Mises, 1996: 257). Non-democratic supranational organisations and treaties to ensure free movement of goods and capital are essential in order to make the most of the earth's natural mineral deposits, which, for Mises, are often 'located in areas whose inhabitants are too ignorant, too inert, or too dull to take advantage of the riches nature has bestowed upon them' (ibid.: 686). Historically, liberals have been far more paternalistic than they care to admit (Hochuli et al, 2021; Zevin, 2021).

Nevertheless, in Berlin's eyes, we should detach positive liberty from any particular conception of flourishing. The language of self-mastery is retained in Berlin's formulation, but it is a far more individualistic self-mastery that is quite distinct from the positive liberty of antiquity. It is to 'wish my life and decisions to depend on myself, not on external forces of whatever kind'. It is to 'be moved by reasons, by conscious purposes, which are my own, not by causes which affect me, as it were, from the outside' (Berlin, 2002: 178). There are a number of problems here which make this account of 'positive liberty' unsatisfactory and incoherent. First, by detaching positive liberty from any conception of the *telos*, Berlin significantly diminishes any meaningful distinction between positive and negative liberty. Berlin himself acknowledges this when he writes that 'the freedom which consists in being one's own master, and the freedom which consists in not being prevented from choosing as I do by other men, may, on the face of it, seem concepts at no great logical distance from one another' (Berlin, 2002: 178). To have positive liberty is to possess the power and resources to do as one chooses. It is simply the means to enact one's negative liberty, and both positive and negative forms of liberty operate together quite comfortably within the broader liberal frame. Secondly, Berlin prioritises negative liberty over and above positive liberty. There's not much point to positive liberty or choosing who governs you when they are forced, by the prioritisation of negative liberty, to leave everything alone. Indeed, this is precisely how neoliberal politics works today. Economic elites and cultural libertarians vote for and support whichever candidate promises to leave them alone to the greatest degree.

Thirdly – and an issue that relates back to liberalism's anthropological assumptions more generally – is the idea that one's decisions and desires are entirely one's own, that they are autonomously chosen and authored without any external influence. One of the fundamental lessons of Lacanian psychoanalysis is that this is an impossibility; that our desire is always the desire of the Other. Our desires are never entirely our own, and we are never truly the masters of our own house. As we saw in Chapter 3, the subject, desperate to escape the terror of the Real, actively solicits the Symbolic Order's system of signs, values, customs, and meaning that provide a frame of reference and fixity with which we can identify, orient ourselves, and make coherent sense of who we are in relation to the world. The formation of subjectivity simply is not possible without this submission to the Big Other. Therefore, as Žižek (2006) explains, when we desire, we do so within the confines of the symbolic space in which we dwell. When we are asking 'what do I want?', what we are *really* doing is asking the Big Other, 'what do you want from me?' In the Christian Symbolic Order, for instance, when we ask 'what should I do?', we are really asking 'What does God want from me?', exemplified by the popular W.W.J.D. (What Would Jesus Do) bracelets. In the world of consumerism, we desire according to what is popularly accepted by the Big Other as 'cool' and 'fashionable'. Our enjoyment or desire for a particular sports car or luxury watch would be diminished if others would not envy or admire our purchase. None of this is to say that we do not have the freedom or agency to make choices and shape our social and symbolic environment. It is simply to say that the choices we do make are always informed and constrained by the symbolic space in which we live. The notion that our desires can autonomously spring from within ourselves independent of our wider socio-symbolic environment is the disavowed lie at the heart of liberal-postmodernism. Even when our desires are transgressive, they are nevertheless dependent upon the very thing they transgress (Žižek, 2006).

Given that we are imagined to be isolated, egoistic, and non-relational creatures who have a profound distrust of all power and authority, and whose highest value is the liberty to autonomously choose our own ends, it is of little surprise that a further domain assumption of liberalism is the belief that conflict is inevitable and harmony impossible. The liberal writer Edmund Fawcett, quoted at the outset of this chapter, goes even further. For him, liberalism's 'desirable picture of society' is that of 'an unfraternal place without natural harmony from which clashing interests and discordant beliefs could never be removed but where, with luck and wise laws, unceasing conflict might nevertheless be turned to welcome ends in innovation, argument, and exchange' (Fawcett, 2014: 6). 'Social harmony', he argues, 'was not achievable, and to pursue it was foolish […] for harmony was not even desirable' (ibid.: 10) due to its tendency to stifle liberalism's appetite for blind progress for its own sake. As such, there is to be little to no agreement on what we should and should not do, on what our energies should and not be directed towards, or on what the ends of life should be. This belief in the inevitability of conflict is what drives liberalism's obsession with developing *a priori* principles of justice or morality which can establish the ground rules of fair play between otherwise discordant wills. It is what influenced Kant's philosophy which in turn shaped John Rawls' principles of justice, which we will turn to in a moment. But it also informs later forms of leftist political and social scientific thought around intersectionality in subtler ways as well.

These domain assumptions firmly reject any notion of the *telos*. Together, they act as a bouncer on the door of the club that doesn't just marginalise a Neo-Aristotelian ethics but ejects them into the alleyway, slams the door in their face, and issues them a lifetime ban from re-entry. Indeed, these domain assumptions discussed above are implicitly and explicitly present in a range of intellectual and political thought that both wittingly and unwittingly has had a substantial influence on contemporary thinking around the concept of social harm and the critical criminological and zemiological research landscape more broadly. Namely, the liberal egalitarian philosophy of John Rawls; the philosophy and thought of the post-war new left in the UK, US, and Europe; and the literature and ideas surrounding postmodernism and intersectionality. Through looking at these strands of thought, the remainder of this chapter endeavours to tease out the influence of these liberal domain assumptions on social harm research in critical criminology and zemiology, and how it has created a zemiological culture that is simultaneously and paradoxically deontological, sentimentalist, and emotivist in ways that prohibit coherence around the concept of social harm.

Zemiology in the Shadow of Justice

Virtually all of the domain assumptions discussed above are present in Rawls's theory of justice as fairness, which eventually expanded to become an entire doctrine of liberal egalitarianism. From the very first pages of Rawls's treatise on justice, he demonstrates the first two domain assumptions of liberalism. Firstly, he asserts a conception of the human self that is antecedent to and more important than any of their inherited and acquired social roles, occupations, and relationships, and this is reiterated throughout. As Sandel (1982) argues, this is a possessive rather than a constitutive conception of the self. It is the difference between saying that we *have* x, y, and z – where x, y, and z represent certain social roles, relationships, and occupations – rather than saying that we *are* x, y, and z. In the latter formation, saying that we *are* x, y, and z closes the gap between the self and their roles, such that they are definitive of our being and demand things of us. In the former formation, they do not. Therefore, Rawls argues that 'the structure of teleological doctrines is radically misconceived' because 'the self is prior to the ends which are affirmed by it'. Consequently, he argues that '[w]e should ... reverse the relation between the right and the good proposed by teleological doctrines and view the right as prior' (Rawls, 1971: 560). What logically follows from this is that the antecedent self is understood to be in possession of an inviolable freedom to author their own 'life plan' or conception of the good independent of anything external to the antecedent self. It is a 'purely formal' definition of the good, in which 'a person's good is determined by the rational plan of life that he would choose with deliberative rationality from the maximal class of plans'.

These basic domain assumptions dictate that Rawls must develop some *a priori* principles of justice that are independent of any particular notion of the good. It is in this sense that Rawls developed his theory of justice in opposition to both teleological and utilitarian ethics. For Rawls, justice is not a virtue by which one achieves one's *telos* or eudaimonia, or through which society may achieve something that is deemed beneficial to the majority. Like duty in Kant's deontological moral philosophy, justice for Rawls is conceived as an end in itself. It is not merely one value among many others but is rather the measuring stick by which the legitimacy of all other goods, purposes, values, and ends are assessed. Each individual is free and entitled to autonomously design and pursue their own particular conception of the good, provided that it conforms to the *a priori* principles of justice. In this sense, justice is the 'value of all values' (Sandel, 1982). But in order to act as a standard by which the legitimacy of various conceptions of the good are evaluated, there must be an 'Archimedean point' which is distinct from and external to that which it measures.

This standard is established by the thought experiment of Rawls' 'original position'. As we have mentioned in previous chapters, the original position imagines a radically isolated self that is divorced from and antecedent to all social roles, occupations, relationships, and characteristics. In the original position, the individual about to enter society is stripped of all their social characteristics and are completely ignorant as to their position in society. They do not know their class, race, gender, age, nationality, or religion. They do not know what their specific aims are or what their 'rational life plan' will be. All that they do know is that people's aims and plans for life will be markedly different from one another and will therefore inevitably come into conflict – a further domain assumption mentioned above – and that there is a moderate scarcity of resources in which there is enough for everyone to have a reasonable share of resources but not enough for everyone to get everything that they might want. Rawls also concedes that there must always be what he describes as a 'thin theory' of the good; a basic set of primary goods that we can assume a rational person in the original position would want more of rather than less. These are a set of basic necessities for individuals to carry out their life plans, and Rawls assures us that they do not take precedence to the right but are rather guaranteed by them. For Rawls, a rational individual in the original position would want more rather than less liberty as it is conceived in the liberal-individualistic sense. They would want the basic freedom to autonomously author and pursue their own 'life plans', freedom of movement and choice, freedom of speech, and the opportunity to hold political office and exercise political sovereignty. They would rationally prefer more income and wealth rather than less, and they would rationally desire self-respect and a sense of self-worth as a basis for carrying out their privately defined notions of a good life plan. While not originally included in Rawls' list of primary goods, other things such as health or access to medicines and healthcare, access to education, and so on have been added comfortably without altering the core premises of Rawls' theory.

From here, the individuals in the original position must decide on principles of justice that could govern between these various conflicting wills and ensure a just and equitable distribution of wealth and primary goods. Rawls argues that rational individuals in the original position would arrive at two basic principles of justice. The greatest equal liberty principle – in which all would have a right to the most extensive system of basic equal liberties – and the difference principle, in which social and economic inequalities are structured such that they benefit the least advantaged in society. The principles of justice that are derived from the thin theory of the good thereby give us the means to assess the validity or goodness of various things and ends and develop what Rawls describes as a full theory of the good. It is claimed that the principles of justice can determine what the qualities of a good doctor, good parent, good spouse, or a good judge would be, and it does so independent of any *particular* conception of the good. For example, Rawls argues that 'a good doctor is one who has the skills and abilities that it is rational for his patients to want in a doctor' (Rawls, 1971: 403). The skills and abilities that a good doctor would have would be those that conform to the principles of justice and provide patients with the primary goods that all rational beings in the original position would want.

But what I wish to argue is that this claim that the principles of justice can inform and guide a full theory of the good is false, for it fails to account for how we are to decide or prioritise between conflicting primary goods, not to mention the ambiguity of some of the primary goods themselves. Continuing the above example of a good doctor, let's look at the cosmetic surgery industry as a more specific example. How would we assess the 'goodness' of this industry and the 'goodness' of doctors working in it according to the principles of justice and the 'thin theory' of primary goods which inform them? On the grounds of one of the primary goods in the original position, that of affording the individual's the greatest liberty possible, we can say that the cosmetic surgery industry and cosmetic surgeons are good and just. They afford individuals the freedom to make choices about their appearance and their bodies. However, on the grounds of another primary good, that of self-respect and self-worth, it is more ambiguous. The very fact that an individual wants a cosmetic surgical procedure indicates that they are lacking a degree of self-respect and self-worth which they intend to address through cosmetic surgery. But it is far less clear as to whether the cosmetic surgery industry is resolving or contributing to this absence of self-respect or promoting a good and positive understanding of self-respect and self-worth. On the one hand, we can say that cosmetic surgery provides individuals with the means to boost their self-respect, self-esteem, and sense of self-worth by altering their appearance. On the other hand, the message being sent by providing the individual with the procedure is that one's self-worth is to be established through one's physical appearance, a message that is subsequently spread and reinforced throughout the social body more widely. Given that psychoanalytic theory has established that all desire is rooted in lack, and that we consistently fail to apprehend the nature of our desire by mislocating the true locus of our enjoyment, the procedure is unlikely to address this absence of self-worth for long. The promise of the procedure's effects on the individual's sense of self-worth is short-lived and some other aspect of one's appearance is then targeted as the key to achieving lasting sense of self-worth, and this can be repeated *ad infinitum*, to the point that it is directly harmful to the individual's physical health. Indeed, there is plenty of academic research to indicate that this is the case, and that cosmetic surgery can actually have a negative impact on both one's mental and physical well-being (see for example, Hall, 2019, 2020).

Therefore, we have problems to resolve. First, we must ascertain the true nature of self-respect and self-worth and how it is to be attained. Rawls gives us little to no guidance here. For him, these are matters for the individual to decide. Then we must decide how to prioritise between the freedom of the individual to autonomously author their life plan and the need for self-respect. But in the rejection of the *telos*, and the absence of a clearer conception of human flourishing that can serve as that *telos*, we have no means for doing so; and like all good liberals, Rawls' anthropological assumptions leads him to err on the side of individual freedom.

A similar problem arises when it comes to what makes a good university lecturer. Following Rawls' example of a doctor, a good university lecturer is one who has the qualities and characteristics that it is rational for their students to want. But according to the primary goods desired by rational individuals in the original position, what qualities and characteristics is it rational for students to want? It is assumed by Rawls that a rational individual in the original position would want more rather than less wealth and income, and attaining the highest possible degree classification that looks good on one's resumé and can appear attractive to employers has always been seen as one way to achieve these primary goods. But in a highly competitive graduate labour market, would it therefore be rational for an individual to want an educator that truly pushes them, demands high standards of them, challenges them, and rigorously marks and assesses their work such that there is a significant risk of potentially failing or achieving lower marks? Or is it more rational for the individual in the original position to want university lecturers that do not demand they do a great deal of reading, that spoon-feed them the answers to their assessments, and are lenient markers who inflate the grades of their students such that there is a greater likelihood of their students achieving a high degree classification. According to those individuals in Rawls' original position, it is more arguably more rational for them to prefer the latter. But we would be inclined to argue that these are not the qualities of a 'good' teacher, and that while such teachers would ensure students would receive the degree classification that would help them achieve their primary goods, they are not necessarily helping students in the wider sense. These are the problems we run into when we attempt to derive a notion of the good from a prior conception of 'right' that is independent of any particular notion of the good.

This is one of the key issues with Rawls' theory of justice. In the absence of the *telos*, emphasis is placed on procedure rather than on outcome. The question of justice does not necessarily refer to the outcome, but the way in which the outcome is produced. The emphasis on individual freedom, self-respect, and self-worth thereby prohibits us from understanding things such as gambling, aspects of social media culture, or even the fast-food industry as harmful. Indeed, gambling is one of the examples Rawls uses when discussing procedural justice (Rawls, 1971: 86). For Rawls, if an individual participating in a bet does so of free volition, is fully cognisant of the terms of the bet, and nobody cheats, it can be considered just or fair. How then are we to understand gambling addiction and the gambling industry as harmful? Under this model, to prohibit or discourage gambling would be to risk stigmatising individuals and degrading their sense of self-worth.

Given Rawls' commitment to philosophical liberalism, the presence of these domain assumptions within his thought is entirely unsurprising. But what is more surprising and often unacknowledged[2] is that, despite continued claims of zemiology's opposition to liberalism, these domain assumptions find their way into and structure what is perhaps the most advanced, highly regarded, and widely drawn upon conceptualisation of social harm within critical criminology and zemiology. I am referring of course to Simon Pemberton's human needs approach. Doyal and Gough (1984, 1991), to whom Pemberton's approach is heavily indebted, are explicit in their use of Rawls' theory of justice more broadly and his list of primary goods more specifically as the foundations of their theory of human needs. Indeed, in summarising Rawls' liberal egalitarian philosophy, we actually get a relatively accurate description of Pemberton's conceptualisation of social harm. Like Rawls, Pemberton's is an approach that is characterised by an effort to develop some *a priori* principles of harm that, while based upon a 'thin theory of the good', are nevertheless independent of any *particular* or more robust notion of the good, such that it sits comfortably within liberal individualist conceptions of freedom and autonomy, the compromising of which is itself considered to be a form of social harm. It seems, therefore, that Forrester (2019) was right when she argued that whether we are aware of it or not, wide swathes of philosophy, ethics, and the social sciences continue to operate in the shadow of justice theory.

But in adopting an *a priori* approach in which something can be considered legitimate so long as it does not compromise these basic human needs, it runs into a range of problems. As I have suggested in both in earlier chapters and above, it excludes a vast array of socially harmful practices; it struggles to understand how certain institutions and collective social practices are harmed themselves; and it cannot resolve conflicts between various primary goods or human needs. I have already outlined the specific problems and limitations thrown up by a basically Rawlsian approach to social harm in the first two chapters of this book, and it would be unnecessarily repetitious to revisit these arguments again in any detail here. But looking at Rawls in more depth and its relationship to zemiology nevertheless serves to drive home a broader point. Namely, that while zemiologists have often emphasised their rejection of what they claim to be criminology's 'liberal individualistic notion of harm as embraced by conventional jurisprudence' (Canning and Tombs, 2021: 51), one which focuses on acts committed by individuals against other individuals, it is quite clear that they have not abandoned a more liberal individualist ethics or philosophy more broadly. On the contrary, it would seem that a great deal of zemiological and social harm research is underpinned by a disavowed commitment to certain aspects of philosophical liberalism, a point that we will explore further in the sections that follow. Where Pemberton's extremely influential approach to social harm is underpinned by Rawls' liberal egalitarianism, other aspects of social harm research in critical criminology and zemiology are underpinned by a cultural libertarianism that was a hallmark of the post-war new left.

The New Left

The political and intellectual thought of the post-war new left has had an undeniable impact upon both critical criminology and zemiology. There will likely be objections to the inclusion of the new left in a chapter on liberalism on the grounds that the new left were not liberals but committed Marxists. Specifically, they were cultural Marxists. While 'cultural Marxism' is often used today as a term of denigration by the far-right, it was not, in its original usage, a creation of the far-right nor was it considered a derogatory term. Rather, it was an accurate reflection of the diversification of interests on the political and intellectual left, which was expanding its critical lens beyond what was experienced as the dull realms of economy and class and towards the more vibrant field of culture. I include the new left here because I wish to argue, as others have, that as the new left diversified their interests, their work and ideas took on a culturally libertine and postmodern bent which reflects and echoes many of liberalism's domain assumptions, particularly those around individual autonomy and distrust of power, authority, customs, and traditions (Hall, 2012; Milbank and Pabst, 2016; Winlow and Hall, 2022). These assumptions have not only thrown popular notions of what is or is not harmful into significant contestation but also have found their way into a great deal of social scientific research which invokes the terminology of harm.

Across the UK, Europe, and the US, a common belief of the post-war new left was that the boundaries of politics had to expand beyond the traditional realms of economism, electoral politics, and the working class (Marcuse, 1969; Wolin, 2010). Revelations of the atrocities of the Soviet Union meant that the idea of state communism was no longer electorally viable, and many among the left sought to distance themselves from the barbarism of order thrown up by Soviet state communism (Winlow et al, 2017). Compared to previous generations, affluence was rising as a result of post-war nation states' interventions into the economy, and trade union activism was achieving sufficient benefits and concessions to satisfy the working class. Things were not perfect, but they were good enough that revolutionary consciousness among the left's traditional electoral base was waning. In the eyes of many on the new left, the traditional working class had become the 'integrated majority' of the capitalist system (Marcuse, 1969: 51). It seemed that the kind of radical transformation that the intellectual figures on the left yearned for was not going to be forthcoming through the traditional avenues of leftist politics, and overall, it was felt that leftist politics was becoming stale, fatigued, and needed a jump-start. As Stuart Hall wrote in the editorial of the inaugural issue of the *New Left Review:*

We are convinced that politics, too narrowly conceived, has been a main cause of the decline of socialism in this country, and one of the reasons for the disaffection from socialist ideas of young people in particular. The humanist strengths of socialism—which are the foundations for a genuinely popular socialist movement—must be developed in cultural and social terms, as well as in economic and political. What we need now is a language sufficiently close to life—all aspects of it—to declare our discontent with "that same order".

The purpose of discussing the cinema or teen-age culture in *NLR* is not to show that, in some modish way, we are keeping up with the times. These are directly relevant to the imaginative resistances of people who have to live within capitalism—the growing points of social discontent, the projections of deeply-felt needs.

(Hall, 1960: 1)

Therefore, the solution for the intelligentsia of the post-war new left was to expand the horizons of politics and begin to politicise culture and everyday life. The target for their critique would no longer be confined to the grey and dreary realms of capitalism's economic system but would be extended to a critique of 'the system' in its entirety. The issue was not just economic power, but also power in a more generalised sense. Its interests were not exclusively or even primarily oriented towards how the majority were economically exploited but how various groups and lifestyles were marginalised, excluded, or oppressed and how their individual choices and desires could be liberated (Zamora, 2015). 'The system' was seen to be enforcing a stifling uniformity through the eradication of any kind of difference and insidiously repressing individual freedom not just in economic terms but culturally, sexually, domestically, educationally, medically, and ethically.

This is nicely captured by the Frankfurt School philosopher Herbert Marcuse – who came to be described as the 'Father of the new left' – in *Eros and Civilisation*. Freud had argued that human survival and the development of harmonious civilisation had required a degree of repression and regulation of the base instincts and drives of the id, particularly sexual instincts. The instincts and drives of the pleasure principle are regulated by the reality principle – represented by the ego in the individual's psyche – which encourages the subject to move away from base gratification and instructs the subject on what is and is not socially acceptable. In *Eros and Civilisation*, however, Marcuse endeavoured to distinguish between 'basic repression' and 'surplus repression'. Basic repression was the kind necessary for the perpetuation of human civilisation. But under capitalism, Marcuse argued, there was a significant degree of surplus repression which mutated the reality principle into the 'performance principle'. In a fusion of Marx and Freud, Marcuse argued that just as workers were alienated from their own labour, capitalism alienated individuals from their own desires. The system structured and organised their desires for them, such that they 'do not live their own lives but perform pre-established functions' (Marcuse, 1974: 45). Even beyond work, their lives, interests, morality, and customs are structured by the apparatus of capitalist society. The individual under capitalist society, 'desires what he is supposed to desire' (ibid.: 45), such that 'neither his desires nor his alteration of reality are henceforth his own: they are now "organised" by his society. And this "organisation" represses and transubstantiates his original instinctual needs. If absence from repression is the archetype of freedom, then civilisation is the struggle against this freedom' (Marcuse, 1974: 14–15). *Eros* – the realm of sensuality, pleasure, and libidinal love – should not be subordinated to *Logos* (reason). Instead, the 'performance principle' must yield to the pleasure principle and fuse with the reality principle in order to establish a rationality of pleasure which could allow the subject to attain true freedom.

Leftist politics, therefore, began to shift from a politics of solidarity geared towards economic revolution and the material improvement of the lives of the working classes, to a politics of emancipation from and resistance to social authorities, institutions, shared traditions, identities, customs, and traditional morality (Milbank and Pabst, 2016; Wolin, 2010). All of these things were part of the apparatus which created surplus repression and alienated individuals from their own lives. Marcuse described such a politics as 'libertarian socialism'. As he and many others argued, given that the traditional proletariat were a culturally conformist and integrated majority, true radicalism and resistance to the broader system was more likely to be found among the 'middle-class intelligentsia', 'students', 'ghetto populations', and 'minorities' of all kinds (Marcuse, 1969: 51). It was not the factory or the pit but the fields of culture and everyday life that seemed to be bursting at the seams with revolutionary agency, organic resistance, and non-conformist countercultural trends.

This was paralleled and even presaged in some respects in British and American social sciences. Prior to the full-fledged emergence of the new left, authors such as David Riesman (2001) and C. Wright Mills (1951) were wrestling with the sense of dissatisfaction in American middle-class life and an unfulfilling and culturally authoritarian uniformity it engendered. In British and US sociology and criminology, an immense amount of energy and interest was poured into the study of youth and youth cultures as sites of politicised resistance (Hall and Jefferson, 1976; Hebdige, 1979). Through their experiments with music, fashion, leisure interests, drugs, sexual habits, and hedonistic lifestyles, these young people were kicking back against the surplus repression generated by a capitalism that was seen to be up-tight, hierarchical, old-fashioned, and conservative. Attracted to the new left's accounts of repressed freedom, it was felt that to change the world the really radical thing to do was to transform the self. The established structures, institutions, morality, and customs were a kind of all-encompassing prison from which the individual needed to be liberated. Being 'political' was increasingly about self-expression, style, and individual identity in everyday life (Echolls, 1994; Epstein, 1991; Lasch, 1979). As Hayward and Schuilenberg (2014: 32) summarise, 'change was taking place through pleasure rather than power'. These political and philosophical reflections merged with an increased social scientific interest with social constructionism and symbolic interactionism. What was considered 'deviant' was not bad or deviant in itself but rather the mere expression of the dislikes, values, and interests of the powerful and dominant groups in society (Becker, 1997). Concerns around deviance or harmful practices were just sensationalised moral panics about behaviour which diverged from dominant socio-cultural norms and values (Cohen, 1972). Others argued that condemnation, prohibition, or policing of these forms of 'difference' would likely only result in deviancy amplification as individuals internalised the labels society ascribed to them and their practices (Lemert, 1967). This was creating harmful and problematic forms of stigmatisation, labelling, othering, exclusion, and criminalisation. The overall conclusion is that all or most forms of difference should be unequivocally accepted, tolerated, and embraced. It is not hard to detect a heavy dose of liberalism's domain assumptions within this aspect of new left politics.

Of course as we now know, the new left's 'libertarian socialism' and its individualised and libidinally emancipatory modes of 'resistance' did not remotely threaten capitalism in any meaningful way. On the contrary, against its searing critiques of the commodification of cultural life, it arguably gave stimulus to the real economies of the Western world that were becoming rapidly reorganised around leisure and consumerism (Heath and Potter, 2006). As many have argued, resistance at the point of consumption was always a delusional fantasy:

> But rather than a revolutionary vanguard, such consumers are more accurately theorised as participants in a countercultural movement that, working in concert with innovative firms, pursued market-based solutions to the contradictions of modern consumer culture. Consumers are revolutionary only insofar as they assist entrepreneurial firms to tear down the old branding paradigm and create opportunities for companies that understand emerging new principles. Revolutionary consumers helped to create the market for Volkswagen and Nike and accelerated the demise of Sears and Oldsmobile. *They never threatened the market itself.* What has been termed 'resistance' is actually a form of market-sanctioned cultural experimentation through which the market rejuvenates itself.
>
> *(Holt, 2002: 89, emphasis added)*

As 'cool' became increasingly associated with transgression and as emphasis shifted to establishing a cool individualism that distinguished the self from the herd, themes of rebellion and resistance were easily incorporated as dominant marketing tropes (Heath and Potter, 2006). This has happened to such an extent that today, such themes can be understood as a form of *precorporation* (Fisher, 2009). Here, Fisher argues that what we are dealing with is not the incorporation and appropriation of cultural formations that had originally subversive potential. Rather, many contemporary forms of so-called transgression and resistance are, in reality, hyper-conformist as they are pre-emptively shaped by a consumer capitalism fully geared towards an emancipatory form of liberal individualism. Indeed, such a politics labours under the assumption that our desires and interests can ever be entirely autonomous. In fact, the prioritisation of the pleasure principle which was key to much of the new left's emancipatory politics has itself morphed into a cultural injunction to enjoy through the reorientation of the cultural superego (Žižek, 2002), a reorientation that the radicals of the new left played an unwitting but not insignificant role in shaping. The good life increasingly became one in which the subject had denied themselves nothing, tasted extreme indulgence, experienced new thrills and sensations through sex, substances, and other lifestyle activities, and checked off places and experiences as items on bucket lists. There is a growing and ample body of research which suggests that this generates significant anxiety among contemporary consumer subjects who, should they fail to accumulate such 'rare' experiences, feel like they are somehow living something less than life (see Dean, 2009; Hall et al, 2008; Raymen and Smith, 2017; Smith, 2014 for examples). Even for those who do manage to accumulate such experiences, the superego can never be satisfied, and the enjoyment that is promised through obedience to the superego is never quite forthcoming (McGowan, 2020).

What's more, the emphasis on individual liberty and the extreme aversion to any possibility of stigmatisation, labelling, or othering effectively facilitate the assumption of harmlessness discussed in Chapter 2. Winlow and Hall summarise this cogently when they write that in this sense, this kind of 'asocial libertarianism fits neatly with the doctrine of neoliberalism: nothing exists beyond the immediate freedoms of the subject and no legitimate authority exists that can justifiably curtail those freedoms. By extension, of course, if nothing is sacred there is nothing that cannot be enjoyed, and nothing that cannot be sold on commercial markets' (Winlow and Hall, 2013: 156–157). Any criticism or moral approbation can be dismissed in the name of individual liberty from archaic and parochial normative ethics. Criticism or calls for prohibition could themselves be condemned as unnecessarily stigmatising and an infringement upon the rights and freedoms of expression of the individual. As sympathisers of the new left have written, 'the gauchistes came to realise that human rights and the values of libertarian socialism, rather than operating at cross-purposes, were complementary' (Wolin, 2010: 5).

Parallel developments in philosophy on the new left also gave them a new enemy: the state. Nowhere was this captured better than in the philosophy of Michel Foucault. Perhaps the most notable intellectual on the left in the 1970s and 1980s, he went on to become one of the most cited philosophers in the world and has certainly exerted a significant influence over critical criminology, zemiology, and social harm research. While traditionally thought of as a thinker who is critical of liberalism and specifically neoliberalism, more recent analyses of Foucault's oeuvre – particularly his later work – make the convincing argument that he was deeply committed to a number of liberal or libertarian ideas and was equally seduced by many neoliberal ideas as well in ways that are reflective of the more general libertarian turn taken by the new left.

Akin to the view of new left Frankfurt School scholars such as Adorno and Horkheimer (1997), Foucault believed that western progress was a myth. But where their focus was upon the subtle forms of unfreedom within the culture industry, Foucault's focus was upon the nature and operation of power, which he conflates with domination. His philosophy challenged the left to think about power in a new way. Rather than thinking in terms of top-down power exerted by a sovereign state or a monarch, Foucault was concerned with the diffuse forms of micro-power that were everywhere in society. People were not becoming freer, western society was not becoming more tolerant or humane. Rather, there was an insidiously domineering form of control operating throughout the vast apparatus of the state and social institutions that was constantly refining its means and mechanisms of controlling and guiding the individual. Overall, he was struck by:

> The attention that the state brings to bear on individuals; one is struck by all the techniques that have been established and developed so that the individual in no way escapes either authority, or supervision, or control, or the wise, or training, or correction. All major disciplinary machinery – barracks, schools, workshops and prisons – are machines that permit the identification of the individual, know who he is, what he does, what we can do, where to place him, how to place him among the others'
>
> *(Foucault cited in Zamora, 2015: 68)*

Schools, hospitals, prisons, families, the welfare state. All of these things are forms of governmentality and biopower, a vast *barbarism of order* (Hall, 2012) whose purpose is to normalise, manipulate, and control the individual. This is what led to Foucault's sympathy and seduction by neoliberal ideas around the social security and the health system – albeit for different reasons than those espoused by neoliberals themselves. For Foucault, both social security and national health systems were just another mechanism of governmentality and biopower that standardises and normalises the conduct of individuals (Zamora, 2015). The welfare state in its entirety was not just an extension of disciplinary power but also a new mode of power in its entirety. In its pervasive concern and 'welfare' for the individual, the welfare state could exert a diffuse and pervasive control as both caregiver and guarantor of security. In neoliberalism, Foucault actually saw a potentially refreshing break from moralistic normalisation that had characterised modern societies up to this point (Whyte, 2019). In his 1978–1979 lectures, he argued that in neoliberalism:

> you can see that what appears on the horizon … is not at all the ideal or project of an exhaustively disciplinary society in which the legal network hemming in individuals is taken over and extended internally by, let's say, normative mechanisms. Nor is it a society in which a mechanism of general normalization and the exclusion of those who cannot be normalized is needed. On the horizon of this analysis we see instead the image, idea, or theme-program of a society in which there is an optimization of systems of difference, in which the field is left open to fluctuating processes, in which minority individuals and practices are tolerated, in which action is brought to bear on the rules of the game rather than on the players, and finally in which there is an environmental type of intervention instead of the internal subjugation of individuals.
>
> *(Foucault, 2008b: 259–260)*

Much of his work followed similar lines. In *Madness and Civilisation* (2001), the overwhelming message was that madness or mental illness was essentially a myth, a social construction of the post-enlightenment age. Those deemed 'mad' or diagnosed with mental illness were not necessarily dangerous, ill, or in need of a cure or control. They simply did not adhere to typical social conventions. They were different. Foucault even flirts with the idea that madness was not a negative thing at all. Perhaps there was wisdom in the difference of the so-called mentally ill? Who got to decide what was normal and pathological anyhow, and on what basis? An undercurrent of the Foucault's entire intellectual corpus is that perhaps 'normality' is the most destructive and harmful notion of all. In contemporary society, anything different is perceived as a threat and can therefore not only be ignored, but controlled, detained, and hidden from view. The general structure of this argument is replicated in other works such as *Discipline and Punish* (1991) and *The History of Sexuality* (2008a).

We continue to see these trends in the critical criminological and zemiological corpus of social harm research today. Work around stigma, labelling, and othering are key watchwords in academic and popular discourse in ways that throw up difficulties for the concept of social harm. The difficulty of course lies in how and where one draws the line around what is legitimately and illegitimately stigmatised in the absence of a coherent conception of the good and in a discipline which increasingly views all normative standards as an arbitrary social construction. For example, a 2017 article in a prominent criminological journal argues that 'minor attracted persons' (MAPs) – people who are sexually attracted to children – are unduly stigmatised, othered, and excluded in harmful ways (Walker and Panfil, 2017). Drawing directly on Foucault, they argue that by treating sexual attraction to children as something which can and should be cured, society and criminal justice systems are marginalising MAP populations and inflicting harms of misrecognition upon them. Parallels are even drawn between discourses around sexual attraction to children and discourses in the not-so distant past about homosexuality, effectively placing homosexuality and minor attraction on a level playing field as equally legitimate sexualities in ways that echo the Foucauldian scepticism towards all existing modes of normativity.

Indeed, for Foucault, one of the key features of governmentality and biopower is its use of knowledge. His notion of power-knowledge, at its most basic, is the idea that power is at once based on knowledge but is also used to create knowledge as well. What we call 'knowledge' are just regimes of truth that are a simple reflection of power and existing power relations and the means for their perpetuation. Foucault drew upon Nietzsche's *Genealogy of Morals* – in which Nietzsche argues that morality is nothing more than the will to power – and applied it to the realms of knowledge. He saw his task as two-fold. First was the deconstruction of knowledge, revealing the mythical and arbitrary nature of much knowledge and human ideals, eventually arriving at the conclusion that knowledge was nothing more than the will to power (Foucault, 2008a). Consequently, the task of politics and even aspects of philosophy and social research was to allow people to speak for themselves and express their own truth; to unearth a diverse and pluralistic array of subjugated knowledges. In his view, all those who presented themselves as founts of truth, knowledge, and wisdom, and who positioned themselves as spokespersons for others were a key cog in the vast machine of power that perpetuated forms of power-knowledge that both repressed a vast array of marginalised others and kept many of them in a state of bondage and dependency (Wolin, 2010). In their anti-statism, their distrust of convention, normativity, and all forms of authority, Foucault and the new left were dogged adherents the idea that power could not be trusted, that the social corrupted the inherently good individual, and a deeply liberal notion of freedom.

The new left, the Frankfurt School, and Foucault have all left an indelible mark on politics, activism, ethics, popular culture, intellectual life, and the broader zemiological and moral culture we currently occupy. Their terms, language, and ethos are implicitly and explicitly embedded throughout popular and intellectual culture, and zemiological and critical criminological research on social harm are no exception. This is the disavowed liberalism at the core of a significant portion of social harm and zemiological research, which I argue throws up significant problems for establishing coherence and consensus around the concept of social harm, not to mention a good deal of inconsistency and internal contradiction within this broad corpus of work.

It is not uncontroversial to claim that within both popular culture and much contemporary social harm research, there is a noted distrust of authorities, institutions, customs, and traditions, and a highly ambivalent relationship to the state. This is one of the more curious features of social harm research, and zemiology in particular. On the one hand, there are searing critiques of neoliberal governments and an express desire for the state to get involved in the spheres of education, health, employment, housing, and so on in order to equip the individual with the positive liberty and resources to fashion their own lives. There is also an explicit denunciation and aversion to the negative liberty of elite actors in the economic sphere. But on the other hand, it would also seem that there is a healthy distrust of the state and other sources of authority and a profound attachment to negative liberty in virtually all other areas of life which, as we have already established throughout this book, makes coherence around the concept of harm extremely difficult. Limits upon negative liberty risk the harms of stigmatisation, labelling, and othering, terminology with which the social harm and zemiological literature is saturated. Most major zemiological texts speak of 'autonomy harms' in their various typologies, and they do so in such a way that is not exclusively limited to positive forms of liberty nor outlines limits on negative liberty in the non-economic realms. This kind of autonomy, therefore, is intimately connected to 'human flourishing', the systemic compromising of which is considered to be socially harmful.

The problem is that, in contrast to positive liberty, negative liberty is an extremely vague and open-ended notion of freedom. It imagines the 'good' as arriving when one is sufficiently free from all external authorities, ethics, and normative constraints. But, as we noted in Chapter 3, the moment this freedom is achieved, one has to confront the emptiness of the ideal. The enjoyment and utopia that were imagined are never forthcoming in the way it is anticipated, and the conclusion at which the subject arrives is that we are not sufficiently free, that there is still a lingering normativity that is stigmatising and labelling certain practices and oppressing our identities and desires from which we need to be further liberated. But in the absence of a collective notion of the good life, how much freedom is enough, what are its limits, and how are we to resolve zemiological issues when these 'freedoms' come to be more widely understood as actively harmful and detrimental to cultural and moral fabric of social life?

Large parts of zemiological and critical criminological social harm research also retain an enduring attachment to the Foucauldian belief that discourses of knowledge are the socially constructed products of power rather than truth (see Canning and Tombs, 2021; Copson, 2016; Hillyard and Tombs, 2004). Indeed, this is the precise perspective from which zemiology has critiqued criminology and the concept of crime and advocated for a more ontologically robust concept of harm. This is another one of the more curious features and inconsistencies within the contemporary landscape of social harm scholarship. It is possible to critique the socio-legally constructed nature of 'crime' while simultaneously maintaining

that we can establish a real and truthful ontological and epistemological basis for the concept of social harm. But it is not possible
to do so when committed to a postmodern Foucauldian perspective that all knowledge and truth discourses are manifestations and
reflections of power, what Foucault called power-knowledge. It is
not possible to do so when advocating postmodern ideas around
intersectionality which would challenge the very notion of harm
as having any ontological truth. This means that when trying to
progress beyond its original critique of crime and criminology and
establish coherence around the concept of social harm and knowledge around what is harmful, zemiology is trapped by the nature of
its original critique. It can progress no further. By virtue of the fact
that the zemiologists drew upon postmodern influences means that
the same questions and criticisms that are applied to the concept
of crime can, by the same logic, be endlessly applied to discourses
of social harm. What harm? From whose perspective? According
to what values and in whose interests? This is not to say that such
questions are unimportant. But the zemiologists' use of the likes of
Foucault and his postmodern scepticism towards truth means that
they are, from the outset, impossible to answer, effectively negating
the value and purpose of going 'beyond crime' in the first place.
Perhaps this is because those writing within zemiology do not see
themselves to be in positions of power or authority. Therefore, they
view themselves as emancipating the 'truth' from systems of power
and unearthing 'subjugated knowledges' (Copson, 2016: 90). But
for starters, Foucault was highly critical of the idea that truth could
be established at all, irrespective of whether it was divorced from
regimes of power. Secondly, it is difficult to deny that the liberal
left now occupy an increasingly dominant position of power within
the social sciences, particularly critical criminology and zemiology.

The situation is even more confusing when one observes that
in prominent zemiological texts there is an endorsement of both
postmodern Foucauldian ideas around the power-knowledge nexus
and Rawlsian models which believe we can derive an objective
understanding of harm through *a priori* principles of social justice
or human needs. For instance, Canning and Tombs (2021: 44–45)
remind us to take heed of Foucault's lesson that 'discourse, not least
language and linguistic terms, is saturated in power: the power
to name, to produce or use certain words, or influence what we
know or prioritise as knowledge'. But they also endorse Pemberton's

human needs approach to the concept of social harm as the most sophisticated and definitive account of social harm (ibid.: 51). Two conflicting perspectives are at work here. Are the Rawlsian principles that underpin Pemberton's work just another manifestation of Foucauldian knowledge-power that are to be endlessly deconstructed, unpicked, and critiqued? After all, the Rawlsian principles on which Pemberton builds his conceptualisation of harm were developed by a white upper-middle class Ivy League professor deeply committed to a particular brand of liberalism and had serious flirtations with laissez-faire liberalism early in his career; and his theory of justice is undeniably reflective of the politics and interests of a very particular time and space, as demonstrated by Forrester's (2019) forensic analysis of Rawls' work. Or are they to be accepted as truth, or at least closely proximate to truth, thereby negating the Foucauldian critique? This is an internal contradiction that has not even been acknowledged within the extant zemiological literature, let alone resolved.

Postmodernism and Intersectionality: A Zemiological Terminus?

The work of the new left and Foucault was, in many respects, a flight from the Symbolic Order. More than this, it was an effort to destroy the idea of truth and liberate ourselves from its myths. Its express goal was a destabilisation of all institutions, authorities, and normative understanding. This was part of the wider trend and discourse of postmodernism that was gaining traction in philosophy. Foucault and the postmodernists were exposing the truth about the Big Other and the Symbolic Order, namely that they are collective fictions. As Žižek rightly argues, these things are only real and exist so long as we suspend our disbelief and act *as if* they exist. A favoured example of this for Žižek is the folktale of the emperor's new clothes. In the tale, con artists promise to provide the emperor with the most magnificent clothes imaginable, clothes so magnificent they are in fact invisible to those who are stupid or unworthy of viewing them. They 'make' the clothes for the emperor and pretend to dress him in this splendid, but of course non-existent, sartorial ensemble and send him out into the streets. Afraid of appearing stupid or inferior, both the emperor and the people collective participate in the pretence, acting as if they can see these magnificent clothes. This collective fiction is working just fine until an impetuous child, unaware of the social dynamics at play, blurts out that the emperor is in fact naked.

Traditionally, Žižek argues, we were those in the crowd who agreed to participate in such collective fictions. While essentially fictitious, the Symbolic Order and its manifestation in the Big Other nevertheless gave meaning, order, structure, and coherence to our lives and our place in the world, providing the subject with a platform of existential security. The aforementioned movements and thinkers, on the other hand, were the child boldly declaring the emperor to be naked. For the radicals of the new left, such collective fictions were not sources of nourishment, meaning, or security, but impediments upon our freedoms. It was not a case that they were imperfect and in need of improvement of reform. Rather, they must be abolished entirely. While the traditional symbolic order functions through the suspension of disbelief, the likes of the new left, Foucault initiated a postmodern suspension of belief in a way that went beyond healthy scepticism, such that the only thing we could believe in was our own cynical disbelief (Winlow and Hall, 2013).

Postmodernism, for one of its most significant voices, was best understood as a sweeping 'incredulity toward metanarratives' (Lyotard, 1984: xxiv). Nobody believed anymore in the grand narratives and systems established by philosophers to explain the world, history, politics, ethics, justice, and so on. And how could they? After all, the world was far too diverse and pluralistic to be susceptible to such grand explanatory systems which endeavoured to apply their ideas and logic universally. People were different, they evolved, and they inherently resisted such universal logic. Truth, reason, ethics, morality; they were all rooted in myth and enforced by authorities vested with arbitrary power. Moreover, the myths in which they were rooted often had no relation to the specific heritages and traditions of the increasingly diverse array of groups and people who now composed society. As such, all of these things required very careful deconstruction, although the deconstruction was from the outset an end in itself rather than the means to a *re*construction; and in the cracks opening up in the edifice of Western modernity, the individual could discover creative opportunities for freedom. Rather than grand narratives, the postmodern era would be defined by the proliferation of a diverse array of micronarratives which defied modernity's universalism and captured the true breadth and multiplicity of human experience.

This kind of postmodernism and post-structuralism had a significant influence on popular analytical frameworks such as intersectionality as well (Hancock, 2016). Rooted in standpoint theory, the starting point for advocates of intersectionality as an analytical framework is that knowledge must be grounded in lived experience. The problem for intersectionality is that science, philosophy, ethics, and so on have historically been overwhelmingly written from the perspective and position of white men but have nevertheless been presented as universals. This presents only a partial view of the world. Since it is assumed that the views, knowledge, and lived experience of people will be fundamentally different according to their intersecting identities of sex, race, sexuality, gender, class, religion, and a whole host of others, what currently counts as 'truth' actually excludes the vast majority of the human race. These perspectives are fundamentally impenetrable to those not from the same intersectional group. A white man will never be able to truly understand the way in which a black man experiences the world. The same is true for a white woman and a black woman; a white cisgendered heterosexual and a transgender bisexual of Pakistani or Jamaican heritage. These intersecting identities mean that there is a fundamental and inescapable difference in how various persons experience, interpret, and feel about basic social interactions, situations, and encounters with various institutions and authorities. Furthermore, the principle of epistemic privilege argues that the most accurate knowledge about the world is most likely to be garnered from those in marginal social positions (Sweet, 2020: 925). Intersectionality, therefore, rejects entirely the notion of absolute truth and affords a great deal of weight to the experiences, perceptions, and interpretations of the individual. What is experienced as a perfectly normal or innocuous interaction for a white male may be experienced as a deeply traumatising and damaging 'harm of misrecognition' for an individual from a different intersectional background.

The example of the student at Smith College discussed in Chapter 1 is a good example of this, but a document from Imperial College[3] listing examples of microaggressions provides further examples. Some are pretty cut and dry and would be perceived by most reasonable people as harms of misrecognition – such as the assumption that a female member of medical staff is a nurse rather than a doctor or staring uncomfortably at a same-sex couple holding hands as they walk along the street. Others, however, are more ambiguous. One example given is remarking to an East Asian person that they are very quiet in a meeting or a seminar and that they should speak up and be more verbal as the group wants to know what they think. Some would interpret this as a welcoming and inclusive action, encouraging the individual to know that their opinion is valued and that they're in a safe space to voice their thoughts. It might even be said in an effort to gauge how well a particular student is grasping certain material in precisely the same way a lecturer might encourage a quiet white British student to be more vocal in class. The document, however, argues that this can be a harmful microaggression. The East Asian person, it argues, is being forced to assimilate to the dominant culture in a way that denigrates their own cultural values and styles of communication and positions white/Western communication styles – which are assumed to homogenously be outspoken and opinionated – as 'normal' and 'ideal'. Another example is remarking on how articulate a BAME colleague is. Again, this might be a compliment that had nothing to do with the individual's ethnicity, but merely a remark upon how clearly and articulately they communicate their thoughts and ideas. For the authors of this Imperial College document, however, this can be experienced as a harmful microaggression which assumes BAME persons are intellectually inferior and expresses surprise when they display communicational competence.

As I alluded to in Chapters 3 and 5, we could understand all of this – postmodernism, Foucault, the new left, intersectionality – in Lacanian terms as a regression from the Symbolic Order into the Imaginary. If you recall, the Imaginary is characterised by illusory misidentifications with images in the external world. There is a certain amorphousness to the Imaginary, in which there is no genuine distinction between self and other. In the mirror stage, the self is the image and the image is the self, and the subject endeavours to manipulate, master, and control the mirror image and govern its movements. In the Imaginary, reality is as you *feel* it. The Symbolic Order, by contrast is a realm of genuine otherness. The subject must be prised apart from the misidentifications of the Imaginary and take up a place in relation to the systems, roles, prohibitions, customs, and laws that make up the Symbolic Order.

However, the argument that this is a regression into the Imaginary is incomplete, for it is important to acknowledge that the Imaginary and the Symbolic Orders are not entirely divorced from one another but are codependent. As we established earlier, in order for the feelings, interpretations, and misidentifications of the Imaginary to acquire any wider salience or legitimacy, they must first be recognised by the Big Other, the network of institutions that make up the Symbolic Order. Earlier I used the example that while I can feel like an academic, I cannot legitimately claim to be so until I am recognised as such by the Big Other and have gone through the processes and procedures required for such recognition. Similarly, the feelings, interpretations, and perceptions of harms of misrecognition or microaggressions cannot acquire any wider salience or power until they are recognised by the Big Other. Consequently, we increasingly see activist groups lobbying employers, government, and legislators to make it such that personal interpretations or feelings are recognised and respected as sovereign in law. A slightly absurd example is that of a 69-year-old man in the Netherlands who applied to have his age legally changed because, despite identifying as 20 years younger than his biological age, he is constantly being rejected by women on dating apps and websites on the basis of his age, which he claims amounts to a harmful form of ageism and misrecognition (Cockburn, 2018). Here, this particular man is trying to make the Symbolic Order the servant and protector of his misidentifications. He refuses to accept the reality of his age, and endeavours to coerce the recognition of the symbolic order. But it is arguably also the logic and aim of having ideas such as epistemic privilege – as they are used in the postmodernist intersectionality literature – recognised at an institutional level by organisations and employers. When the institutions that make up the Symbolic Order – employers, legislatures, and so on – recognise that knowledge is rooted in experience and that the most accurate and privileged knowledge-experience is garnered from those in positions of greatest marginalisation (Collins, 2000; Sweet, 2020), the feelings, interpretations, and perceptions of individuals begin to acquire a wider salience and privileged authority. As a result, individuals can lose their jobs, be forced to undergo disciplinary proceedings, or even be convicted of criminal offences or a violation of one's rights based upon the feelings and interpretations of the individual. Certain cultural forms and traditions can be banned, and classic texts can be removed from circulation. In an inverted way, such ideas arguably reproduce the same problems and shortcomings of communitarianism.

Given postmodern intersectionality's incredulity towards 'truth', its tendency towards endless deconstruction, and its commitment to epistemic privilege and the belief that knowledge is ultimately rooted in personal experience, we can never fully discount the validity of the personal experiences and interpretations of the individual. Consequently, as we stated back in Chapter 1, when it comes to harm, feelings and perceptions can trump or be considered on a par with any set of ontologically or ethically grounded principles or values. The problems this raises for a zemiological project whose primary critique of the concept of crime was that it has no ontological reality are, I hope, obvious to see. How are we to establish coherence around the concept of harm when there is commitment to a philosophical perspective which categorically denies the idea of shared reality and grand narratives? Intersectionality maintains that various intersecting groups can never experience the world in the same way. The very same interaction, the very same experience and treatment will, for some, be interpreted as perfectly normal and legitimate while for others it is an unquestionable microaggression and a harm of misrecognition.

Therefore, while intersectionality has opened up a vast terrain for social harm research and has been extremely influential on the fields of critical criminology and zemiology, it is also a kind of zemiological endpoint when it comes to establishing any coherence around the concept of social harm. Its incredulity towards truth, reality, and morality means that establishing consensus on the reality of harm is prohibited from the outset. Furthermore, its elevation of individual experience and interpretation to the highest seat of authority – not to mention the assumption that intersecting groups have inescapably diverging experiences and understandings of what is and is not harmful – means that we are also pre-emptively denied any means for resolving zemiological disagreement. This produces an interminable zero-sum game in which arguments are flung back and forth over whose position and standpoint is most valid, over who should be given epistemic privilege – something we are currently seeing in the disputes between gender critical feminists and transgender scholars and activists around issues of gender self-identification. Consequently, zemiological debate becomes a manipulative clash of wills in precisely the way that MacIntyre (2011: 28) described. The will of one must be coercively aligned with the attitudes, feelings, and preferences of the other. Frederic Jameson (1992) famously argued that postmodernism is the cultural logic of late capitalism. But it is equally the philosophical logic of a culture of emotivism. In this respect, the influence of liberal-postmodernism and intersectionality on the contemporary study of social harm creates a zemiological terminus that its own logic cannot transcend.

★ ★ ★ ★

Zemiologists, critical criminologists, and everyday non-academic people who study or talk about 'social harm' differ as to what can and cannot be legitimately considered harmful. To a certain extent, this is inescapable, although I would argue that we should strive to differ to a much lesser degree than is currently the case and, as above, try to find a means for resolving zemiological disagreement in a rational rather than emotivist way. But despite these differences, they all use the word harm. Consequently, it is of significant importance as to whether they should all mean the same thing when using this word, and whether they are all asking broadly analogous questions when considering whether or not something is social harmful. Arguably, this chapter has uncovered is that they are not. They are in fact asking very different questions.

The deviant leisure perspective and ultra-realist criminology, for example, have critically interrogated consumer culture and particular leisure activities from both criminological and social harm approaches (Ayres, 2019; Briggs and Ellis, 2016; Gibbs, 2021; Hall, 2019; Hall et al, 2008; Raymen and Smith, 2016, 2017, 2019; Smith, 2014; Winlow and Hall, 2016). It should be acknowledged that neither the deviant leisure perspective nor ultra-realism is explicitly Neo-Aristotelian, and there is nothing within either of these approaches which dictates commitment to this ethical position. Nevertheless, I would argue that whether they are aware of it or not, the work that has been done on this subject from these positions have been implicitly underpinned by questions that are Neo-Aristotelian in nature. Questions such as: what is it to live well? Is what I am spending my money, leisure time, and energy on truly good? Are they hurting others? Do I have good reason to desire what I happen to currently desire, or are my pursuits and desires misdirected? Is consumer culture hindering my ability to truly flourish not just as a spouse, parent, or member of a community or some other social role or practice, but as a human being more generally? If so, what systems, actors, and forces are contributing to this misdirection of desire and what do such systems and actors gain from such misdirection? Quite simply, they are enquiring as to the nature of a good life, of human flourishing in its fuller sense. Although a shortcoming of this work is that it has yet to arrive at a more fleshed-out, systematic, yet sufficiently flexible understanding of human flourishing which could provide a barometer of understanding when someone or something is being harmed.

Despite Pemberton's (2015) use of the language of human flourishing, his approach is much different. As we have established, he does not enquire in any detail as to what constitutes human flourishing – stating only that it is the autonomy, in the liberal-individualist sense, to exercise life choices – and simply identifies some of the resources or basic human needs that he convincingly argues such flourishing requires. The Neo-Aristotelian approach questions what we should do with our lives, what constitutes meaningful human activity that will lead to true flourishing and *eudaimonia*. But within the postmodern liberal universe, such questions are proclaimed unanswerable and unnecessarily totalising and are therefore reformulated to something along the lines of 'what preferences and desires should I indulge to make me happy?' The sovereignty of the unique individual with all of its wants and desires is at the centre of such questions, and the question of harm becomes whether one has all the basic needs and resources required to make choices around their preferences and desires, irrespective of their goodness. Therefore, in some respects, Pemberton's approach confuses ends and means, treating some of the material *means* to human flourishing as a guarantor of flourishing in itself. The broadly Rawlsian underpinnings of his approach mean that when looking at issues of social harm, people working from Pemberton's perspective are effectively asking: what do the principles of justice require? Are the individual's basic human needs being met? And if not, why not? These are undoubtedly important and valid questions which must form a key part of any conceptualisation of social harm. But in the absence of a more robust notion of human flourishing, the perspective itself struggles to deal with a whole host of other zemiological issues which we have already discussed at length at various points throughout this book.

Those working from more recognition-based perspectives or liberal-postmodern positions are often asking whether the individual is being afforded sufficient respect and integrity. Are the freedoms, choices, cultures, and identities of autonomous individuals being validated and respected by social institutions and the social body more widely, or are individuals are being stigmatised, manipulated, targeted, or oppressed in various ways? Who is controlling the discourses around harm, crime, and justice? How do they apply to various diverse groups and do these discourses exclude certain harms from view or actively harm certain groups? Again, these are important questions, but they are often approached in such a way that endeavours to deconstruct discourses about what is and is not harmful while prohibiting the construction of universal principles that can take their place, given their scepticism about objective truth.

These are vastly different questions which can yield vastly diverging and sometimes directly opposite answers and conclusions around the harmfulness of various practices and actors. For instance, Neo-Aristotelian questions from scholars working in the deviant leisure or ultra-realist tradition around whether we should really be directing our energies and efforts towards certain types of social activity, or whether such activities are actually compromising our human flourishing, may be interpreted by some working from a more liberal-postmodern tradition as harmful questions in and of themselves, stigmatising and invalidating the choices and preferences of sovereign individuals. Such positions are not speaking remotely the same language. Therefore, as suggested in Chapter 2, we need a *shared* question from which social harm research can begin. How can we know, with confidence and good reason, that a person institution, community, practice, or environment is being harmed? In order for this question to be functional, we need a way of knowing whether or not individuals, institutions, communities, and practices are flourishing, and such an account cannot be weighed down by the pluralist individualism of philosophical liberalism or the all-consuming cynicism of liberal postmodernism.

Notes

1 It is worth noting that Berlin was born into a wealthy Russian family in Riga and then Petrograd (modern-day St Petersburg) eight years prior to the Russian Revolution. As a child, he witnessed the violence of the Bolshevik revolution first-hand, with his family identified as bourgeoisie and enemies of the Bolshevik regime. He spoke publicly about

how his memories of the revolution sparked his opposition to violence, and there is no doubt that the events witnessed, and his own family's fortunes, deeply shaped his politics and thought.

2 I make this claim on the grounds that Rawls' name does not appear anywhere in Pemberton's *Harmful Societies'* text or other zemiological texts discussing Pemberton's approach, despite the fact that his conceptualisation of social harm is heavily indebted to Rawls' liberal egalitarianism. I am not suggesting that Pemberton or other zemiologists are committed to every aspect of Rawls' thought. I imagine many would take umbrage with his difference principle, which argues that inequalities are permissible insofar as they benefit the least advantaged members of society. I am merely observing that the domain assumptions which underpin Rawls' work are nevertheless present within this highly regarded conceptualisation of social harm.

3 The document can be found at the following link: https://www. imperial.ac.uk/media/imperial-college/faculty-of-engineering/ public/Resource-Examples-of-Microaggressions.pdf

References

Adorno, T. and Horkheimer, M. (1997) *Dialectic of Enlightenment*. London. Verso.

Ayres, T. (2019) 'Substance Use in the Night-Time Economy: Deviant Leisure?' in T. Raymen and O. Smith (Eds) *Deviant Leisure: Criminological Perspectives on Leisure and Harm*. Cham. Palgrave MacMillan: 135–160.

Becker, H. (1997) *Outsiders: Studies in the Sociology of Deviance*. New York. Free Press.

Berlin, I. (2002) *Liberty*. Oxford. Oxford University Press.

Briggs, D. and Ellis, A. (2016) 'The Last Night of Freedom: Consumerism, Deviance and the Stag Party'. *Deviant Behaviour*. DOI: 10.1080/01639625. 2016.1197678.

Canning, V. and Tombs, S. (2021) *From Social Harm to Zemiology: A Critical Introduction*. Abingdon. Routledge.

Cockburn, H. (2018) 'Man, 69, Applies to Legally Change Age because He "Identifies as 20 Years Younger"'. *The Independent*. 8th November 2018. Available at: https://www.independent.co.uk/news/world/europe/ man-change-age-netherlands-emile-ratelband-court-arnhmen- gelderland-a8623421.html.

Cohen, S. (1972) *Folk Devils and Moral Panics*. London. Routledge.

Collins, P.H. (2000) *Black Feminist Thought: Knowledge, Empowerment and Consciousness*. New York. Routledge.

Constant, B. (2011 [1816]) *The Liberty of the Ancients Compared with That of the Moderns*. Indianapolis. The Online Library of Liberty.

Copson, L. (2016) 'Realistic Utopianism and Alternatives to Imprisonment: The Ideology of Crime and the Utopia of Harm'. *Justice Power and Resistance*. 1: 73–96.

Dean, J. (2009) *Democracy—And Other Neoliberal Fantasies*. Durham. Duke University Press.

Deneen, P. (2018) *Why Liberalism Failed*. New Haven. Yale University Press.

Doyal, L. and Gough, I. (1984) 'A Theory of Human Needs'. *Critical Social Policy*. 4(10): 6–38.

Doyal, L. and Gough, I. (1991) *A Theory of Human Need*. Basingstoke. Palgrave Macmillan.

Echolls, A. (1994) 'Nothing Distant about It: Women's Liberation and Sixties Radicalism' in D. Farber (Ed) *The Sixties: From Memory to History*. Chapel Hill. University of North Carolina Press: 149–174.

Embery, P. (2021) *Despised: Why the Modern Left Loathes the Working Class*. Cambridge. Polity.

Epstein, B. (1991) *Political Protest and Cultural Revolution*. Berkeley. University of California Press.

Fawcett, E. (2014) *Liberalism: The Life of an Idea*. Princeton. Princeton University Press.

Fisher, M. (2009) *Capitalist Realism: Is There No Alternative?* Winchester. Zero Books.

Forrester, K. (2019) *In the Shadow of Justice: Postwar Liberalism and the Remaking of Political Philosophy*. Princeton. Princeton University Press.

Foucault, M. (1991) *Discipline and Punish*. London. Penguin.

Foucault, M. (2001) *Madness and Civilisation: A History of Insanity in the Age of Reason*. Abingdon. Routledge.

Foucault, M. (2008a) *The History of Sexuality: The Will to Knowledge*. London. Penguin.

Foucault, M. (2008b) *The Birth of Biopolitics: Lectures at the Collège de France 1978–1979*. Basingstoke. Palgrave Macmillan.

Gibbs, N. (2021) '"No One's Going to Buy Steroids for a Home Workout": The Impact of the National Lockdown on Hardcore Gym Users, Anabolic Steroid Consumption and Image and Performance Enhancing Drugs Markets'. *Journal of Contemporary Crime, Harm, and Ethics*. 1(1): 45–62.

Graeber, D. (2015) *The Utopia of Rules: On Technology, Stupidity, and the Secret Joys of Bureaucracy*. London. Melville House.

Hall, A. (2019) 'Lifestyle Drugs and Late Capitalism: A Topography of Harm' in T. Raymen and O. Smith (Eds) *Deviant Leisure: Criminological Perspectives on Leisure and Harm*. Cham. Palgrave Macmillan: 161–186.

Hall, A. (2020) 'The Dark Side of Human Enhancement: Crime and Harm in the Lifestyle Drug Trade' in R. Atkinson and D. Goodley (Eds) *Humanity Under Duress*. Sheffield. Multitude Press.

Hall, S. (1960) 'Introducing *NLR*'. *New Left Review*. 1(1). Available at: https://newleftreview.org/issues/i1/articles/stuart-hall-introducing-nlr.

Hall, S. (2012) *Theorising Crime and Deviance: A New Perspective*. London. Sage.

Hall, S. and Jefferson, T. (1976) *Resistance Through Rituals: Youth Subcultures in Post-War Britain*. London. Hutchinson.

Hall, S., Winlow, S. and Ancrum, C. (2008) *Criminal Identities and Consumer Culture: Crime, Exclusion and the New Culture of Narcissism*. Abingdon: Routledge.

Hancock, A. (2016) *Intersectionality: An Intellectual History*. Oxford. Oxford University Press.

Hayward, K. and Schuilenberg, M. (2014) 'To Resist=To Create?' *Tijdschrift over Cultuur & Criminaliteit*, 4(1): 22–36.

Heath, J. and Potter, A. (2006) *The Rebel Sell*. Chichester. Capstone.

Hebdige, D. (1979) *Subculture: The Meaning of Style*. London. Routledge.

Hillyard, P. and Tombs, S. (2004) 'Beyond Criminology' in P. Hillyard, C. Pantazis, S. Tombs and D. Gordon (Eds) *Beyond Criminology: Taking Harm Seriously*. London. Pluto Press: 10–29.

Hobbes, T. (2017) 'De Cive' in D. Baumgold (Ed) *Three Text Edition of Thomas Hobbes' Political Theory: The Elements of Law, De Cive, and Leviathan*. Cambridge. Cambridge University Press.

Hochuli, A., Hoare, G. and Cunliffe, P. (2021) *The End of the End of History: Politics in the Twenty-First Century*. London. Zero.

Holt, D. (2002) 'Why Do Brands Cause Trouble? A Dialectical Theory of Consumer Culture and Branding'. *Journal of Consumer Research*. 29: 70–90.

Jameson, F. (1992) *Postmodernism: Or, the Cultural Logic of Late Capitalism*. London. Verso.

Lasch, C. (1979) *The Culture of Narcissism: American Life in an Age of Diminishing Expectations*. New York. Norton.

Lemert, E. (1967) *Human Deviance, Social Problems and Social Control*. Englewood Cliffs. Prentice Hall.

Losurdo, D. (2011) *Liberalism: A Counter-History*. London. Verso.

Lyotard, J. (1984) *The Postmodern Condition: A Report on Knowledge*. Minneapolis. University of Minnesota Press.

MacIntyre, A. (2002) *A Short History of Ethics*. Abingdon. Routledge.

MacIntyre, A. (2011) *After Virtue*. London. Bloomsbury.

Marcuse, H. (1969) *An Essay on Liberation*. Boston. Beacon Press.

Marcuse, H. (1974) *Eros and Civilisation: A Philosophical Inquiry into Freud*. Boston. Beacon Press.

McGowan, T. (2020) 'Superego and the Law' in Y. Stavrakakis (Ed) *Routledge Handbook of Psychoanalytic Political Theory*. Abingdon. Routledge: 139–150.

Milbank, J. and Pabst, A. (2016) *The Politics of Virtue: Post-Liberalism and the Human Future*. London. Rowman & Littlefield.

Mill, J.S. (2003) *On Liberty*. New Haven. Yale University Press.

Mills, C.W. (1951) *White Collar: The American Middle Classes*. Oxford. Oxford University Press.

Pabst, A. (2019) *The Demons of Liberal Democracy*. Cambridge. Polity Press.

Pemberton, S. (2015) *Harmful Societies: Understanding Social Harm.* Bristol. Policy Press.

Rawls, J. (1971) *A Theory of Justice.* Cambridge. Harvard University Press.

Raymen, T. (2019) 'The Enigma of Social Harm and the Barrier of Liberalism: Why Zemiology Needs a Theory of the Good'. *Justice, Power, and Resistance.* 3(1): 134–163.

Raymen, T. and Smith, O. (2016) 'What's Deviance Got to Do With It? Black Friday Sales, Violence, and Hyper-Conformity'. *British Journal of Criminology.* 56(2): 389–405.

Raymen, T. and Smith, O. (2017) 'Lifestyle Gambling, Indebtedness and Anxiety: A Deviant Leisure Perspective'. *Journal of Consumer Culture.* Retrieved from https://doi.org/10.1177/1469540517736559.

Raymen, T. and Smith, O. (Eds) (2019) *Deviant Leisure: Criminological Perspectives on Leisure and Harm.* Cham. Palgrave Macmillan.

Riesman, D. (2001) *The Lonely Crowd: A Study of the Changing American Character.* New Haven. Yale University Press.

Sandel, M. (1982) *Liberalism and the Limits of Justice.* Cambridge. Cambridge University Press.

Siedentop, L. (2014) *Inventing the Individual: The Origins of Western Liberalism.* Cambridge. Harvard University Press.

Smith, O. (2014) *Contemporary Adulthood and the Night-Time Economy.* London. Palgrave.

Sweet, P.L. (2020) 'Who Knows? Reflexivity in Feminist Standpoint Theory and Bourdieu'. *Gender & Society.* 34(6): 922–950. DOI: 10.1177/0891243220966600.

Visnjic, J. (2021) *The Invention of Duty: Stoicism as Deontology.* Boston. Brill.

Von Mises, L. (1996) *Human Action: A Treatise on Economics.* San Francisco: Fox & Wilkes.

Walker, A. and Panfil, V. (2017) 'Minor Attraction: A Queer Criminological Issue'. *Critical Criminology.* 25: 37–53.

Whyte, J. (2019) *The Morals of the Market: Human Rights and the Rise of Neoliberalism.* London. Verso.

Winlow, S. and Hall, S. (2013) *Rethinking Social Exclusion: The End of the Social?* London. Sage.

Winlow, S. and Hall, S. (2016) 'Criminology and Consumerism' in P. Carlen and L. Ayres França (Eds) *Alternative Criminologies.* Abingdon. Routledge: 92–109.

Winlow, S. and Hall, S. (2022) *The Death of the Left.* Bristol. Policy Press.

Winlow, S., Hall, S. and Treadwell, J. (2017) *The Rise of the Right: English Nationalism and the Transformation of Working-Class Politics.* Bristol. Policy Press.

Wolin, R. (2010) *The Wind from the East: French Intellectuals, the Cultural Revolution, and the Legacy of the 1960s.* Princeton. Princeton University Press.

Zamora, D. (2015) 'Foucault, the Excluded, and the Neoliberal Erosion of the State' in D. Zamora and M.C. Behrent (Eds) *Foucault and Neoliberalism.* Cambridge. Polity: 63–84.

Zamora, D. and Behrent, M.C. (Eds) (2015) *Foucault and Neoliberalism.* Cambridge. Polity.

Zevin, A. (2021) *Liberalism at Large: The World According to the Economist.* London. Verso.

Žižek, S. (2002) *For They Know Not What They Do: Enjoyment as a Political Factor.* London. Verso.

Žižek, S. (2006) *How to Read Lacan.* New York. W.W. Norton & Company.

7

WHERE DO WE GO FROM HERE?

All disciplines and fields of study experience periods of stasis or regression. For a time, they cease to generate new insights, theories, and discoveries. They start to move away from the questions that are of most central importance to their field and give it their reason for being, thereby requiring a critical review or internal evaluation that can get it back on track. However, most disciplines have significant periods of progression, development, and forward movement before they begin to ossify and veer off course. Criminology is arguably a good example of this. It progressed past its early positivist and classical phases and developed strong post-positivist aetiological commitments to developing depth theories which attempted to understand and explain the motivations for criminal behaviour as they occurred in their social, economic, and cultural contexts. But from around the 1960s onwards, criminology increasingly began to shift from aetiology to what Jason Ditton (1979) dubbed 'controlology', becoming disproportionately concerned with systems of criminalisation and control in which almost any kind of troubling or problematic behaviour could be explained away as nothing more than a 'moral panic'. In the shift from aetiology to controlology, criminology stopped producing sufficiently sophisticated theories which even attempted to address the fundamental criminological question of 'why individuals or corporate bodies are willing to risk

DOI: 10.4324/9781003098546-7

the infliction of harm on others in order to further their own instrumental or expressive interests' (Hall, 2012a: 1). Developments at the margins of critical criminology have identified this problem and are now trying to breathe new life into the field by developing novel theoretical perspectives that can address criminology's aetiological crisis, albeit with significant difficulty (Ellis, 2016; Hall, 2014; Hall et al, 2008; Hall and Winlow, 2015; James, 2020; Kuldova, 2019b; Lloyd, 2018; Raymen and Smith, 2016; Treadwell et al, 2013; Tudor, 2018; Winlow, 2014).

The study of social harm, however, is arguably different. While it certainly has its intellectual forebearers and influences (see Canning and Tombs, 2021; Pemberton, 2015 for a useful review), as a field, the systematic study of social harm as we currently understand it was born in the eyes of many with the edited collection *Beyond Criminology* (Hillyard et al, 2004). Since this time it has undergone rapid growth and progress in the volume and diversity of work conducted under its banner. But in important respects, the systematic study of social harm has arguably regressed more or less from the moment of its birth. In that original collection, one of the stated goals of this new field or approach was the development of a more ontologically robust concept of social harm that could combat the somewhat arbitrary and socio-legally constructed nature of 'crime'. But in less than 20 years – a stage of early infancy when it comes to academic disciplines – the field has arguably moved *away* from, rather than towards, that primary goal. Rather than developing ever more sophisticated and robust conceptualisations of harm, the field increasingly finds itself endorsing pluralist positions which reduce harm to whatever the individual empirically experiences as harmful and adopting epistemological principles which do not aspire to universalism, but rather privilege the intersectional experiences of selected demographics. Those working in this field find themselves espousing philosophical positions which reject metanarratives, objective truth, and universal ethics; questioning whether we can establish a coherent set of ontological principles of social harm at all. Or, as is true for most people working in this field, they avoid the question altogether.

On the surface of things, this sounds like the actions of an opponent of zemiology, an external enemy that has infiltrated its ranks from the outset and endeavoured to undermine zemiology's project by taking it away from its stated goal and even denying that such a goal is achievable. But this is not the work of an enemy. Much like criminology's aetiological crisis, it has been self-inflicted from within and even celebrated as a kind of progress. As this book has endeavoured to show, this has much to do with the ethical, cultural, and social scientific context in which the systematic study of social harm was born, and some of its consequent intellectual inheritances. Firstly, it was born in an ethico-cultural context committed to liberal individualism and a social scientific context dominated by social constructionism, postmodern liberal pluralism, and a weighty degree of cultural libertarianism and fear of all authorities. Relatedly, it was also born in an emotivist culture that, in many scenarios, struggles to establish coherence around what is and is not harmful. The problem of emotivism is arguably only intensifying as society becomes increasingly divided in economic, political, and sociocultural terms. Whether it's Brexit; Covid-19; Black Lives Matter; debates around academic freedom; or various forms of political protest, there seem to be an increasing number of domestic and international flashpoints which carry with them questions about social harm, and these flashpoints are increasingly becoming screens onto which our ever-deepening divisions are projected. The intensity and malevolence of the ensuing emotivist arguments demonstrate just how at odds we are with one another in our own societies and cultures, and how desperately we need shared ethics that can transcend an emotivism that feels like it is rapidly descending into a kind of secular Manichaeism.

Most problematically of all, it was born in an intellectual and moral philosophical context which had long since marginalised Neo-Aristotelian ethics which is crucial to the development of a robust conception of human flourishing, and by extension crucial to the coherence of social harm as a concept. This book has worked from the position that before the all-important study of social harm can move forward, we must do two things. First, we must fully reveal and confront such internal contradictions, inheritances, and shortcomings; and secondly, we must explain how they came to exist. Hopefully, such confrontations and explanations can provide us with an idea of where things have gone wrong and the pitfalls to avoid as we move forward.

But while critique is a necessary first step, I would be remiss if I did not offer up some direction as to a way out of the doldrums of emotivism. Failure to offer even some suggestions as to how to develop a more robust conceptualisation of social harm that can address these aforementioned shortcomings would make me guilty of purely negative critique. I would be pulling something down without attempting to build anything in its place. As I have stated repeatedly throughout this book, conceptualising social harm is a task that is intimately bound up with developing a shared notion of the Good, of what it means to truly flourish and live good and meaningful lives. A fully fledged conceptualisation of human flourishing is obviously an enormous task which would require a book (or series of books) to develop. While this is a task that I intend to undertake in future books, I nevertheless want to offer up by way of conclusion some thoughts as to where we go from here.

However, before we get to this, there is a lead-in question that requires our attention: How are we to deal with the issue of relativism? Alasdair MacIntyre's (1985) essay 'Relativism, Power and Philosophy' offers us a useful place to start. Here, MacIntyre presents the problem of relativism as the problem of an individual who is well versed in two or more contrary worldviews that, conceptually, speak different languages and interpret social issues and problems in radically different manners. These two contrary worldviews speak in their own language, individuals judge according to the customs, standards, and traditions of their particular worldview, and each of these worldviews is incommensurable and incompatible with one another. With regard to taxation, to provide a classic example, what is from the one point of view a legitimate and equitable redistribution of wealth, is from the other point of view an illegitimate act of theft of what one has earned or has been bequeathed to them and is rightfully theirs. To use MacIntyre's example around private property, 'what is from the one point of view an original act of acquisition, of what had so far belonged to nobody and therefore of what had remained available to become only now someone's private property, will be from the other point of view the illegitimate seizure of what had so far belonged to nobody because it is what *cannot* ever be made into private property—for example, common land' (MacIntyre, 1985: 8; original emphasis).

While each language or worldview remains strange to the other, relativism is not a problem. People can continue on judging and evaluating issues within their particular worldview. Relativism only becomes a problem in societies such as our own when an individual is aware of and can comprehend the claims of two or more conflicting worldviews or traditions. Since this imagined individual can justify her choices according to either worldview which is internally coherent but fundamentally incommensurable with the other, she is unable to justify the choice of one worldview rationally and objectively over the other. Therefore, MacIntyre argues, there appear to be two ways to respond to this deadlock of relativism.

The first is that an individual or community simply seeks to impose their worldview upon those advocates of rival perspectives or traditions until their rivals simply submit out of exhaustion, are overwhelmed by the sheer volume and number of their opponents, or are coerced into silence to the extent that their perspective or worldview is more or less extinguished from the landscape of credible debate. This is the culture of emotivism described at various points throughout this book that in many important respects reflects our own. Instead of employing reason, emotivists manipulate, accuse, and belittle their opponents. They besmirch their name and draw upon emotive arguments and feelings of guilt to make their case. Emotivists coerce their opponents into allegiance, rather than convincing them, and this constitutes a 'truth-making enterprise, not a truth-seeking one' (Wight, 2021: 439). The use of the language and concept of social harm in both politics and social sciences, and in everyday life, has arguably become increasingly emotivist in nature (Scheffer et al, 2021), undoubtedly a product of certain philosophical trends in the social sciences that have discarded the idea of objective truth and instead committed to a position which believes 'truth' is a function and expression of power. It creates a world in which there is only 'my truth', 'our truth', or 'their truth' (Wight, 2021: 444), and claims as to the harmfulness or harmlessness of something can be rejected or dismissed on the grounds that such claims are designed, consciously or unconsciously, to maintain existing power relations and therefore constitute a certain form of bigotry or prejudice. This is what drives the shrill tone of much contemporary debate in the realms of politics, academia, and social media, but it is hardly a desirable or adequate response. It is a culture which reduces moral, political, and zemiological disagreement to a manipulative clash of antagonistic wills despite purporting to appeal to objective standards and consequently fails to resolve the issue of relativism at the level of thought, providing only the *appearance* of resolution and the establishment of truth. Unfortunately, as the last chapter pointed out, such philosophical trends have been embedded in the study of social harm since its birth. Whenever one critiques the socially constructed nature of crime from a Foucauldian perspective that views *all* accounts of truth as arbitrary power-knowledge (Canning and Tombs, 2021; Hillyard and Tombs, 2004), it effectively renders the task of establishing the truth about harm impossible. After all, if there is no objective truth and if all zemiological truth claims are a mere reflection of power, why should anyone listen to us? How could our claims ever acquire a wider salience? This kind of Foucauldian postmodern cynicism is something that we must completely abandon if we are to establish greater coherence around the concept of social harm.

The second approach is to seek 'impersonal standards of judgment, neutral between competing claims' (MacIntyre, 1985: 12) by developing a 'third language' which transcends the situated particularity of perspectives and traditions. This neutral language or conceptual scheme can provide an objective standpoint from which to judge the claims of rival and opposing traditions. This has arguably been the approach taken by some of those in social harm studies who have attempted to conceptualise social harm. Yar's (2012) recognition-based conceptualising; Pemberton's (2015) Rawlsian needs-based approach; and Lasslett's (2010) strict ontological approach have all endeavoured to develop a new and neutral language which can establish principles that can transcend such disagreement. This book has offered extensive critiques of each of these approaches and their shortcomings. But MacIntyre's more salient point is that adopting an artificially neutral 'third language' does not resolve the issue of relativism any more effectively than the individual who can comprehend two opposing worldviews and arbitrarily chooses between them, or the culture of emotivism that manipulates its opponents into submission in order to create a coerced consensus. In truth, it *exacerbates* the problem of relativism, as 'each inhabitant of this artificially neutral culture is committed either to one of the partisan standpoints that it comprehends or to the neutral standpoint that comprehends them all' (Lutz, 2012: 177). It merely adds another perspective that one must choose to adopt or reject.

So if a culture of emotivism is inadequate to deal with the issue of relativism, and if the development of an allegedly neutral 'third language' merely exacerbates the problem, what is the solution? We avoid the temptation of relativism or emotivism, MacIntyre argues, not by trying to develop a third 'neutral language' but by critically interrogating alien conceptual traditions by the standards of our own tradition, and most crucially, allowing those alien conceptual traditions to raise questions for our own perspectives:

> Rationality, understood within some particular tradition with its own specific conceptual scheme and problematic, as it always has been and will be, nonetheless requires *qua* rationality a recognition that the rational inadequacies of that tradition from its own point of view ... may at any time prove to be such that perhaps only the resources provided by some other quite alien tradition ... will enable us to identify and to understand the limitations of our own tradition; and this provision may require that we transfer our allegiance to that hitherto alien tradition.
>
> *MacIntyre, 1985: 19*

As Christopher Lutz has written about this approach, 'the criterion of truth is not some metaphysical principle, but the world itself' (Lutz, 2012: 178). It is by testing our theories against the world that we discover their truthfulness and their inadequacies, and the approach MacIntyre advises in his essay is the approach that has been taken throughout this book. It has endeavoured to interrogate social harm approaches and traditions – which as I have attempted to display are significantly underpinned by philosophical liberalism – through the otherwise alien lens of Neo-Aristotelian ethics and philosophy. It has done so in order to raise rational and logical questions for those approaches and traditions. What social harm issues do these approaches struggle to address? What conflicts can they not resolve? What internal contradictions hinder their approach? And how might a Neo-Aristotelian perspective address these issues more effectively?

Take Pemberton's (2015) human needs approach as an example. Despite the criticisms that have been made of Pemberton's approach throughout this book, I nevertheless maintain that it is the best account of social harm that has been produced to date by quite some distance. This is the precise reason I have consistently singled it out for scrutiny, not because it is an easy target but because it is quite a *difficult* target and I have wanted to test and check the veracity and reliability of the very best approach to social harm in a variety of zemiological scenarios. Indeed, it does a number of things very effectively. It outlines a vast array of basic human needs which are essential for any individual or community to flourish, and therefore the framework it offers is capable of addressing quite inclusively a wide range of core harms in contemporary neoliberal capitalist society around housing, austerity, employment, environmental harm, and so on. Moreover, even though it is described in terms of *human* needs, many of the needs discussed could equally apply to non-human animals, plants, and species, something that is imperative in an era of climate change. Nevertheless, it does not provide any developed account of human flourishing, and in the absence of such an account, it struggles in at least two important ways.

First of all, as outlined in Chapter 2, it struggles to account for when institutions, roles, and social practices are themselves harmed. It can more than adequately identify when particular institutions or practices compromise the basic human needs of individuals, groups, or environments, and such tendencies may well be indicative of the fact that the institutions themselves have been harmed and are being prevented from pursuing their *telos* and the goods internal to their practice. But by evaluating the health of institutions in this roundabout way, we can only say institutions or practices are experiencing harm themselves when the telos of those institutions or practices happen to be that of ensuring the basic human needs of individuals or communities are being met. This limits us quite significantly. To a certain degree, it offers us an understanding of how the practice of, say, governance or politics and their related institutions are being harmed by austerity policies that prevent them from fulfilling some of the goods internal to their practice such as meeting basic human needs. But it does not provide us with the means of understanding how politics more generally is being harmed, or how other crucial practices which are not bound up with meeting basic human needs are being harmed. Practices and institutions such as journalism, the arts, sport, the legal profession, the university and academia, and so on. Given the current state and problems within such institutions and social practices, this is a significant problem.

The second thing that it struggles within the absence of a more comprehensive notion of human flourishing is the ability to suggest that certain practices, industries, or choices are fundamentally harmful in and of themselves and compromise human flourishing more generally. As with the examples in Chapter 2 of gambling and social media, the best it can do is show how they harm *some* individuals, in some situations, and under particular circumstances. But we can do no more than this. For so long as there are a sufficient number of individuals who do not experience such harms and who (mis)understand such practices as central to their human flourishing; and so long as we have no account of what genuine human flourishing actually is and of what it is to live well that can contravene such claims, then we cannot describe such industries and practices as fundamentally harmful. We have no means for saying that individuals should not be directing their time and energy towards such pursuits. If we were to ask an individual why they might engage in gambling, or taking recreational drugs, or spending vast swathes of their time on social media, we would likely be met with responses such as 'because I want to', 'because I enjoy it', or 'because it makes me feel good'. Such reasons are not particularly good reasons and are deeply liberal-individualistic reasons. But without a more comprehensive notion of human flourishing, we are powerless against them, and we have no means of saying that a particular practice, industry, or market should not exist or have any place in our society. The best we could do is warn the individual that such practices might one day end up compromising their basic human needs such as their economic security or their mental and physical health, to which this imaginary individual would simply respond, 'but that won't happen to me', or 'but that only happens to x number of people in the population'. Consequently, the practices, industries, and markets that inflict these harms can stay in place by default, and their legitimacy – while perhaps slightly tainted – is not entirely ruined, protected as it is by the sovereign choice of the autonomous individual. The more extreme harms they produce continue, and we can only cross our fingers and hope that individuals avoid them. Again, given the harms generated by leisure and consumer markets and the sovereign choices of their autonomous consumers, this is also a significant problem. Therefore, what we need is an approach to human flourishing and social harm that can do all of the things and address all of the problems that Pemberton's approach does well, while also doing things and addressing the problems that Pemberton's approach cannot.

Establishing a true account of human flourishing requires us to think about the human subject and human flourishing in a significantly different way than we are accustomed to in liberal modernity. First of all, we need to resist the temptation to think of human flourishing as something that is a given, provided that we have certain material resources or basic human needs at our disposal. This is a product of liberal Enlightenment thinking, which tends to imagine the human subject entering the world and more or less automatically becoming a fully constituted rational, autonomous creature with various preferences and desires, and who uses their rationality to determine the best means to satisfy those preferences and desires. Basic human needs like access to education, secure and well-paying employment, suitable housing, healthcare, and a living environment conducive to good health, and so on are vital prerequisites to human flourishing, but they are not sufficient. To say that an individual, group, or community is flourishing is to say far more than simply observing that their basic human needs have been met (MacIntyre, 1999). Therefore, rather than being thought of as a given, human flourishing must instead be thought of as something that must be achieved. Although, as discussed in Chapter 3, we must think of human flourishing as an achievement in a way that avoids falling into the repetitious trap of the death drive. This will be discussed further at a later point in the chapter.

Secondly, in order to establish a richer account of human flourishing, we must also ditch the tendency of liberal philosophy and the social sciences to think of the human subject isolated from their social roles, practices, relationships, and memberships. Rather, we need to think of the subject in a more socially embedded way. Human beings are not 'mushroom people' (Hobbes, 2017). We enter the world as sons and daughters, brothers and sisters, members of a particular family and community with its own tradition and past. As we grow up and develop, we become a part of other relationships, we take on various social roles and become practitioners of particular social practices. The good for a particular individual is inextricably bound up with their various social roles and practices. But as part of a web of social relations, the good of the individual is also intimately bound up with the good of others. Indeed, it is only as a socially embedded subject who is part of such a web of relations that the question 'what is the good life for me' can develop into and be thought about as part of the wider question of 'what is the good for human persons?' As Badiou (2001) and MacIntyre (2011) both observe, such questions as to whether or not we are flourishing can only be properly asked on social fields and within social practices. 'Am I a good father?' 'Am I a good student?' 'Am I a good teacher, politician, housing administrator?', and so on. If we are to establish an understanding of what constitutes human flourishing, we must start looking at this web of relations as *guides* to the discovery and achievement of a shared understanding of human flourishing and resist the liberal temptation of always viewing them as potential impediments to privatised and pluralised notions of flourishing.

A third thing we must avoid when thinking about human flourishing and the end state of *eudamonia* is conflating it with mere 'happiness' or 'enjoyment', as has been the unfortunate tendency of some of Aristotle's translators. 'For in contemporary English' MacIntyre writes, 'to be happy is to be and feel satisfied with one's present state or with some aspect of it, whether one has good reason to be and feel satisfied or not' (MacIntyre, 2016: 54). By contrast, what Aristotle called *eudaimonia* is more accurately understood as 'that state in which one is and feels satisfied with one's condition *only because one has good reason to be and to feel satisfied*' (*ibid.* 54, emphasis added). This is crucial for combatting the assumption of harmlessness that was discussed in Chapter 2 and the scenario above where, when challenging the legitimacy of a particular practice or market on the basis that it actively harms some people, we are rendered impotent by responses which simply claim, 'but I enjoy it' or 'it doesn't harm me'. It challenges the individual to provide more than a liberal-individualist response that one wants to do something just because they like it and that is how they want to exercise their freedom and live their lives. Rather, it challenges them to provide *good reasons* for liking and wanting to do that thing, and that they have good reasons both as an agent engaged in a particular form of activity or social role and as human beings more generally. In exercising these kinds of judgments, one is engaged in true judgments about human flourishing which will provide truer answers as to what it is best for the individual to do in order to live well. It is a way of thinking that is thoroughly antithetical to the standpoint of moral liberal individualism.

Clearly then, the term 'good' and what we mean by it is essential for any account of human flourishing and social harm, and MacIntyre invites us to consider some of the ways in which we ascribe 'goodness'. There is, first of all, an ascription of goodness in which we evaluate something as 'good' only in terms of its means to achieve some other kind of good. Being tall, for instance, isn't good in itself but is good if one wants to be a professional basketball player. Being afforded certain opportunities or being in a particular place at a particular time is good only if one wants to be or do something else that is in itself good and is served by having that opportunity or being in that particular place.

Second, there are goods in relation to social roles and practices, and by 'practices' MacIntyre means something quite specific:

> By 'practice' I am going to mean any coherent and complex form of socially established cooperative human activity through which goods internal to that form of activity are realised in the course of trying to achieve those standards of excellence which are appropriate to, and partially definitive of, that form of activity, with the result that human powers to achieve excellence, and human conceptions of the ends and goods involved, are systematically extended.
>
> *MacIntyre, 2011: 218*

A practice, therefore, is something which has genuine goods internal to itself. Goods that are to be valued as ends in themselves are worth pursuing for their own sake and can only be discovered and achieved by participating in that practice and pursuing those goods according to standards of excellence that are determined by the tradition of that practice (MacIntyre, 1999, 2011). Consequently, these goods internal to these roles and practices and the standards of excellence in attaining such goods are not individually defined but inherited, and they can only be revised or amended collectively by the members of that particular social role or practice.

Politics, academia, basketball, housing administration, or the making and sustaining of a family are all examples of practices. They have genuine goods internal to themselves that are genuinely good for their own sake rather than being good purely for the sake of external goods such as money, fame, or the admiration of others, and we flourish most as human beings when we engage in practices that have such internal genuine goods. To be excellent in achieving these goods or to pursue excellence as it relates to these internal goods is to flourish *qua* politician, *qua* basketball player, *qua* academic, and so on, and one can give good reasons for pursuing such things because they have genuine goods that are worth pursuing for their own sake. Moreover, one can only truly flourish *qua* politician, *qua* academic, or *qua* parent by diligently pursuing these internal goods. This, MacIntyre argues, gives such things an inherently moral quality. A politician can only govern communities wisely by having a clear understanding of the needs of the community more widely and a constancy of commitment to serving their interests. An academic can only move academic thought forward by reading the literature, becoming learned, engaging in hard thinking, and having the courage to disagree with and build upon prevailing intellectual orthodoxy. One can only flourish as a basketball player through an initiation into the standards and skills it requires and practising them with diligence. Therefore, an integral aspect of human flourishing is the pursuit of goods which are good for their own sake through various types of social roles and social practices, and which individuals can provide good reasons for pursuing.

Gambling, to continue with the example used at various points throughout this book, would arguably not qualify. It could not be described as a genuine social practice because, unlike other forms of social practice like politics, academia, basketball, or family, it has no genuine goods internal to itself. The sole purpose of gambling is the external good of money – and in the long run, one is unlikely even to attain this. Card games, by contrast, could be described as good. They require a certain degree of skill or tactical knowledge that could be argued as having genuine goods internal to themselves, and one pursues these goods for the sake of mastering card games and flourishing *qua* card player, but playing cards is not the same thing as gambling. One can play card games successfully and enjoyably for its own sake without wagering on the outcome. I invite the reader to consider what other prominent and popular activities in contemporary social life lack any genuine internal goods.

As alluded to above, there are also goods *external* to social roles and practices. Wealth, fame, prestige, and admiration are all external goods which can be attained through a wide range of practices such as politics, academia, or personal fitness. While such external goods can provide incentives for individuals to pursue the goods internal to social practices, if given too much primacy, they can have a corrosive effect on them as well. As I have argued elsewhere (Raymen, 2019: 153–154), the candidate for political office might lie to voters or endorse policies that will hurt the community they intend to govern in order to secure the support of powerful financial backers required for re-election or ensure a cushy job in the financial sector after they leave their role in politics. The academic might refrain from questioning certain academic orthodoxies in order to maintain the prestige and appreciation of one's colleagues or might avoid certain lines of enquiry to ensure they receive research funding which will lead to a promotion. Instead of pursuing the many goods internal to enhancing one's personal fitness, an individual might place too much emphasis upon winning certain competitions or upon others admiring their physique in both online and offline contexts, and consequently take image and performance-enhancing drugs which are potentially detrimental to their health (Gibbs, 2021; Hall, 2019, 2020; Hall and Antonopoulos, 2016; Van de Ven and Mulrooney, 2017). This has the effect of both harming the social practice in which one is engaged more generally, but also harming one's truer flourishing as a politician, academic, and so on. MacIntyre writes that 'in any society which recognised only external goods, competitiveness would be the dominant and even exclusive feature', and in a society in which the pursuit of external goods became dominant, 'the concept of the virtues might suffer first attrition and then perhaps something near total effacement, although simulacrum might abound' (MacIntyre, 2011: 228).

Arguably, this is precisely what has happened in neoliberal capitalist societies that have become overwhelmingly geared towards the pursuit of goods external to social practices over and above (and often at the expense of) genuine goods internal to those practices. Housing is a favoured example. Housing and property in late capitalism have become a largely speculative affair, in which it is increasingly used as a financial asset and understood and valued in terms of the external good of its exchange value over and above its use value and internal good as a home (Madden and Marcuse, 2016). Consequently, over the course of the last several decades, those in charge of the organisation and regulation of housing have sold off large amounts of social housing in order to boost the private property market, often engaging in underhanded attempts to initially reduce their property and land values prior to their privatisation in order to maximise future profits (Smith, 1996). This has resulted in community decline, and the gentrification and exclusion of local working class populations with property prices and rental rates skyrocketing. In prime real estate areas, properties remain vacant as they are utilised almost exclusively for their external good as a store of wealth, future profit, and a means to launder ill-gotten wealth (Atkinson, 2020). This has precipitated a crisis in the availability and affordability of housing in both large metropolises and rural locales that are attractive for holidaymakers, with numerous associated harms and tragedies (Tombs, 2019).

The external goods of the social practice of housing have been pursued to such an extreme point that scholars such as Madden and Marcuse (2016) have seen it suitable to make distinction between 'real estate' and 'housing', in which the former attacks the latter. As they have written:

> [t]he commodification of housing means that a structure's function as real estate takes precedence over its usefulness as a place to live. When this happens, housing's role as an investment outweighs all other claims upon it, whether they are based upon right, need, tradition, legal precedent, cultural habit, *or the ethical and affective significance of the home.*
> *Madden and Marcuse, 2016: 17; emphasis added*

The last line of the above quote is significant. Madden and Marcuse (2016) echo MacIntyre's broader sentiment that housing as a social practice has an integral moral component, with goods internal to its practice. In this regard, if we were to imagine the social practice of organizing and regulating housing geared towards its internal goods, the picture of housing in contemporary society would look quite different. Emphasis would be placed upon all housing being affordable and well-maintained. Rather than cultivating the lifeless *nonspaces* (Augé, 1995) of gated communities and vacant neighbourhoods of 'prime real estate' in an effort to boost value, focus and funding would be geared towards the cultivation of genuine neighbourhoods and spaces for collective and intimate forms of public and private social life. These are the kinds of locales imagined by Jacobs (1961) in *The Death and Life of Great American Cities*, fundamentally ethical spaces which emphasise affective and emotional place-making through real human ties. We could apply this same idea and logic to countless other examples. Again, I invite the reader to think of their own examples where the goods internal to a particular social practice has been fundamentally compromised, corrupted, or marginalised by its external goods or other forces.

So far, we have goods which are only a means to some other genuine good and we have genuine goods that are internal to social roles and practices, the pursuit of which are integral to our flourishing and are therefore good in and of themselves. But MacIntyre (1999, 2011) argues that there is a third level and a third type of judgment about human flourishing, and this type of judgment begins to tailor ideas of flourishing more closely to given individuals, communities, and practices. It is a type of judgment that allows us to distinguish between what makes a particular good valuable and worthy of pursuit for its own sake, and what makes it good for a particular individual, community, or society in a particular context or when faced with a particular set of circumstances.

Individuals are inevitably engaged in a wide range of social roles and practices with genuine goods internal to themselves, and these roles and practices unavoidably come into conflict with one another, thereby raising questions about the importance of each of these roles and practices in their lives more generally. We can all think of examples where an individual is flourishing in their profession or their hobbies, but they are doing so – or being forced or pressured to do so – at the expense of their family or their community, and consequently, we cannot say that such an individual is truly flourishing. Rather, they are living a compartmentalised life. For example, it may be genuinely good for me as an academic to go away to a week-long conference in Miami or Budapest. But at that particular time, it may not be best for me to go as a parent or spouse, or as a trade union member or a man of religious faith. Consequently, this third level is about ranking, ordering, and choosing between a diverse range of genuine but sometimes conflicting goods and deciding to what extent they should have a primary or subordinate place in an individual's, community's, or society's life, or whether they should have no place at all. To do so is to provide what MacIntyre describes as a narrative unity to one's life. Since we are not just isolated asocial individuals, but agents engaged in various social roles and practices, our personal narratives are always already entangled and interconnected with the lives and narratives of others, such that when we pose questions such as 'what is the good for me?' or 'what am I to do if I am to live well?', we are never really posing them in a liberal-individualistic sense. This broad complex of narratives is the ultimate background against which we pose and answer questions about what it is to truly flourish, and against which we decide what we should and should not be doing or pursuing.

An individual or community that is truly flourishing is one that has successfully become, or is on the journey to becoming, a practical reasoner in the Neo-Aristotelian sense. The practical reasoner has the ability, either individually or collectively, to step back and distance themselves from their basic wants and desires, discriminate between them and discern what it would be genuinely best for them to do, pursue and commit to according to their various social roles, memberships, practices, but also as human beings more generally. This, MacIntyre (1999) argues, is what distinguishes the mature practical reasoner from a child who has yet to learn such skills. Any parent will be familiar with the experience of their young child refusing to take medicine or have an injection due to their immediate base desire to avoid the unpleasant taste of the injection or the pain of the medicine. They will also be familiar with the exasperating sense of frustration that arises when the child is seemingly impervious to the mature logic that there are long-term good reasons for enduring the pain of the injection or the brief unpleasantness of the medicine's taste. This is due to the fact that the young child still has to learn to become a practical reasoner. But arguably, such practical reasoning is precisely what we are deprived of in a liberal-individualist consumer culture geared towards a cultural injunction to enjoy (Žižek, 2002a), in which almost every choice and every desire is indulged and justified by the mere fact that it is desired and wanted by the autonomous individual, irrespective of whether they have good reasons for their desires. To be sure, it is no coincidence that social scientists have started looking much more closely at issues of cultural infantilisation in contemporary society, but particularly in relation to consumer capitalism (Furedi, 2016; Hayward, 2012; Raymen and Smith, 2017; Smith, 2014).

Therefore, in many respects, we can say that the good life for human beings is a life spent deliberating over and seeking the good life for human beings. This was the conclusion of Aristotle (1976) himself, and later Aristotelian thinkers such as MacIntyre (2011). Continued consideration of what it is to flourish is a genuine good that is internal to all social practices, including life itself; and thinking of human flourishing in this way is crucial if we are to avoid the pitfalls of the death drive that McGowan (2013) warned us of in Chapter 3. Somewhat paradoxically, we must avoid thinking of the *telos* of human flourishing in a futuristic sense in which the achievement of human flourishing promises some kind of utopian enjoyment in the future and can only be attained through the elimination of certain external barriers. To do so would be to fall prey to the tendency to mislocate the true locus of our flourishing just as the consumer mislocates the true locus of their enjoyment in the commodity itself rather than in the desire for the commodity. This misidentification of the true locus of our flourishing or our enjoyment is precisely what the repetitious logic of the death drive feeds upon and is precisely what thwarts every attempt to construct a good society and contributes to the relativisation of harm. Consequently, rather than thinking of human flourishing as an end point or state of enjoyment that exists at some far-off point in the future, we must relocate the true locus of human flourishing as to be found in the continuous pursuit of human flourishing itself.

We can therefore understand human flourishing being compromised when an individual, institution, or community fails to pursue, is prevented from pursuing, or is encouraged not to pursue the genuine goods that are internal to social practices and the various social roles they occupy; and when we are systematically prevented from acquiring the means to become practical reasoners who can discriminate among the various wants, desires, and goods in their lives, determine what the good life is for them according to their roles, practices, and present circumstances and context, and subsequently act on such practical reasoning.

I acknowledge that this is quite a wordy and unwieldy definition. But just as what constitutes human flourishing can never be neatly defined by a couple of concise sentences, neither can social harm. Discerning what constitutes human flourishing and social harm requires frameworks more than it requires definitions. Frameworks are flexible structures, whereas definitions tend to be rigid. Given the diversity of scenarios, circumstances, and contexts under consideration, any approach to social harm and human flourishing requires structured flexibility rather than the *a priori* rigidity of a definition. Consequently, any definition built upon a framework will inevitably sound quite vague and unwieldy. I therefore encourage readers to place more emphasis and attention on the broader framework rather than the definition itself, although it should also be re-emphasised that this is not a fully fleshed out framework for conceptualising human flourishing and social harm either. What has been presented in the preceding pages is merely the scaffolding upon which we need to build and develop. Nevertheless, this fledgling approach already allows us to do several things which address a number of the aforementioned issues with existing approaches to social harm and even begins to address some problems which have not been mentioned as well.

Firstly, by understanding human flourishing as connected to social roles and practices and the pursuit of their genuine internal goods, we begin to establish a basis for issuing the demand that the individual provides good reasons for their pursuit of some practice or activity instead of another. When the individual engaged with a particular market or practice justifies their engagement on the liberal-individualistic grounds that they like it and that is how they choose to exercise their freedom, we can dismiss such claims and demand that they provide better, genuine reasons. We can ask what genuine goods are internal to such practices and activities and consider whether or not they are worth pursuing for their own sake. Consequently, we can not only demonstrate that such practices and markets harm *some* other people and that by engaging with them the individual is giving tacit permission for such harms to continue; but we can also demonstrate that such practices and markets contribute nothing to human flourishing in the truer sense, that it is not going to contribute to their living well, and therefore the individual does not have any good reason for continuing to choose this over some other more benign practice that will contribute to their flourishing. More pertinently, we can do the same thing when the purveyors of such products and markets justify their business on the same liberal-individualistic grounds on behalf of their consumers.

Secondly, it provides us with a basis for understanding when practices and institutions are themselves being harmed. Most importantly, this is a basis which is not dependent on the *telos* of those practices and institutions being the meeting of individual's basic human needs. Through such a model, we can understand how practices and institutions like universities, journalism, politics, the arts, the legal profession, and so on are being harmed and damaged. This approach also allows us to do all of the things that Pemberton's human needs approach does effectively, given that all of the basic human needs outlined by Pemberton (2015) and Doyal and Gough (1991) are contingent upon the agents of a particular practice, role, or institution pursuing the goods internal to that practice, role, or institution. When such agents fail to pursue or are systematically prevented from pursuing such internal goods, those basic human needs tend to be compromised.

Thirdly, as alluded to above, it is a flexible framework, and any approach to conceptualising social harm must be structured in such a way that it can be sufficiently flexible to human circumstance without being so malleable that it loses all meaningful structure entirely. This approach allows us to understand what the good is for human beings more generally, but also for individuals in their particular contexts and circumstances. This goes some way to determining how we rank order such goods and how we resolve situations where the goods internal to various institutions, roles, and practices come into conflict with one another. It allows us to think of the human subject in a non-compartmentalised way and as more than just a bundle of competing preferences whose 'rationality' serves those preferences whatever they happen to be. But it also allows the goods internal to social practices to evolve as global and local circumstances change. The example given earlier in Chapter 2 is related to the issue of climate change. The context of the Anthropocene and the climate crisis forces us to re-evaluate the goods internal to our practices. Averting climate change is not merely an external good or an ancillary benefit but is in fact a genuine good that is worthy of pursuit for its own sake and must therefore be embedded in all of our social practices. Engineering, energy supply, food production, or the production of any commodity must therefore take the internal good of environmental sustainability into account and rank it highly on our list of priorities. Social practices must be modified accordingly, or it may well be the case that in the course of our deliberations we conclude that certain practices and goods should have little to no place in our society.

Fourthly, as described above, thinking about human flourishing in this way helps us to avoid the death drive's repetitive trap which arguably plagues all current conceptions of social harm, but particularly those rooted in pseudo-Hegelian ideas of achieving recognition, and which contribute to the erroneous assumptions of harmfulness and harmlessness which result in the relativisation and confusion of the concept of harm more broadly. Fifthly, and along slightly different lines, it allows us to ascertain when a certain degree of harm, pain, or suffering can occupy a *legitimate* place in our lives. The importance of this point should not be understated, and to my knowledge, it has not yet been discussed anywhere in the social harm literature. In the *Ethics,* Aristotle (1976) is clear that the journey to true flourishing is often a difficult, painful, and sometimes

distressing experience. To pursue the goods internal to social practices and to achieve excellence in them will involve setbacks, failures,
and rejections. Arguably, we can never lead a truly good life without some kind of harm, and any systematic study of social harm –
whether that be in critical criminology, zemiology, or some other
academic discipline – must surely have some understanding of when
harm is actually a necessary, beneficial, and positive feature in our
lives. It must have some idea of when enduring a certain degree of
harm, as it is experienced in the subjective sense, is actually essential
to the good. Although understandably, this will be a matter of very
careful debate.

★ ★ ★ ★

Few would argue that we are living through a vitally important
historical moment. Our society is one which faces myriad crises and
harms on all fronts. We are blighted by crises in such crucial areas
of social life such as housing, climate change, work, indebtedness,
mental health, drug abuse, and food and water security; and we live
in a world characterised by subjectivities that are intensely competitive and individualistic, narcissistic, and display a palpable hostility
towards any form of social, political, moral, or religious authority
(Milbank and Pabst, 2016; Winlow and Hall, 2013). The white-
hot intensity of the culture wars has seemingly never been greater.
On all sides of these arguments, traditional hierarchies of harm are
being inverted entirely, and pillars such as the presumption of innocence are casually tossed aside on the toxicity of social media. There
are instances in which very real inflictions of harm – such as taking away individuals' livelihoods, hurling streams of personal abuse
through social media 'dogpiles', and verbal and physical threats – are
being positioned as legitimate responses to the mere expression of
an opinion that upsets a particular group of people (Nagle, 2017;
Wight, 2021). Moreover, when we are witnessing the widespread
use of moral language to *defend* the preservation of social practices,
industries, and institutions that threaten lives, corrode the social,
and jeopardise environmental stability and general human well-
being, it is clear that something has gone very wrong at the deepest
moral, philosophical, and ideological core of our society.

The question of social harm, I hope readers now acknowledge,
is an incredibly knotty issue for which there is no easy resolution.

I also hope readers acknowledge that it is a question that in many respects transcends the social sciences. We cannot hope to discover what constitutes social harm through empirical research alone because the question of social harm is actually a deeply philosophical issue. Therefore, despite the study of social harm's extraordinary growth, we must nevertheless face up to the cold reality that at the precise moment in which we need that ever-elusive coherence around the concept of social harm, there seems to be only increasing confusion and uncertainty as to what is and is not harmful and on what grounds we can call something a genuinely harmful presence which has no business in our society. But resolving this problem is an important task, one that is worthy of our time and collective intellectual effort. It is one that we must undertake if we are to develop a better politics; a more just economy; and a more civilised and reasonable public sphere characterised by rational debate, genuine solidarity, and shared interests rather than atomisation and difference. It is a task to which we must dedicate ourselves if we are to develop a more nourishing cultural sphere that provides individuals and communities with security, meaning, and purpose rather than the mere opportunity to collect a disconnected series of experiences, commodities, and base pleasures which produce only competitive individualism, anxiety, and lack. Progress in this task will require hard empirical graft and detailed research, but it will be equally reliant upon deep moral and political philosophical reflection, the likes of which have largely been avoided in the social harm literature. Above all, however, we must overcome the temptation to take the easy routes of postmodern cynicism and liberalism's pluralistic individualism, which would have us deconstruct everything while constructing nothing, and would have us pre-emptively dismiss any universal principles or framework that might provide concepts of social harm and human flourishing with some meaningful ethical, ontological, and epistemological grounding. The great hope of this book is that the social sciences can overcome such temptations and that a new generation of scholars can get to work in building a more robust concept of social harm, and in due course develop some blueprints for a better world. If we fail to do so, then we fail to do justice to what is one of the most powerful and potentially transformative concepts available to the social sciences, and the concept of social harm's current stasis will be permanent.

References

Aristotle (1976) *Ethics*. London. Penguin.

Atkinson, R. (2020) *Alpha City: How London Was Captured by the Super-Rich*. London. Verso.

Augé, M. (1995) *Non-Places: An Introduction to Supermodernity*. London. Verso.

Badiou, A. (2001) *Ethics: An Essay on the Understanding of Evil*. London. Verso.

Canning, V. and Tombs, S. (2021) *From Social Harm to Zemiology: A Critical Introduction*. Abingdon. Routledge.

Ditton, J. (1979) *Controlology: Beyond the New Criminology*. London. Macmillan.

Doyal, L. and Gough, I. (1991) *A Theory of Human Need*. Basingstoke. Palgrave Macmillan.

Ellis, A. (2016) *Men, Masculinities and Violence: An Ethnographic Study*. Abingdon. Routledge.

Furedi, F. (2016) *What's Happened to the University? A Sociological Exploration of Its Infantilisation*. London. Routledge.

Gibbs, N. (2021) *Insta-Muscle: Examining Online and Offline IPED Trade and Masculine Body Culture*. PhD Thesis. Northumbria University. Newcastle.

Hall, A. (2019) 'Lifestyle drugs and late capitalism: A topography of harm' in T. Raymen and O. Smith (Eds) *Deviant Leisure: Criminological Perspectives on Leisure and Harm*. Cham. Palgrave Macmillan: 161–186.

Hall, A. (2020) 'The dark side of human enhancement: Crime and harm in the lifestyle drug trade' in R. Atkinson and D. Goodley (Eds) *Humanity under Duress*. Sheffield. Multitude Press.

Hall, S. (2012a) *Theorising Crime and Deviance: A New Perspective*. London. Sage.

Hall, S. (2014) 'The Socioeconomic Function of Evil'. *The Sociological Review*. 62(2): 13–31.

Hall, S. and Winlow, S. (2015) *Revitalising Criminological Theory: Towards a New Ultra-Realism*. Abingdon. Routledge.

Hall, A. and Antonopoulos, G. (2016) *Fake Meds Online: The Internet and the Transnational Market in Illicit Pharmaceuticals*.

Hall, S., Winlow, S. and Ancrum, C. (2008) *Criminal Identities and Consumer Culture: Crime, Exclusion and the New Culture of Narcissism*. Abingdon. Routledge.

Hayward, K. (2012) 'Pantomime Justice: A Cultural Criminological Analysis of 'Life-Stage Dissolution'. *Crime, Media, Culture*. 8(2): 213–229.

Hillyard, P. and Tombs, S. (2004) 'Beyond criminology?' in P. Hillyard, C. Pantazis, S. Tombs and D. Gordon (Eds) *Beyond Criminology: Taking Harm Seriously*. London. Pluto Press: 10–29.

Hillyard, P., Pantazis, C., Tombs, S. and Gordon, D. (Eds) (2004) *Beyond Criminology: Taking Harm Seriously*. London. Pluto Press.

Hobbes, T. (2017 [1642]) 'De Cive' in D. Baumgold (Ed) *Three Text Edition of Thomas Hobbes' Political Theory: The Elements of Law, De Cive, and Leviathan.* Cambridge. Cambridge University Press.

Jacobs, J. (1961) *The Death and Life of Great American Cities.* New York, NY. Vintage.

James, Z. (2020) *The Harms of Hate for Gypsies and Travellers: A Critical Hate Studies Perspective.* Switzerland. Palgrave Macmillan.

Kuldova, T. (2019b) *How Outlaws Win Friends and Influence People.* Switzerland. Palgrave Macmillan.

Lasslett, K. (2010) 'Crime or Social Harm: A Dialectical Perspective'. *Crime, Law and Social Change.* 54: 1–19.

Lloyd, A. (2018) *The Harms of Work: An Ultra-Realist Account of the Service Economy.* Bristol. Policy Press.

Lutz, C.S. (2012) *Reading Alasdair MacIntyre's after Virtue.* London. Continuum Publishing Group.

MacIntyre, A. (1985) 'Relativism, Power, and Philosophy'. *Proceedings and Addresses of the American Philosophical Association.* 59(1): 5–22.

MacIntyre, A. (1999) *Dependent Rational Animals: Why Human Beings Need the Virtues.* Chicago, IL. Carus Publishing.

MacIntyre, A. (2011) *After Virtue.* London. Bloomsbury.

MacIntyre, A. (2016) *Ethics in the Conflicts of Modernity.* Cambridge. Cambridge University Press.

Madden, D. and Marcuse, P. (2016) *In Defense of Housing.* London. Verso.

McGowan, T. (2013) *Enjoying What We Don't Have: The Political Project of Psychoanalysis.* Lincoln, NE. University of Nebraska Press.

Milbank, J. and Pabst, A. (2016) *The Politics of Virtue: Post-Liberalism and the Human Future.* London. Rowman & Littlefield.

Nagle, A. (2017) *Kill All Normies: Online Culture Wars from 4Chan and Tumblr to Trump and the Alt-Right.* London. Zero Books.

Pemberton, S. (2015) *Harmful Societies: Understanding Social Harm.* Bristol. Policy Press.

Raymen, T. (2019) 'The Enigma of Social Harm and the Barrier of Liberalism: Why Zemiology Needs a Theory of the Good'. *Justice, Power, and Resistance.* 3(1): 134–163.

Raymen, T. and Smith, O. (2016) 'What's Deviance Got to Do with It? Black Friday Sales, Violence, and Hyper-Conformity'. *British Journal of Criminology.* 56(2): 389–405.

Raymen, T. and Smith, O. (2017) 'Lifestyle Gambling, Indebtedness and Anxiety: A Deviant Leisure Perspective'. *Journal of Consumer Culture.* Retrieved from https://DOI.org/10.1177/1469540517736559.

Scheffer, M., van de Leemput, I., Weinans, E. and Bollen, J. (2021) 'The Rise and Fall of Rationality in Language'. *Psychological and Cognitive Sciences.* https://doi.org/10.1073/pnas.2107848118.

Smith, N. (1996) *The New Urban Frontier: Gentrification and the Revanchist City.* London. Routledge.

Smith, O. (2014) *Contemporary Adulthood and the Night-Time Economy*. London. Palgrave.

Tombs, S. (2019) 'Grenfell: The Unfolding Dimensions of Social Harm'. *Justice, Power and Resistance*. 3(1): 61–88.

Treadwell, J., Briggs, D., Winlow, S. and Hall, S. (2013) 'Shopocalypse Now: Consumer Culture and the English Riots of 2011'. *The British Journal of Criminology*. 53(1): 1–17.

Tudor, K. (2018) 'Toxic Sovereignty: Understanding Fraud as the Expression of Special Liberty within Late Capitalism'. *Journal of Extreme Anthropology*. 2(2): 7–21. https://doi.org/10.5617/jea.6476.

Van de Ven, K. and Mulrooney, K.J.D. (2017) 'Social Suppliers: Exploring the Cultural Contours of the Performance and Image Enhancing Drug (PIED) Market amongst Bodybuilders in the Netherlands and Belgium'. *International Journal of Drug Policy*. 40: 6–15.

Wight, C. (2021) 'Critical Dogmatism: Academic Freedom Confronts Moral and Epistemological Certainty'. *Political Studies Review*. 19(3): 435–449. doi: 10.1177/1478929920942069.

Winlow, S. (2014) 'Trauma, Guilt, and the Unconscious: Some Theoretical Notes on Violent Subjectivity'. *The Sociological Review* 62(2): 32–49. doi: 10.1111/1467-954X.12190.

Winlow, S. and Hall, S. (2013) *Rethinking Social Exclusion: The End of the Social?* London. Sage.

Yar, M. (2012) 'Critical criminology, critical theory and social harm'. In S. Hall and S. Winlow (Eds), *New Directions in Criminological Theory*. Abingdon: Routledge.

Žižek, S. (2002a) *For They Know Not What They Do: Enjoyment as a Political Factor*. London. Verso.

INDEX

Note: Page references with "n" denotes endnotes.